Bill Russell
Vigilant Innovation

De Gruyter Studies in Innovation and Entrepreneurship

Series Editor
John Bessant

Volume 4

Bill Russell

Vigilant Innovation

───

Configuring search and select processes to avoid disruption

DE GRUYTER

ISBN 978-3-11-065334-2
e-ISBN (PDF) 978-3-11-065732-6
e-ISBN (EPUB) 978-3-11-065338-0
ISSN 2570-169X

Library of Congress Control Number: 2020936214

Bibliographic information published by the Deutsche Nationalbibliothek
The Deutsche Nationalbibliothek lists this publication in the Deutsche Nationalbibliografie;
detailed bibliographic data are available on the Internet at http://dnb.dnb.de.

© 2020 Walter de Gruyter GmbH, Berlin/Boston
Typesetting: Integra Software Services Pvt. Ltd.
Printing and Binding: CPI books GmbH, Leck

www.degruyter.com

MIX
Papier aus verantwor-
tungsvollen Quellen
FSC® C083411

Acknowledgements

I come from a family with deep connections with printing and publishing. This book is inspired by my father, Richard Russell, who loved every day of his 50 years as a printer, primarily with the Oxford University Press. His career was supported by my mother, Carol Russell, who has always acknowledged that she was married to both my father, and the world of printing. I am grateful for the support that they have always given me, and I dedicate this book to them.

All writing projects are tough on families. Without the patience and understanding of Cilla, Poppy, Joe, Tommy and Sam this book would never have seen the light of day. Thank you for understanding my general distractedness during the second half of 2019, when the book writing process was at its most intense.

The research study at the heart of the book was guided by John Bessant, and Steve Brown. John's ongoing guidance and friendship as I continue to explore the stories that bring the world of innovation to life is much appreciated. Data collection was supported by many colleagues that I worked with during my own 12 years as a publisher, especially Keith Howard.

The ideas in the book have been developed and polished through working with students and colleagues at the University of Exeter, particularly those involved with the Exeter MBA and in the SITE (Science, Innovation, Technology and Entrepreneurship) Department. I appreciate the humour and enthusiasm that we share in the classroom and beyond.

Lastly, publishing projects are only realised through authors collaborating with publishers in creative ways. Steve Hardman of De Gruyter has supported the book throughout a stretched writing period, and Maximilian Gessl saw the project home. Thanks for publishing a book about innovation in the publishing industry. While many innovations can claim to have changed the world, few can dispute that printing and publishing have created value from ideas, spreading knowledge and supporting learning.

https://doi.org/10.1515/9783110657326-202

Introduction

We are living and working in a period of continual disruption, which we can define as major changes that unbalance and reorganize the ways that individuals, organizations, societies and their ecosystems connect and act. The 21st century is only 20 years old, and we have already experienced significant shocks and change following the 9/11 attacks in 2001, the 2007/2008 financial crisis and the coronavirus pandemic in 2020. The same period has seen the rise of China as a global and economic power. Technology centred firms like Alibaba, Amazon, Facebook, Google and Tencent have harnessed the potential of the internet to create and dominate new markets in the digital era. Concerns over the future of our planet have risen to be central to the discussions of politicians, decision makers in business and society more broadly.

Writing as a management practitioner and specialist in the field of innovation, I continue to find my original degree in history extremely helpful. Due consideration of the past reminds us that the re-ordering of political, technological, social and business systems and much more has always taken place. Understanding how and why organizations are created, how they sustain growth in changing environments, and how they stumble, are the basic concerns of management scholars, consultants and practitioners across the globe – whatever the size or purpose of the organization.

Innovation within established companies

There are relatively few organizations that last a hundred years or more. Those that do have built, adapted, sustained and continually re-invigorated the capabilities required to manage innovation as globalization, rapid technological change and economic interconnectedness have increased. Large organizations are increasingly challenged across a growing range of environments, requiring them to drive forwards a combination of management approaches, constantly adapting their innovation mix to ever changing priorities, problems and ecosystems.

Innovation, and especially technology enabled innovation, is essential for the long-term survival and growth of organizations. This book explores the world of innovation in established firms operating in the business to business (B2B) markets that make up well over half the world's economy. While there are many alternatives, the book uses the definition that "Innovation is the successful exploitation of new ideas" to explore how established organizations manage the critical early stages of the innovation process. The book deep dives into how 10 B2B focused publishers search for and select opportunities for further development in continually disrupting markets. The companies that the book focuses on matter to a knowledge enabled society, because they include organizations that disseminate the latest

https://doi.org/10.1515/9783110657326-203

research in science, technical, medical, and social science subjects from leading researchers at the world's most ground making universities and research laboratories.
The organizations interviewed for the book had survived and thrived for an average
of 178 years at the time that data was collected, making the sample possibly one of
the oldest ever engaged in a consideration of innovation and management more
generally.

To be successful over time, businesses must master both incremental and radical
innovation. The realm of incremental innovation is more straightforward, with fewer
variables and uncertainties than the world of more radical moves. It is clear that one
approach to innovation does not fit all situations. The book will argue that while the
pursuit of incremental innovation is not only simpler than radical innovation, it is
also a "must deliver" area of activity, with a constantly growing literature to guide
practitioners (Danese, Manfè, & Romano, 2018; Womack, Jones, & Roos, 1990).

Leifer et al. (2001) help us through explaining that: "A radical innovation is a
product, process, or service with either unprecedented performance features or familiar features that offer significant improvements in performance or cost that
transform existing markets or create new ones". They suggest that a radical innovation offers one or more of the following:

–   An entirely new set of performance features
–   Improvements in known performance of five times or greater
–   A significant (30% or greater) reduction in cost

Examples include the collapse in costs of analysing text based information leading
to the surge of AI enabled projects, as well as the way that platforms such as
Alibaba and Amazon have revolutionized how SMEs connect with their customers.

Even though new products are more likely to fail than to succeed, competitive
and profit pressures require established firms to invest in new product and service
development projects, even when little is known about the commercial viability of
opportunities in the early stages of the innovation cycle. Firms recognize that product life-cycles are generally shortening, and that competition comes from both obvious and non-obvious sources, including technology enabled startups informed by
the "Lean Startup" movement engaged in trial-and-learning and pivoting.

Scrutiny of Innosight's strategic change rankings for established firms highlights the positive impact on companies of creating new products, services, markets
and business models (Anthony, Trotter, Bell, & Schwartz, 2019). Their ranking methodology gives the highest weighting to the percentage of revenue outside a firm's
core generated from new growth areas. The ranking also focuses on how effectively
an organization has evolved its traditional core to changes or disruptions in traditional areas of strength, giving legacy businesses new life. With the average tenure
of companies on the S&P 500 declining from 33 years in 1964 to 24 years in 2016
(Anthony, Viguerie, Schwartz, & Landeghem, 2018), the indication is that the firms
that thrive through ever-changing times achieve ongoing strategic transformation

through adapting the core to disruptive change while also generating new growth from new products, services and business models beyond the core business.

The original inspiration for the research project which informs the book came from two sources. Firstly, despite 15 years as a senior level leader in large companies (20,000 plus) and a medium sized firm, including being part of a board team that doubled the size of a publishing firm during a time of significant digital disruption, I felt compelled to understand how offerings are best developed in the digital era. Secondly, the work of George Day and Paul Schoemaker introduced me to the development of the capabilities needed for organizations to become more vigilant, particularly through making sense of the uncertainties found in the periphery (Day & Schoemaker, 2006, 2019).

However, while Day and Schoemaker particularly consider vigilance in terms of sensing, probing, and making sense of weak signals both inside and outside the firm, this book focuses on the fundamental offering development processes and routines central to identifying and validating viable new offering opportunities in core markets, and beyond the core. While the importance of pursuing both exploitative (do better) and exploratory (do different) innovation is often emphasised, there is much to be explained about how established organizations coordinate the search and selection stages of the innovation process across a portfolio of new offering opportunities to create their customers of the future. To continue to grow, companies must be effective in searching for and validating opportunities in core markets, and beyond the core. At times this involves looking in non-obvious environments in the periphery of an organization's operational landscape. Vigilant organizations need both the individuals who can join the dots between diverse knowledge sets, and the routines to mobilize insights and turn insights into new offerings.

Portfolio methods aim to solve the problem of how to review a set of projects relevant to both the incremental "do better" and more radical "do different" agendas, considering a balance of economic and non-financial risk/reward factors. Many of these approaches break down opportunities into categories which reflect the level of uncertainty associated with different environments:
- Core – where organizations have significant knowledge
- Adjacent – where customers, users and technologies are less known
- Breakthrough – often at the periphery of the firm's attention and knowledge

While the importance of pursuing both exploitative and exploratory innovation is often emphasised, there is a need to explain how effective ambidextrous organizations coordinate the search and selection stages of the innovation process (Birkinshaw & Gupta, 2013) across a portfolio of innovation opportunities considering core, adjacent and breakthrough opportunities in the periphery of an organization's operational environment (Cooper, 2013; Day & Schoemaker, 2006; Day, 2007; Killen & Hunt, 2013).

Exploring innovation in the publishing industry

While publishing is a sector with a long history, science, technical and medical (STM) publishing was one of the first major proponents of digitally enabled subscription based services in the mid-1990s. The digitally enabled subscription model has upended countless arenas, particularly in the disrupting media sector. The timeline of recent dramatic changes in the entertainment industry where Netflix has disrupted the business models of Hollywood and the television industry can be traced back to the early adopters of digital subscriptions by trailblazing librarians and publishers in the STM publishing ecosystem.

The companies that were interviewed for the study at the heart of the book had all demonstrated extraordinary resilience in sustaining themselves for an average of 178 years. Darwin's often used observation is particularly relevant to the companies that I have studied: "It is not the strongest of the species that survives, nor the most intelligent, but the one most responsive to change." Some of the quotes from respondents bring to life how their organizations are responding: "If you are going to be in the information business, and we live in the information age and the information technology driven age, you need to get really good with software and data, which redefines what it means to be a publisher, in terms of information and in terms of information technology."

When change is needed, diversity of knowledge and experience is valuable. Organizations benefit from building the dynamic capabilities to sense and seize opportunities, and transform themselves. The dizzying speed of change in a wide range of technologies – not just digital technology – means that how firms connect their technology and innovation strategies is increasingly important. An interviewee new to the STM sector observed: "Technology people build "facts" in different ways", suggesting that fresh vigilant eyes approach the innovation search and select process differently to industry insiders.

The cognitive frames of organizations struggling to keep up with the digitally enabled "technology arms race" in what the book describes as "the rapid change core business" were constrained by operational limitations, and the pursuit of cost savings. Comments like: "We're quite conservative. We like the core business", and: "There are certainly opportunities that come up that are outside the core business, but people get very uncomfortable very quickly" show how an organization's strategy, culture and mindset can either open up opportunities through vigilance, or limit it.

Drawing on over hundred years of research into innovation and an in depth research study, the book brings to life the reality of managing established firms – rather than startups or scaleups – to secure advantage through vigilant innovation in disrupting markets.

Contents

1 Creating customers in the digital era

Peter Drucker (1954) famously asserted: "There is only one valid definition of business purpose: to create a customer . . .." The organizations that continue to grow in disrupting environments develop the capabilities to create customers in both core (known) and beyond the core (less known) arenas. Effective innovation strategies typically address both the "do better" development of existing technologies, products and services, and the development of new capabilities, technologies and value propositions in emerging arenas that demand more radical "do different" processes, routines and technology solutions. Innovation involves identifying tools, ideas and opportunities to create knowledge and take new and improved services and products (offerings) to market.

To continue to "create customers", organizations need to develop the search and select routines that enable them to develop what has historically been called their product line-up. While new product development (NPD) has traditionally been seen as the process through which established firms have refreshed what they offer to customers, a quick look at the numbers suggests that we need to update our terminology. Services account for almost 70% of the global economy. In the United States they make up almost 80% of economic activity, and 86% of total employment. I will refer to "offering development", rather than "product and/or service development" as the main focus of the book in recognition of the increasingly dominant role that services take across low, middle and high-income countries.

A challenge for organizations is that the management of traditional activities in low uncertainty environments is still highly influenced by Frederick Taylor's principles of scientific management dating back to the early twentieth century (Furr & Dyer, 2014; Taylor, 1911). Rooted in task analysis, the job of the manager was to make sure that each task was standardized as much as possible, with workers directed to follow prescribed processes. Taylor's principles of task specialization, work standardization, the division of labour and accountability spread through industry and management education, with examples drawn from the likes of Ford and General Motors. Most large firms are still organized around management structures enabling task specialization, e.g. finance, marketing, operations, R&D and procurement/supply chain management.

While Taylor's principles have done much good, they were born of a particular set of principles – which were designed for managing the tasks relevant to sustaining a customer, but they are limited when it comes to Drucker's "central purpose" of business, which is now updated to relentlessly "create" customers in turbulent, digitally enabled environments. Many of the lessons of management research and established corporate routines enable individuals to be good managers of execution, but do little to develop opportunity centred innovation in the core – which is changing faster than ever due to digitalization – as well as beyond the core. There

https://doi.org/10.1515/9783110657326-001

is a need to consider the entrepreneurial management approaches needed for firms to be vigilant in high uncertainty arenas – specifically in the area of opportunity identification and validation.

Successful innovation in digital environments

A key consideration in the study of any aspect of business in the 21st century is the impact of the "digital revolution", facilitated by the exponential rise in processing power and connectivity. We are seeing a profound in change the size and reach of organizations, and how they are organized, managed and connected to customers, users and suppliers. The business world continues to be in a constant state of flux, with the impact of technological innovation arguably the most important factor. However, many commentators argue that the changes society and organizations are experiencing have distinctive characteristics. Brynjolfsson and McAffee (2014, 2015) posit that we are experiencing the "Second Machine Age" involving the automation of cognitive tasks, contrasting with the industrial revolution – "The First Machine Age" – which increasingly saw manual labour operating physical machines in locations such as factories, ships and on railway tracks.

The concept and terminology of the "Fourth Industrial Revolution" (Schwab, 2017) has been rapidly adopted to indicate the novel ways that digital technology is now embedded in society and humans, following on from the earlier three industrial revolutions centred on steam engines, followed by electrification and then widespread deployment of microprocessors. This book will use the "Digital Era" as a means to refer to the pervasive use and integration of digital components, products and services. It is telling that seven out of the top 10 companies on the 2018 Forbes ranking of the world's most innovative companies are digitally centred firms, with the exceptions being Tesla, Hindustan Unilever and Incyte – a biopharmaceutical company (Davenport, 2019b).

Applying the historian's perspective is instructive, as it reminds us that the scale of transformation experienced by individuals, society and organizations over the past 200 years or so has been extraordinary. The initial impetus and then momentum of the industrial revolution was found first in Europe, and then in the US, building from 1800–1920 (Birkinshaw, 2018; Chandler, 1990; Ferguson, 2011). Between 1850 and 1920 seismic changes took place in business and in society, bringing increased mobility, pollution and wealth – much of which was distributed unevenly. Innovation of various kinds also underpinned the growth of large firms driven by entrepreneurial innovators such as Ford, Firestone and Edison.

Birkinshaw (2018) argues persuasively that the scale of change from the industrial to the digital era is as significant as the transformations associated with the transition from the pre-industrial to the industrial age. In the digital era, an increasing proportion of the services and products that organizations and individuals consume are digital – communication platforms, streamed entertainment and games played on digital devices. In the B2C service economy, even physical products are digitally enabled – phones, cookers and cars. In the B2B space that comprises more than half of the world's economy (Lilien, 2016), the digitalization of processes, communication and growth of e-commerce is transforming practice.

The trend towards digitalization involves manufacturing firms integrating their offerings with intelligent digital systems which enable their products to function without human intervention, connecting with other machines. As firms such as Alibaba have risen in importance, suppliers have established digital platforms to automate payments, rebates and invoices, transforming the efficiency of the transaction process. With human-machine, machine-human and machine-machine – or virtual – communication becoming the norm in B2B relationships, internet access enables the efficient working of the B2B economy. The development and expectation of the constant updating of data underpins the Internet of Things (IoT). Progressively inanimate objects will upload data without human involvement. Some have even gone so far as to claim that IoT can change the world (Ashton, 2009).

The digital business environment is fundamentally different from the way that business was organized in the twentieth century and before. Digital technology is changing the structure of firms, and how they are organized. While the industrial age saw the growth of large, hierarchically organized firms such as BMW, GE and Siemens, born digital firms such as Alibaba, Amazon, Google, and Spotify are more open to bottom-up decision making, as shown in Figure 1.1.

Established firms that are digitally mature recognize that the distinctive requirements of managing their organizations and wider ecosystems are changing. They are learning to adapt and win in rapidly changing digital markets. To be successful, firms and their managers recognize that the firms who are setting the pace need to develop leaders with the capabilities suited for the digital era (Kane, Palmer, Phillips, Kiron, & Buckley, 2018). The emerging traits of effective digital management seek to enable organizations through:
- Pushing decision-making further down into the firm
- Developing different cultures and mindsets from traditional business – because digital business is faster, more flexible and distributed
- Experimentation and iteration
- Individuals continually developing their own skills

Offering development in a VUCA world

The world in which today's firms compete has become less certain, riskier and more volatile, uncertain, complex and ambiguous (VUCA). The innovation process essential for success takes place within very different organizations in multiple contexts, varying from steady state to sectors subject to major technological and market

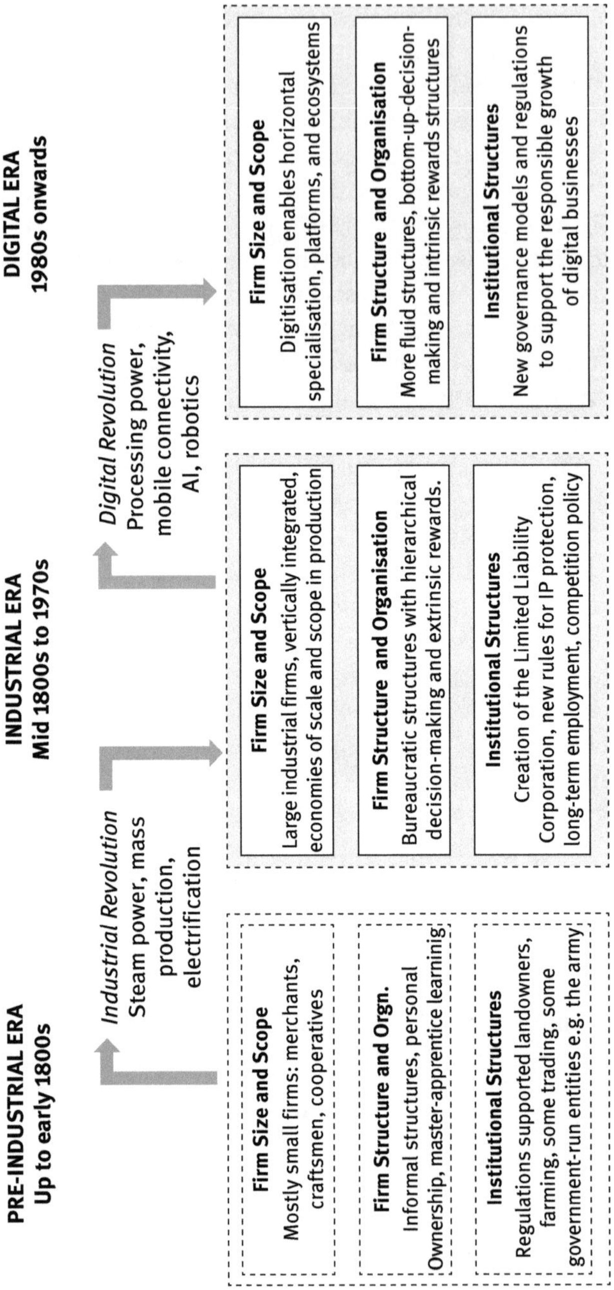

PRE-INDUSTRIAL ERA
Up to early 1800s

INDUSTRIAL ERA
Mid 1800s to 1970s

DIGITAL ERA
1980s onwards

Industrial Revolution
Steam power, mass production, electrification

Digital Revolution
Processing power, mobile connectivity, AI, robotics

Firm Size and Scope
Mostly small firms: merchants, craftsmen, cooperatives

Firm Structure and Orgn.
Informal structures, personal Ownership, master-apprentice learninig.

Institutional Structures
Regulations supported landowners, farming, some trading, some government-run entities e.g. the army.

Firm Size and Scope
Large industrial firms, vertically integrated, economies of scale and scope in production

Firm Structure and Organisation
Bureaucratic structures with hierarchical decision-making and extrinsic rewards.

Institutional Structures
Creation of the Limited Liability Corporation, new rules for IP protection, long-term employment, competition policy

Firm Size and Scope
Digitisation enables horizontal specialisation, platforms, and ecosystems

Firm Structure and Organisation
More fluid structures, bottom-up-decision-making and intrinsic rewards structures

Institutional Structures
New governance models and regulations to support the responsible growth of digital businesses

Figure 1.1: Changes from the industrial to the digital era (Birkinshaw, 2018, p. 191).

disruption. The digital era sees established firms seeking to solve new and often rapidly changing problems for their customers. This is particularly the case when customers and users are experiencing their offerings in changing, digitally dependent environments. Established firms, challenged by both startups and experienced competitors, are changing what they manage, and how they manage processes, people, customers, ecosystems and technology.

The need to search for innovation options, and then select the most promising opportunities, is central to classic and contemporary innovation theories, as these steps support the processes designed to "create the customer." This book is primarily concerned with how established organizations manage innovation search and select activities considering new offering development opportunities across core, adjacent and breakthrough settings in disrupting digital environments. We will use the lens created by a study into the innovation search and select processes in the higher education centred STM publishing industry to see how established organizations, with an average age of 178 years at the time of data collection, have adjusted to the complexities of searching for and selecting opportunities in the digital era.

Increasingly complex markets, cultures and job roles can benefit from over a hundred years of research into innovation, with Gabriel Tarde's first plotting of an S-shaped technology diffusion curve in 1903 a great example of how long scholars have been reflecting on the path of innovation and its ever twisting partner – technology. In the 1980s researchers developed their thinking about new product development, moving from the exploration of new product design options under uncertain conditions through to the emergence of a dominant design. Once a dominant design has been accepted by product designers, customers, and suppliers, the logic was that established firms focused less on product innovation, and more on the process aspects involved with delivering physical products and the standardization of production techniques coupled with the integration of supply chains (Utterback & Abernathy, 1975).

The 1990s heralded major consideration of disruptive technologies, a concept introduced and popularised by Clayton Christensen in the Innovator's Dilemma (Christensen, 1997). He argued that even when established firms are well managed and focus on their customers, they remain exposed to competition from unexpected sources. Christensen's concept of disruptive innovation has secured a powerful and persistent influence with practitioners, while scholars have probed further to challenge some of its central theoretical arguments (Christensen, Mcdonald, Altman, & Palmer, 2018; Gans, 2016b). "Disruptive innovation/disruption" has often been used as a synonym for new threats and/or significant ongoing change. Consultants, journalists and writers across social media – particularly LinkedIn and Twitter – use the phrase "disruptive innovation" to bring to life the potential of new technologies and startups to reshape industries and change for ever competitive patterns. When established firms are confronting major difficulties in their established, core markets, they are said to be disrupted.

The current century can be seen as experiencing a "digital revolution," driven by the exponential growth of computer processing power and connectivity. This digital era sees organizations experiencing fundamental changes in size, how they serve customers, and how they operate within business ecosystems. The big, vertically integrated organizations of the industrial period are being replaced by more focused, specialised companies linking sellers and buyers through digitally enabled platforms. This is an era of continual disruption, with technologically centred innovations and associated new business models transforming individual companies, whole industries and ecosystems. (Kumaraswamy, Garud, & Ansari, 2018)

The theory of disruptive technologies emphasises how challengers – who may be startups or established firms, can offer disruptive technologies (or innovations) to take sales and influence from established firms managing well refined activities in what can be seen as their core markets. Christensen's argument is that new entrants start out with offerings lacking the features and performance of established firms, and that these new offerings are cheaper or more accessible than established products and services in mainstream markets. The "inferior" innovations offered by challengers are attractive initially to niche market segments which are either overserved, or not served at all, by established firms. The lack of attention of the established firms on emerging opportunities enables challengers to be considered by customers outside the selection environments of established markets (Kumaraswamy et al., 2018).

In Clay Christensen's final interview before he died in early 2020, he describes three types of innovation, all of which have a different type of impact on an organization:

– Sustaining innovation: The process of making good products better
– Efficiency innovation: Trying to do more with less, which does not create new growth, as the aim is to squeeze out more than is being put in
– Market-creating innovations: Developing simple products for unserved populations who – up until now – have not been able to afford or have access to something

He saw market-creating innovations as the source of growth in economies and companies, as they mobilize resources, investment, operations, staff, and infrastructure to serve new and larger populations of customers (Christensen & Dillon, 2020).

While established firms may well be in a position to offer innovations that match or exceed those of the challengers, competing with the offerings of new competitors or responding to emergent, digitally enabled habits and expectations can cannibalize profitable offerings in established markets. Confronting this "innovator's dilemma," established firms regularly don't pay serious attention to the challenger and their innovation, as they continue to focus on developing the sales and performance of their established offerings. Christensen argued that at some point the disruptive innovation becomes good enough to meet the needs of core customers, who then switch to the more affordable or more easily accessible offering. Incumbents, with well established routines, budgets and cultures connected to core market offerings and business models then struggle to compete with challengers, and see sales decline. Christensen's original advice was to set up separate business units to manage innovation activity (Christensen, 1997).

This theory of disruption has been subjected to criticism, with a range of challenges including Christensen's definition of the concept (King & Baatartogtokh, 2015; Lepore, 2014; Sood & Tellis, 2011). Christensen and colleagues engaged with these criticisms and responded with clarifications, and broadened the definition of disruption to include the emergence of fresh market footholds and new business models alongside low-end disruptions (Christensen et al., 2018; Christensen, Raynor, & McDonald, 2015). Despite these modifications, Christensen's theory does not fully explain a number of high impact disruptions during the digital era such as the success of Apple's high-end iPhone or Uber's taxi-challenging platform. As The Economist put it (2015), the theory of creative destruction reaches back to Schumpeter (1942b), and while Christensen has done much to advance our understanding of the field, we need to look at other well established literatures to frame our understanding of how markets become disrupted, and what influences how organizations respond to the need for change both within the organization, and beyond.

The rise in consideration given to the inter-relationships between stakeholders has seen greater prominence for the individual and business networks that increasingly support both incumbents with established business models and the generation of new offerings being developed by challengers with fresh ecosystem configurations (Adner, 2017). The importance of complementary assets to the commercialization of innovations was established by Teece (1986), who recognized that innovators can secure value from their new offerings without managing all the complementary assets themselves, with external firms regularly providing the assets. Through working together organizations create a collective business model including the value proposition presented to buyers, value creation and delivery, and value capture. Other players such as regulators and industry bodies also play an important role in ecosystem dynamics.

Business ecosystems are particularly important in systemic industries which incorporate technologies and product platforms offered by different firms. The offerings of different firms need to be compatible to generate utility for users, and deliver value to a complex network of stakeholders. A change to one part of the ecosystem can alter relationships and the roles that players take with each other (Garud & Munir, 2008). A complicating factor is that the boundaries are becoming blurred between humans and machines through Artificial Intelligence (AI), mobility ecosystems and the physical and the digital e.g. the Internet of Things (IoT).

Novel innovations can re-order and adapt relational interdependencies across entire ecosystems (Adner & Kapoor, 2010; Jacobides, 2018). A good example of this is where the relationships between readers, funders, universities, authors and publishers have been changed by the Open Access model of academic publishing, as free and un-limited access to some elements of scholarly research co-exists uncomfortably with paid for access to other outputs from the scholarly research process (Johnson, Watkinson, & Mabe, 2018). A pre-condition to the creation of an alternative to the traditional scholarly publishing model was the creation of a digitally enabled content submission systems designed to meet the workflow requirements of publishers, editors and authors. The development of industry standards for digital cooperation around usage metrics, Digital Object Identifiers (DOIs) and citation engines such as Mendeley helped to build an efficient and inter-operable ecosystem challenged by a fundamental belief of many authors, funders readers and universities, which is that research generated knowledge should be free to access.

A major challenge for disruptors in ecosystem centred industries incorporating multi-sided platforms is how to create a fresh and viable ecosystem wrapped around the disruptive innovation (Gawer & Cusumano, 2014). This is a particularly difficult challenge, as new entrants regularly require access to the complementary assets of the ecosystem established firms that they intend to challenge. This is often described as the disruptor's dilemma (Ansari, Garud, & Kumaraswamy, 2016; Gans, 2016b). Good lessons in how to play this game come from assessing how disruptors such as TiVo and Spotify have had to cooperate closely with established firms. Frequently the ongoing challenge sees different organizations within the ecosystem focusing on a platform, with priorities and objectives that diverge – while the different firms actually create value together.

Established firms in ecosystems with functioning business models hope that they have the resources to play the ecosystem game. They look to see which way the cooperation is headed, accepting that the outcomes of disruptive innovations are difficult to predict. However, by its very definition, the trajectory of innovation is uncertain, particularly in the case of ecosystems. Startups operating in ecosystems often have much to offer, but they can't wait for the ecosystem to "settle down," as they may well run out of money. This leads to ongoing tensions within ecosystems, as disruptors – established firms or startups – jostle forwards promoting the vision of the ecosystem that best matches their hopes and capabilities.

Directly relevant to the research project at the heart of this book are questions about why established firms are unable or unwilling to acknowledge and respond to the danger of disruption in real time, and then succumb to disruption over the life cycle of their offering. Cognitive explanations indicate that organizations engaged in the development of new offerings under conditions of uncertainty are frequently guided and limited by the prior industry affiliations on the framing of new projects (Benner & Tripsas, 2012; Kaplan, 2008). Explanations rooted in behavioural psychology indicate that established firms can be limited by core rigidities and mental models (Danneels, 2011; Leonard-Barton, 1992; Levinthal & March, 1993). Christensen's early work emphasised the financial dilemma facing established firms when introducing disruptive innovations that are not well connected to prevailing business models and which threaten the cannibalization of the revenues flowing from current offerings. It is no surprise that questions as to why established firms so frequently fail through missing opportunities to build new offerings persist, with no "silver-bullet" answers coming from intense research into why established firms fail to renew.

A recent study explains that digitally maturing organizations – the firms that really "get" how to innovate in the digital era – are run differently from their rivals who are at an early-stage in terms of digital maturity. They innovate at much higher speed than their less capable competitors. They spend more on innovation than less digitally mature enterprises, with the innovation activity across the enterprise at all levels, rather than relying on labs and R&D centres. Progressive, digitally enabled organizations engage with external partners more – and less formally – than firms who are less advanced digitally. Cross-functional teams are given greater autonomy than more traditional firms, with cross-functional work being supported by senior management. While digitally maturing firms operate in more innovative and agile ways than their rivals who have adopted digital approaches more slowly, they recognize that there is a need for greater governance in areas such as the social and ethical implications of operating in a more in digitally mature way (Kane, Palmer, Phillips, Kiron, & Buckley, 2019).

There is a significant danger that we over-simplify the change activity associated with digitalization. MIT's Center for Information Research conducts field-based research into the challenges of leading dynamic, global and information-intensive organizations, providing guidance as to how established organizations can re-equip themselves for the digital world. Jeanne Ross is leading MIT's work in the area, and emphasises that two different transformations are taking place within established enterprises. On one side, there is a need to digitize existing processes to secure operational excellence – and cost savings. In addition, there is a need to develop and scale new digital business models for rapid company and arena changing innovation. Both transformations are required for ongoing business success, but she stresses that digital technology is the only thing that digitization and digital transformation share (Ross, 2019).

In core operations, where efficiency and service delivery are preeminent, top-down, highly structured approaches and accountabilities remain essential, as the automation of workflow seeks to free up staff to engage in new, value adding activity. It is not surprising that the pursuit of operational excellence involves process optimisation, clear metrics, and the development of structured business cases. The use of digital technologies for the digitization of core market focused activities builds on previous cycles of enterprise resource planning (ERP) and customer relationship management (CRM) initiatives. Digital technologies such as AI, IoT, and robotics all increase the opportunities for operational excellence.

Digitized processes extend the visibility of service delivery – e.g. tracking a parcel – all the way to a smartphone. Service offering providers are now expected to provide a seamless service to customers from opening an account, paying for the offering itself, changing service levels, and seeing charges while sitting on a train. Standardized business processes that deliver security, reliability and predictability as a part of internal and external customer interactions are the goal. The digitization of the core business accepts individual discretion being limited by precise decision rules. Process owners are measured on how efficiently they manage processes to ensure cost savings and high customer service ratings – visible to all through online scoring services.

But these strict, standardized process focused activities do not work in the less certain world of identifying and then solving new, digitally enabled problems through market-creating innovations. Digital companies such as Spotify, Tencent (the world's biggest gaming company) and Amazon develop successful offerings through identifying and delivering fresh, information enhanced customer value propositions. New digital offerings open up new revenue streams.

The identification of monetizable digital offerings requires experimentation. While an organization's leadership may recognize the need to solve digitally experienced problems, they need to empower small, agile teams to conduct the experiments needed to search for and validate opportunities. The book emphasises the importance of moving from general problem statements (useful and essential) to the identification of the detailed digital jobs-to-be-done that underpin contemporary offering development practice. The teams that manage search and select processes focused on digital offerings need to be managed differently from the teams driving through efficiency focused digitization projects in the core business.

Organizations are therefore facing the need for managerial ambidexterity. On one hand they need to drive through clearly defined standard processes to secure cost-cutting and near-term profitability, while also developing a future focused capability and structure to support their "next" growing businesses based on agility and the flexibility to change. Senior teams are struggling to manage both aspects of their organizations. The business metrics that guide a business to operational excellence such as process optimization and clear business cases actually get in the way of identifying and then delivering emergent digital business models.

MIT's research indicates that established companies find it impossible to operate in the fresh new world of digital value propositions if they have not yet established a firm control on the digitization of their core processes. Even when the core operation is humming efficiently, developing and implementing the new routines and governance approaches for digital innovation beyond the core is proving difficult. Developing digitally centred value propositions requires organizational change. One of the greatest areas of change comes down to the need for speed when making decisions, and running experiments to generate maximum learning through a series of development sprints. The central tension is that digitization relies on top-down leadership approaches with accountabilities all the way up the hierarchy, while success in fast moving digital arenas needs the empowerment of agile teams, with distributed accountabilities (Ross, 2019).

In this chapter we have considered how Drucker's guidance to companies – to focus on the creation of customers – has developed through different stages of economic, social and technological development. Christensen in particular has reminded us of the importance of market-creating innovations. Informed by literature on disruption and the challenges of managing efficiency and growth in digitally enabled organizations, it is now useful to look more deeply at how innovation processes work, before learning from the case studies detailed in Chapters 4 and 5.

2 The innovation process in disrupting environments

Innovation has long been considered to be an engine of growth. It can also enable growth independent of the larger economy. Schumpeter (1942a) focused on the importance of new products as a generator of economic growth, arguing that the competition created by new products was far more significant than the marginal changes in the prices of existing products. Established companies regularly fail, or only achieve slow growth. Before getting into the detail of the research project into how publishers are managing the early stages of the offering development process in disrupting environments, it is helpful to review the innovation management literature regarding the core themes affecting how organization manage their innovation activities.

Invention vs. Innovation

Thomas Edison, the holder of over 1,000 patents, understood that the real challenge in innovation is not invention, but the process of making good ideas work technically and commercially (Dyer, Furr, & Lefrandt, 2019; Israel, 1998). He recognized that innovation is not just coming up with good ideas, explaining: "Anything that won't sell, I don't want to invent. Its sale is proof of utility, and utility is success" (Daum, 2016). The process of growing the ideas so that they can be applied into practical use lies at the very pragmatic centre of successful innovation activity.

A consistent finding in the research literature is that innovation, in the majority of cases, relies deeply on external sources, summarized succinctly as: "Popular folklore notwithstanding, the innovation journey is a collective achievement that requires key roles from numerous entrepreneurs in both the public and private sectors" (Van de Ven, Polley, Garud, & Venkataraman, 1999, p. 149). Over the past 100 years, scholars have developed a significant body of academic research and writing on innovation. Much of the research has focused on different aspects of technological innovation (e.g. Henderson & Clark, 1990; Utterback, 1994), but the last 20 years have seen the exploration of other aspects of innovation, such as process innovation, (Benner & Tushman, 2003; von Krogh, Netland, & Wörter, 2018) service innovation (Weinstein & Gallouja, 1997), and strategic innovation (Pisano, 2015).

A significant stream of research has explored how the marketing function influences the organization's approach to survival and growth (Jaworski & Kohli, 1993; Kohli & Jaworski, 1990; Prabhu, 2014). A major finding of this research is that firms that are more rather than less market orientated are typically more innovative

https://doi.org/10.1515/9783110657326-002

(Frambach, Prabhu, & Verhallen, 2003; Ottum & Moore, 1997) and have greater levels of profitability over time. Market orientation involves: "Organization-wide generation of market intelligence, dissemination of the intelligence across departments and organization-wide responsiveness to it" (Kohli & Jaworski, 1990).

The failure of established firms to overcome inertia when challenged by discontinuous technological change has long been an area of interest. A major reason for this is that established firm failure is so prevalent. It is also intriguing that these failures take place so regularly when managers are aware of change that will affect their organizations (Eggers & Park, 2018; Johnson, 1988). Through seeking to understand how the innovation process functions in different environments, considering the position of established firms and disruptive organizations, the author acknowledges that managing the innovation process touches all aspects of the organization, and the networks that they operate within.

Defining innovation

There are many definitions of innovation, but all emphasise the need to complete the development and exploitation of new ideas, converting new knowledge into benefits for stakeholders. A regular challenge in researching, discussing and carrying out innovation is the confusion between innovation and invention. Innovation comes from the Latin – innovare – meaning "to make something new."

Drucker helps us with defining innovation, observing that: "Innovation is the specific tool of entrepreneurs, the means by which they exploit change as an opportunity for a different business or service. It is capable of being presented as a discipline, capable of being learned, capable of being practiced" (Drucker, 1985, p. 19). However, the emphasis on entrepreneurship, which is conducted in many different ways by challenger companies, established firms and networks, limits the utility of this definition.

Porter emphasised the importance of newness, writing: "Companies achieve competitive advantage through acts of innovation. They approach innovation in its broadest sense, including both new technologies and new ways of doing things" (Porter, 1990). In the current, highly networked business environment, the emphasis on companies is a limitation of this definition, as is the focus on competitive advantage, which is becoming increasingly short lived, as companies and products sustain themselves for progressively shorter periods.

Recognizing that innovation is best managed within an overall process, the definition of innovation guiding the book is pragmatic, and focuses on the utility of innovation:

"Innovation is the successful exploitation of new ideas"
     Innovation Unit, UK Department of Trade and Industry (2004)

Innovation and the product development funnel

The product development funnel concept is based on the understanding that most products are developed following a logical and standard sequence, with activities, tasks and routines that are consistent across development projects across different sectors and product types.

At defined stages, projects are either supported for further development, or cancelled, narrowing down the number of projects over time. Starting from a broad set of possibilities, organizations end up with a small set of implementations. The development funnel emerged from earlier phased NPD approaches, such as the high profile "Phased project planning" approach deployed by NASA in the 1960s, which led to project scrutiny through the defined "gates" that projects needed to pass through to progress to the next stage of development. The stage-gate process popularised by Cooper (1985, 2011) is one of the most widely adopted product development funnels.

This book adopts a model of innovation as: "The process of converting ideas into a state of reality and then capturing value from them" (Tidd & Bessant, 2018 p. 16). The innovation process can be seen as having four main phases, each of which must deal with particular challenges.

The first phase involves the search for new ideas. The ideas can come from new technologies, societal change, government standards, competitors, R&D, culture – to identify just a few sources. However, the challenge for both incumbent firms – those already established well in a market, and new organizations wanting to grow, is how to organize a search process that delivers an ongoing stream of opportunities, giving organizations improved chances of both continuing to deliver value to stakeholders, and growing new and previously unmet market opportunities.

The second phase is about selecting the ideas from the options generated that offer the greatest opportunities of success. The selection process demands that organizations make strategic choices about where to focus their activities. Factors that directly influence selection include the development of a differentiated value proposition, and how organizations can build on existing capabilities.

The third phase is concerned with implementation, and allocating resources and energy to turn ideas into reality. Implementation involves managing an increasing commitment of resources – time, money, emotion and knowledge of different types to a project, while the outcomes are uncertain. Organizations are betting that they can make the idea work for stakeholders inside and outside the firm, that they can manage the project(s) to plan, and that the returns will be greater than the resources put into it.

The fourth phase is all about capturing value from the innovation project(s). How can organizations ensure that all the work and effort has been justified, either in financial terms or in the creation of social value. How can the organization make sure that competitors do not just adopt the idea, and make it work for them?

The organization will consider what it has learned from the innovation initiative, and how it can deploy the learning in the future to best effect.

The approaches that organizations take to innovation vary significantly. However, the product development funnel process described above operates widely. Firms like Procter and Gamble seek to pick up signals about potential needs and technical options, develop a strategic concept, finalise a range of products, and then seek to capture the value from all this work through an integrated and high impact launch process. Sustaining innovation is typically driven forwards by established firms, and involves changing internal processes, following the same basic process, triggered by perceiving and validating needs through signals that identify both the need for change, and the options for change. The majority of product centred innovation involves relatively incremental changes to existing products, or new variants that exploit established knowledge sets.

The innovation paradigm includes products and services, an organization's supply chain, public service delivery such as the NHS in the UK through over a million staff, small/medium sized enterprises (SMEs) and large companies with formal R&D operations, organizational and market ecosystems. The paradigm has been extended by the digital revolution, which transforms products into interactive offerings (music, written media, film and entertainment) and how people communicate (digital social media, e-mail, voice and face to face communication services e.g. Zoom).

The degree of innovation being contemplated affects how the innovation process works, as does the size of firm, sector or wider technological or societal context. A significant and influential number of researchers have emphasised the need to take the degree of novelty in an innovation into account. The approach to managing the incremental improvements vital to sustaining innovation differs from the management of radical projects that demand cross-functional collaboration both within the firm, and across a company's ecosystem. Organizations often need to develop different routines and organizational structures to manage innovation as they encounter discontinuous conditions, when the "rules of the game" change. When a disrupting sector is shouting "do different things" to organizations due to major technological, user, social and political shifts – as was the case in STM publishing markets – then organizations may have to search for trigger signals and pervasive opportunities in less defined and unfamiliar places. Firms seek to be vigilant and identify the weak signals early enough for them to move in to areas of high opportunity (Day & Schoemaker, 2006, 2019).

Search

Organizational processes and capabilities are needed to be effective at searching for innovation opportunities. The study draws on general models of information processing and organizational learning, but has a particular focus on the unclear and uncertain signals that come from adjacent markets and the periphery of a business (Haas & Ham, 2015; Ocasio, 2011; Schoemaker & Day, 2009), and compares the processes and capabilities needed by established businesses to search peripheral, adjacent and focal areas of activity. The era of digital turbulence changes the search process. The amount of information to be considered during the search process has exploded due to digitalization, and the process of turning information into insight that informs decision making has become far more complex.

The search phase within the innovation process sees organizations scanning their environment, internally and externally, and trying to make sense of the relevant signals about opportunities, threats and competitive activity. Triggering the innovation process is about much more than occasional moments of inspiration. Knowledge push, needs pull, needs from the "bottom of the pyramid" (Prahalad, 2004b), lead users (von Hippel, 2005), ethnography (Cayla & Arnould, 2013), the observation of users in digital environments known as netnography (Kozinets, 2002, 2015), learning from big data (Brynjolfsson, Hitt, & Kim, 2011), design thinking (Kelley, 2001), seeking to do more with less (Radjou & Prabhu, 2015), mistakes and intelligent failure (McGrath, 2011; Schoemaker, 2011) and many other activities can be deployed to search for opportunities for innovation. Ideas are not in short supply. Most of these sources of innovation reflect both push and pull elements, and there are risks in focusing overly on either push or pull drivers of innovation.

The challenge for organizations is that the search space is multi-dimensional, expanding fast, and unfamiliar – even in the core business. An important contribution of Henderson and Clark (1990) was their finding that search activities were not just about searching close to, or at a distance from core knowledge concepts, but also involve searching across configurations and presenting the "component/architecture challenge". They argued that innovation is more often about developing and managing a bundle of knowledge which needs to be turned into a configuration to deliver a product or service, and that innovation is rarely about a single technology or market. Effective innovation management requires firms to source and deploy knowledge about components, and to be adept at connecting up the components to deliver value. Their work brought consideration of the architecture of innovation to the fore, and this concept has been further developed to reflect the importance of networks and changing technology (Kapoor & Adner, 2011). The problem solving approach of the firm influences their innovation management, and affects whether organizations are bounded by firm and industry norms, or manipulate both components and architecture (Hargadon, 2002; Nickerson & Zenger, 2004).

There are dangers in not listening to market needs. Counter intuitively, there are also dangers in listening to markets and customers too closely and limiting the quest for new product opportunities to better solutions for existing problems (Verganti, 2016). How companies search for options matters – summed up by Henry Ford, who is alleged to have said: "If I had asked the market they would have said that they wanted faster horses!" Christensen's research has demonstrated the dangers of relying on customers for innovation signals to great effect (Christensen, McDonald, Altman, & Palmer, 2018). Market research tends to explore versions of products that already exist, rather than helping people to respond to concepts beyond their existing experience (Lafley & Martin, 2013). Ethnography has come to the fore as a powerful input to the market research process, and Cooper and Edgett (2008) have identified that ethnography is more effective in the "ideation" phase than customer visit teams, focus groups or other market research techniques.

A key dimension that influences the search for triggers is the Abernathy and Utterback model of the innovation life cycle, which sees innovation at the early fluid stage concerned with significant experimentation and the focus being on the product and the creation of a radical new offering (Utterback & Abernathy, 1975). As a dominant design becomes established, attention moves to more gradual developments around the core trajectory, with the development of the touch screen smart phones since the launch of the iPhone in 2007 showing how quickly an offering can shift from a radical to sustaining innovation. With the maturation of an industry, innovation focus moves to process and service centred innovation to deliver a competitive value proposition focused on characteristics like quality, cost and connectivity.

In addition to choices between exploit and explore search activities, businesses need to decide where to search. Christensen identified that organizations often conduct "explore" search activities, but in areas which reinforce the boundaries between their focal markets and new innovation spaces. He found that high rates of R&D investment pushed technological frontiers further in existing product categories, resulting in "technology overshoot" that did not help the companies to compete in emerging markets (Christensen, 1997; Christensen et al., 2018).

Outside a focal market other groups of potential users often exist, with different needs – typically for simpler and cheaper products – which help users to get something done (Christensen, 1997). While the popular view is that startups typically identify and exploit new opportunities, this is far from the truth, with established firms increasingly adept at moving into new arenas (Tellis, 2013). The pattern is of disruption, and the rules of the game constantly changing in a market, with new market segments frequently being created, with winners and losers along the way. Disruptive innovation examples of the kind identified by Christensen demonstrate the requirement for organizations to identify needs which are not being met, are being partially met, or where there might be technology overshoot creating opportunities for simpler and cheaper products (Christensen, Hall, Dillon, & Duncan, 2016; Ulwick, 2005). All or any of these needs could be the trigger for innovation, and they often initiate disruption because existing organizations do not see the different or new patterns of needs. This thinking underpins the concept of "Blue Ocean Strategy" (Kim & Mauborgne, 2005), which argues that companies should define and explore uncontested market spaces through identifying latent needs that are not well satisfied. It is in these area that fast growth and healthier margins are in prospect.

The innovation search literature recognizes that the breadth of external search supports the identification of new ideas (Baumann & Schmidt, 2019; Jeppesen & Lakhani, 2010; Laursen & Salter, 2006; Leiponen & Helfat, 2011; March, 1991; von Hippel, 1988). The "variance hypothesis" suggests that access to a wide range of information provides the "requisite variety" of knowledge required to develop innovations (Owen-Smith & Powell, 2004; Powell, Koput, & Smith-Doerr, 1996). Innovation activities are risky and uncertain, and a wider external search increases the likelihood of overall NPD success (Leiponen & Helfat, 2011). Firms typically take a distributed approach, allocating resources to explore a range of domains (Dahlander, Mahony, & Gann, 2014).

Searching for new ideas is carried out by individuals, as organizations cannot "search," even though the firm's leadership and strategic plans will typically set the objectives of search activity (Li, Maggitti, Smith, Tesluk, & Katila, 2013). The actual process of a successful search depends: "On the individuals who stand at the interface of . . . .the firm and the external environment" (Cohen & Levinthal, 1990, p. 132). Despite the search for new opportunities being an established activity, the search processes of individuals are not well understood (Gruber, Harhoff, & Hoisl, 2013; Maggitti, Smith, & Katila, 2013). Boundary spanners play a critical role in building the credibility and social capital to make the necessary linkages between internal capabilities and external networks. This linking process plays a key role, underpinning the effectiveness of the external knowledge generation process, with further research in the area much anticipated (Monteiro & Birkinshaw, 2016).

Innovations created by a firm are, in essence, a result of the organization's capability to create value from knowledge. From a resource based view (RBV) perspective, mergers and acquisitions (M&A) can be seen as a means to bring new resources and capabilities into an organization to enhance innovation (Ahuja & Novelli, 2014). Acquisitions are a process through which routines or uncodifiable knowledge can be brought in to the acquiring firm, providing an alternative to the internal development of resources, with the potential to shorten development time. Acquisitions have the advantage of potentially giving a firm rapid access to resources in comparison to other approaches to inter-organizational knowledge sourcing relationships (Hagedoorn, 2002; King, Slotegraaf, & Kesner, 2008).

The book investigates innovation search considering offering development specifically, in the context of both exploit (do better) and explore (do different) innovation. M&A represents an option within the search toolset.

Select

Organizations encounter triggers for innovation internally and externally, in their core business, adjacent markets and in areas that often seem peripheral to their focal activities. However large or profitable, they never have the resources to explore all of them. The options they consider, particularly in the early stages of the innovation process, are rarely well defined, or easy to compare. Innovation concerns opportunities to do something new. The process always involves uncertainty, and the further an organization moves from the focal business, the more it feels like driving through fog. The only way to increase certainty about an opportunity is to get a project started, and learn through exploring and refining the product or service idea while considering costs, market size, technology and wider organizational capabilities.

Stage-gate approaches support the process of limiting uncertainty and moving to informed risk-management. At the end of each phase, projects are reviewed and need to pass specified criteria, before they can be progressed to the next stage. The reviews typically involve formalised project evaluation meetings, and consider market and customer feedback, strategic fit, technical feasibility, resource availability and potentially much wider considerations. The stage-gate process is better suited to low-uncertainty, incremental innovation projects in core markets, rather than high-uncertainty projects where flexible learning is required.

The effectiveness of the implementation of stage-gate processes varies, as does the overall operationalization of innovation processes and "best practice." There is a danger that a "one-size-fits-all" or "traditional" approach is taken when considering innovation and offering development stage-gate processes, with challenge coming particularly from the project management field. Shenhar (2001) argued that multiple project management approaches should be deployed when managing traditional stage-gate NPD processes, with multiple types of innovation processes and associated contingencies also found to be successful. A wide range of assessment criteria can be used to review and select projects.

When the innovation approach is focused on exploitation, organizations like Toyota practice high involvement innovation, with improvement programmes based on staff and supplier generated ideas, with considerable supporting information often building impressive results over time. The further the distance from well understood focal markets, the greater the degree of technological and market uncertainty, which in turn increases levels of innovation project failure. The increased involvement of external players using open innovation techniques on incremental innovation initiatives, particularly with service products, is making incremental innovation more dynamic and complex.

Offering development projects beyond core environments are characterized as having significant novelty, complexity and dynamism. These factors combine to make the development of new products inherently high risk, and the capabilities required to manage risk are essential to successful innovation management. Project teams develop persuasive business cases to support rigorous decision making, using tools such as simulation and prototyping. The range of tools available to generate and evaluate ideas both inside and outside the organization continues to develop (Coyne, Clifford, & Dye, 2007; Dodgson, Gann, & Salter, 2005; Heising, 2012). Certain approaches enable an extended "play" step, postponing innovation selection as late in the process as possible to increase knowledge – and decrease uncertainty – as much as possible (Dodgson & Gann, 2014).

The tools and routines to support decision making advance in step with technology and networked product development, but selection and ongoing support (or "kill" decisions) regarding innovation opportunities continue to be subjective, political, and influenced by the cognitive frames of key players (Block & Keller, 2009; Eisenhardt & Bourgeois, 1988; Killen & Hunt, 2013; Ocasio, 1997; Van de Ven et al., 1999).

Innovation portfolio management

An article by Nagji and Tuff (2012) from Deloitte has particularly influenced both the book and research project. They considered what a well-balanced innovation portfolio should look like, proposing that than an innovation portfolio can be characterized by what they described as an "Innovation ambition matrix." They also suggested that a balanced innovation portfolio for a firm could be seen as having a "Golden ratio." The driving force behind their thinking is that established firms need to work out how to operate in a structured manner to develop a portfolio offering considering core, adjacent and transformational (breakthrough) markets. They proposed that there are three levels of ambition for innovation:

Core

The existing offering designed to serve current customers. The assets used currently in the core can be extended to other customers with similar needs who have been just beyond the firm's focus up until now. This is what most effective businesses are able to do month in, month out, as this is how they generate reliable turnover and profits

Adjacent

Firms can expand from a position of strength, both through leveraging customer relationships to offer a different value proposition to them, or by leveraging core capabilities and assets to stretch into adjacent customer groups – with firms sometimes doing both at the same time

Transformational (or breakthrough)

Through the development of new assets and capital, firms should strive to discover new market needs before customers even know that they have them – developing "new to the world" offerings

This structured approach builds on the classic work of the mathematician Igor Ansoff, who developed a matrix to help firms to allocate resources between growth initiatives. His matrix pushed companies to change their tactics depending on whether an organization is launching a new product, targeting a new market, or both. Nagji and Tuff's matrix modifies Ansoff's binary choices of product and market (new vs. old) to consider a range of values, balancing the novelty of the offering (on the X axis) with the novelty of its customer markets (on the Y axis).

Figure 2.1 is a helpful, but not particularly surprising representation of how firms might consider where to place their innovation bets. Where Nagji and Tuff really help those looking for ways to improve innovation management is that they researched into where companies across the consumer, industrial and technology sectors allocated their innovation focused resources. They found that most established firms, even the most financially aware, did not have a sure grip on where they spend their innovation resources, as they do not have the systems in place to recognize how they spend money and allocate staff across Core/Adjacent/ Transformational activities. All the companies involved Nagji and Tuff's research vastly overestimated how much they were innovating beyond the core, with more than 90%, and usually more than 95%, of innovation funding focused on

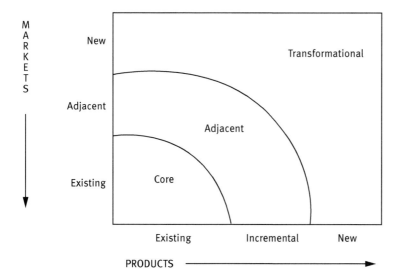

Figure 2.1: Mapping core, adjacent and new opportunities (after Nagji and Tuff).

existing markets and customers. Unsurprisingly they found that the allocation of innovation resources was different across different industries and geographies. For example, technology companies allocated fewer resources to enhancing core offerings, and spent more on pursuing the next technology hit.

We know that organizations and individuals are highly influenced by incentives, but it is often difficult to articulate clearly what the rewards from innovation are. Nagji and Tuff looked to see if there were any patterns contrasting where innovation resources are allocated, and the return that organizations get from their innovation activities in terms of share price. They found that firms that balanced their innovation activity performed better. Organizations that carried out 70% of innovation activity in the core, 20% in adjacent areas and 10% in transformational spaces outperformed their competitors. They also found that core market innovation activities typically deliver 10% of the long, cumulative returns on innovation spend. Initiatives focused on adjacent opportunities delivered 20% of innovation investment return, while transformational projects provided 70% of the benefits from innovation investment.

The "golden ratio" in terms of the return on investment in innovation is therefore highly skewed in terms of increasing focus on both adjacent and breakthrough opportunities. In fact, the returns are the inverse of how innovation resources are allocated. This is consistent with 70/20/10 principle in place for many years at Google, encouraging all staff to spend 70% of their time on their core role, 20% as a member of another team, and 10% on blue sky projects. Nagji and Tuff's findings are supported by Innosight's 2019 report on the "Transformation 20," which saw the best performing firms adapting the core through using digital technologies to create new types of digital experiences and offerings that create new value for customers, as well as pursuing growth beyond the core in adjacent and breakthrough arenas. The winners are deploying new business models that rely on the cloud, IoT, AI and other technologies.

Growth beyond the core sees firms creating a higher-purpose mission that takes them into new territory such as sustainable business. To grow in new areas firms must not be afraid to let go of the past, but exploit core capabilities to enter new growth markets. They seize digital opportunities through new platforms and business models, and operate in a way that ensures that innovation is not isolated in a department or division, but becomes a strategic capability across the whole organization – including core, adjacent and breakthrough activities.

Disrupted and disrupting environments

The Shorter Oxford English Dictionary defines "disrupt" as: "To interrupt the normal continuity of (an activity); throw into disorder." The management literature has focused extensively on disruptive innovation (Bower & Christensen, 1995; Christensen et al., 2018; Gans, 2016), and disrupted environments (Markides & Oyon, 2010; Sood & Tellis, 2011). Consideration of disrupting environments, i.e. markets, processes and the jobs-to-be-done that are in the process of being disrupted, is now securing increased attention. Disrupting environments provide dynamic conditions for established firms and challengers to identify, evaluate and pursue opportunities. Operating in disrupting environments is challenging, requiring companies to deal with uncertainty, complexity, resource allocation and uncertain cognitive frames.

The title of "The Upside of Turbulence" (Sull, 2009) challenges established firms who run their organizations in an incremental "exploit" manner, identifying three factors that drive turbulence and affect strategy decisions, all of which have increased in recent decades:

1. **Dynamism:** The frequency and magnitude of change influence a firm's ability to create value. The psychological effect of changes can magnify their influence, e.g. 9/11, the financial crisis of 2007/2008, and the coronavirus pandemic of 2020
2. **Complexity:** The number of forces that influence value creation, and the level of interaction between them, is increasing. With more interconnectedness, there is greater exposure to unanticipated changes from multiple directions. Technology also diffuses faster across multiple sectors
3. **Competition:** Extends beyond product markets to include clashes over scarce resources e.g. capital, distribution partners, & talented employees

Sull considers that the distribution of opportunities and threats across markets and industries follows an "inverse power law", where "golden opportunities" caused by turbulence typically occur once or twice a decade for most companies, and often in downturns. The pattern is common across a wide range of complex systems. He also saw that the constant exploitation of small opportunities provides the organizational wherewithal to seize "golden opportunities" – where timing is essential, and opportunities usually come about through external forces.

The business environment is fast changing and uncertain because of economic interconnectedness, globalization, and rapid technological change. The diversity and range of business environments has increased. Large firms are especially under pressure, as they stretch across a growing set of environments that are changing rapidly over time. All of this requires: "Businesses not only to choose the right approach to strategy or even the right combination of approaches, but also to adjust the mix as environments shift. One (strategy) size does not fit all" (Reeves, Haanæs, & Sinha, 2015, p. 2).

The end of sustainable competitive advantage

The cycles within which organizations identify, develop, exploit and retreat from markets are shortening, so they need to innovate more quickly, reliably, and efficiently, through exploitation activities in focal markets which continue to offer strong returns, and exploration beyond core environments.

Strategy researchers have been challenged by McGrath, who argues: "Virtually all strategy frameworks and tools in use today are based on a single dominant idea: that the purpose of strategy is to achieve a sustainable competitive advantage. This idea is strategy's most fundamental concept. It's every company's Holy Grail. And it is no longer relevant to more and more companies" (McGrath, 2013a, p. xi). This is in contrast to previously accepted strategy objectives, where researchers sought to understand how a firm can create: "Enduring firm differences in above-normal returns" (Oliver, 1997, p. 697).

McGrath argues that for organizations and their leaders to be successful in volatile and uncertain markets, they need to develop transient competitive advantage, so that they can take advantage of short-lived opportunities rapidly and decisively (McGrath, 2013a). With the main objective of strategy under attack, the structures, routines and processes that leaders depend upon to secure maximum value from competitive advantage become liabilities in fast-moving competitive environments. The experience of RIM (Blackberry), Nokia, Xerox et al., and their failure to build their next wave of competitive advantage, are good examples of how quickly dominant positions and strong profitability can erode (Binns, Harreld, O'Reilly, & Tushman, 2014).

Much of the limitations of earlier work in the strategy discipline go back to the roots of Michael Porter and others in industrial organization economics, with firm performance largely predicated on the structure of the underlying markets where firms compete, and the different positions that firms take in these markets. A central assumption was that, as Porter observed, the structure of an industry demonstrated relatively stable technical and economic dimensions, enabling researchers to analyse performance over extended periods of time (Porter, 1981).

Scholars adopting the Resource Based View concentrated far more on issues within firms, rather than what was going on in the environment surrounding them. Associated research streams considering capabilities within the firm have included organizational learning (Cohen & Levinthal, 1990); organizational evolution and adaptation (Adner & Levinthal, 2004); the management of knowledge (Helfat & Raubitschek, 2000); path dependent development of assets (Dierickx & Cool, 1989); and organizational structure (Robins & Wiersema, 1995). These scholars saw processes and internal structures as being key influences on performance.

The 1990s saw a mounting challenge to the idea of sustainable competitive advantage (D'Aveni & Gunther, 1994), initiating a flow of research questioning the dominant logic of sustainable competitive advantage. The emphasis was that markets exist where hypercompetition is the norm, rather than competitive equilibrium (Gimeno & Woo, 1996; Ilinitch, D'Aveni, & Lewin, 1996). Going back to the roots of the study of innovation in the modern era, the assumption made by these researchers is that all positions of advantage are temporary, as they will inevitably be swept away by "waves of competitive destruction" (Schumpeter, 1942).

The RBV and economic views of strategy both adopt certain assumptions. Firstly, that industries have distinct boundaries, change slowly, and are relatively stable.

Secondly, they both assume that the most important competitor for any company comes from other organizations within the same industry, from organizations offering similar products. The third assumption is that resources (with some exceptions) are properties of firms and are linked to them.

This book argues that these assumptions do not reflect the intense and rapidly changing contexts within which a company's competitive advantage, business model or profitability requirements are challenged more rapidly and regularly, and from different angles than before. Factors including globalization and the digital revolution are reducing entry barriers, empowering new competitors, rapidly changing the balance of power in technology, and creating an era of hypercompetition for firms in an increasing number of markets.

The coronavirus pandemic upended markets, health systems and communication norms, triggering a major rethink across startups, scaleups and established firms.

McGrath's conception of transient rather than sustainable competitive advantage pushes firms to develop a methodology considering where to compete, how to compete and how to make profits, when competitive advantages are temporary. She also considers how to move from one wave of competitive advantage to another (McGrath, 2013a). While there are many markets where sustainable advantage can be secured over long periods, where taking advantage of deep customer relationships and insights in core markets continues to pay dividends, or major ecosystems with focal firms persist, the argument is that an increasing number of existing and developing sectors, served by companies large and small, do not operate or prepare for future growth in stable markets with clear boundaries. Music, entertainment, clothes retailing, mobile phones, mobile payments and education are some of the markets where advantage can be copied quickly, and dominant technology platforms shift.

As will be seen when we consider cognition, the presumption of stability lets inertia into an organization, and organizational power structures are built up around existing business models and leadership attention. The assumption of little change in the future activities of people and organizations is undermined by research the Oxford Martin School (Frey & Osborne, 2013) considering the future of employment. They propose that technology will increasingly replace non-routine tasks such as statistical analysis replacing cancer diagnostics, prefabricated construction replacing typically dexterous building work, and driverless taxis replacing the mini-cab driver. Machines are powerful, intelligent, and they affect what people do, changing the products and services that consumed in both business to consumer (B2C) and business to business (B2B) markets.

Segmentation will move from demographics and product characteristics to "jobs-to-be-done" in an increasingly service dominated economy. New categories will emerge, which McGrath prefers to see as arenas: "Characterized by particular connections between customers and solutions, not by the conventional description of offerings that are near substitutes for one another" (McGrath, 2013a, p. 9). The scope of the arenas: "Will in all likelihood be the outcomes that particular customers seek ("jobs-to-be-done") and the alternative ways those outcomes might be met. This is vital, because the most substantial threats to a given advantage are likely to arise from a peripheral or nonobvious location" (McGrath, 2013a, p. 10).

MacMillan saw transient advantage "waves" (1988). With competitive advantage being transient, the different phases need to be managed (McGrath, 2013b), with different skills needed at different stages of the process. A major challenge for many firms, particularly SMEs, is that moving resources from a successful activity generating good returns in exploitation mode to unproven innovative opportunities is difficult in power terms, politically, for the organizations and individuals involved. Very few companies have worked out how to do this on an enduring basis.

When firms accept the arguments supporting the concept of transient advantage, in disrupting environments at times of hypercompetition, the management of the innovation process becomes even more critical to an organization. The implications of transient advantage are that:

1. The development of advantage in firm, product and geographic arenas will happen in waves over shorter time periods than before
2. The ability to pick up on early warnings, and to get the organization to be vigilant to developments within the ecosystem and beyond will become more important, and will need to happen more regularly – as the advantage lasts for less time
3. Strategy management in the transient context increases the importance and value of acquiring uncomfortable, disconfirming information both at the firm and individual level. This is in contrast to the confirmation bias typically found in "exploit" companies.
4. The people who often see changes coming (technologists, scientists, pattern recognizers) are not the members of the board, who have the ultimate responsibility for making decisions about an increasingly changing and uncertain world
5. Diversity is becoming more critical. Homogeneous teams with limited cognitive bandwidth will be increasingly flat-footed
6. Business strategies will need to be precise, with the driver of categorization being the outcomes that customers seek – "jobs-to-be-done", developing different ways to deliver these outcomes
7. Most significant threats to a prevailing advantage are likely to come from peripheral or nonobvious locations

Hypercompetition and the existence of disrupting markets undermine the traditional concept of sustainable competitive advantage and industry level analysis. The study of innovation must consider how organizations develop sustainable advantage where it is achievable, and transient advantage where they see profitable opportunities within a more limited timeframe. The pursuit of transient advantage demands detailed research at the firm and offering level.

Strategy development and implementation in complex environments

Reflections inspired by Clausewitz in military contexts persuasively pinpoint how strategy is enacted in the moment, and it is relevant to consider how strategy development, decision making and execution take place in increasingly service orientated, chaotic, global, culturally diverse and complex environments. Eisenhardt and latterly Sull have particularly driven forward research in the strategy area considering volatile and complex environments, and how best to deal with them (Sull & Eisenhardt, 2015). Brown & Eisenhardt (1998) identified that successful firms in competitive markets have fast and high quality strategic decision making processes, with Shona Brown deploying her learning from her PhD at Stanford through a 10 year career at Google where she was responsible for building both the People Operations and Business Operations groups. They found that:

1. Leadership teams build collective intuition
2. Conflict is stimulated by assembling diverse teams who are challenged through frame-breaking exercises
3. Effective decision makers focus on maintaining decision momentum, with strategic decisions taking two – four months. If it takes longer, the decision is too big, or the group are procrastinating
4. Politicking is seen negatively, particularly because it includes withholding information

Subsequent research has emphasised the importance of heuristics to strategy development, supported by effective routines (Bingham & Eisenhardt, 2011). Heuristics support problem-solving or self-discovery through using practical - simplifying - methods that are not guaranteed to be optimal or rational. They can be mental shortcuts that ease the cognitive load of making a decision and implementation needs both structure and heuristics. Established firms typically have too much decision making structure, as they tend to focus on efficiency. However, without sufficient structure, it is impossible to improvise effectively and so to capture opportunities. The challenge can be framed as being the trade-off between: "The flexible capture of widely varying opportunities vs. efficient execution of specific opportunities. Less structure opens up the organization to the possibility of addressing a wider range of opportunities that serendipitously occur, but it also hinders the rapid, mistake-free execution of those opportunities."

"Conversely, more structure enables the efficient execution of particular opportunities that can be anticipated. But too much structure is more than just too rigid. It also narrows the range of possible opportunities, suggesting that structure is most valuable" (Davis et al., 2009, p. 439). This viewpoint is key to the book, as core, adjacent and breakthrough environments are all often unpredictable at the same time. As executives plan and execute diversification into unpredictable environments, issues of how best to structure organizations and decision making in the core, and beyond the core operations are often major challenges for established organizations.

Davis et al. (2009) recommended reducing structure in the core, and adding structure in entrepreneurial environments. The second, subtler challenge is the need for a dramatically altered mindset. This mindset entails vigilantly managing the amount of structure (not just its content), improvising to capture fresh opportunities, and quickly rebounding from mistakes at the edge of chaos, where firms can at best capture only a few opportunities and gain an unstable or dissipative equilibrium. Simply put, managing in unpredictable environments is different, harder, and more precarious than in predictable environments. Overall, the irony of adaptation is that, as it becomes more crucial for organizations to adapt, it also becomes more challenging to do so, due to rigidity in resource allocation and inertia within organizational routines.

Decision making is a high impact activity within modern firms. Established organizations often find that the structure built up to manage their "exploit" operations mitigates against seeing and responding to innovation triggers from the periphery, just as the cognitive frames and attention of established firms are generally focused on "do better" rather than "do different" opportunities.

Sull has argued that to sustain corporate renewal, organizations must develop the habit of successfully both identifying and exploiting small opportunities, so that they have the organizational capability to identify and respond to the "golden opportunities" when they arise (Sull, 2009, p. 32–35). Organizations need to seek information so that they can develop mental maps, as people and organizations cannot: "Seize the upside of turbulence by ignoring the provisional nature of knowledge. All mental maps are static representations of a shifting situation, simplifications of a complex world made without the benefit of knowledge that will only emerge in the future. They remain always and everywhere provisional, subject to revision or rejection in light of new information" (Sull, 2009, p. 65–66).

Sull and Eisenhardt emphasise that strategic decision making does not need to be time consuming and complex, but effective, and promote the use of simple rules that evolve with the experience of the company. To support decision making using simple rules, the provision of too much information actually slows down decision making, as individuals feel overwhelmed by the choices that they face. Industry clock speed influences how companies are developing and exploiting transient advantage. In high clock speed industries such as the modern entertainment arena, both small and "golden" opportunities may fleetingly become opportunities to be evaluated, be grabbed by rivals, or be eclipsed by running the core business or other new opportunities.

Therefore, to support "simple rules" decision making, established firms face a challenge as to how to move the attention of the strategy decision-makers to the issues that are critical to support both incremental (relatively easy) and radical (very hard and organizationally indigestible) decisions. The level of complexity is also increasing, as the development of strategy management and innovation in the knowledge era is increasingly shaped by the value of collaboration and networks. Strategy development and implementation has become more complex, the level of (hyper) competition is intensifying, and the need for a company's innovation process to deliver winning value propositions that give them transient competitive advantage has never been greater.

Challenges in responding to disrupted and disrupting environments

Within the extensive strategy literature, significant research has taken place to understand differences in how organizations respond to change, and the explanations are often based on differences in either incentives or capabilities. Economists have argued that the degree of response to change, e.g. technology, can be explained as rational responses to differential incentives. RBV researchers (Barney, 1991) argue that companies often find it difficult to respond to change because of the path dependence connected with initial endowments, or firms possess dynamic, managerial capabilities that allow resources to be reconfigured. The development of a firm's dominant logic also informs how narrowly established firms can travel looking for new innovation opportunities. Studies on the temporal management of innovation also reflect deep organizational habits in terms of how much innovation an organization performs over time (Kaplan & Orlikowski, 2013; Turner et al., 2012), and how difficult it is for organizations to change the rhythm of their innovation activities.

A qualitative study of Polaroid's failure to move from analogue to digital imaging technologies highlighted the paradox of the firm's early development of technical capabilities but subsequent failure to be competitive in the digital camera market (Tripsas & Gavetti, 2000). Their contribution demonstrated that the presence or absence of capabilities was not a satisfactory explanation of organizational inertia, and that cognition was a major contributor to outcomes. They amplified the findings of an earlier, product development orientated study (Dougherty, 1992), which showed that the "thought worlds" of departments, and organizational product routines interact to limit the acquisition of new technology and market insights.

The attention-based view of the firm (Ocasio, 1997, 2011; Ocasio, Laamanen, & Vaara, 2018) argues that one group of the contextual factors influencing the allocation of attention in a firm are the "rules of the game", the routines and incentive systems that structure the process and lenses through which interpretations are made. Christensen (1997) identified the influence on attention of sales and marketing incentives to focus on immediate opportunities. Routines can be seen to respond to both cognitive and motivational elements. They embed in the organization both an understanding of how things should be done, and what gets rewarded.

Kaplan and Henderson (2005) considered the concepts of incentives and cognition together and: "Suggest that incentives and cognition coevolve so that organizational competencies or routines are as much about building knowledge of "what should be rewarded" as they are about "what should be done"". Due to the strong influence of routines on individual and organizational behaviour, both incentives and cognition can reinforce "attention traps."

Laamanen and Wallin (2009) built on these foundations, to show how capability development trajectories aligned with the cognitive paths of managers. They found that where there are shifts in how managers thought about the business, they were able to build the required capabilities. In fact, it was the ability of managers to select which capability bottleneck to focus on which made adaptation to changing conditions possible. This connects back to Herbert Simon's observation in 1947 that: "Organizations and institutions provide the general stimuli and attention-directors that channelize the behaviors of the members of the group, and that provide the members with the intermediate objectives that stimulate action" (Simon, 1947, 100–101).

Fast Second: How do established firms successfully commercialise radical innovation opportunities?

Markides & Geroski, (2004, p. 26) challenge companies to answer the question: "Where do radical new markets come from, what are their structural characteristics, and what skills are needed to create and compete effectively in them?" The full extent of what established firms need to change to become effective pioneers is so significant that they developed the notion of "Fast Second" after considering the long debated themes of first mover advantage, and the position of second movers.

The "Fast Second" thesis is based upon innovation research findings that show:

- Radical innovations creating new-to-the-world markets disrupt users, customers and producers
- Radical innovations are not driven by demand or immediate customer needs, but come from a supply-push process
- Radical innovations usually lack champions, as there is no other market leader, and there are no lead users
- Supply-push innovations are typically developed haphazardly, without a clear customer need, involve multiple research projects and actors, and require a long gestation process when little seems to be happening
- Radical innovations need to create user groups and niches on the periphery of established markets – and these niches initially appear unattractive to established firms, as they are too small, and disrupt the dominant logic of the firm

However, research shows that since the second world war large firms and established firms have introduced the majority of radical product innovations (Chandy &

Tellis, 2000; Tellis, 2013). How can this be the case, considering factors influencing the successful introduction of radical innovations detailed by Markides and Geroski?

The key to unlocking this mystery is through understanding the pre-diffusion literature which explains the pathways to a dominant design. Typically small, entrepreneurial driven companies and their networks (or ecosystems) engage in exploration and development work, linking up with organizations (often established firms) when a dominant design is in prospect. Established firms can be highly effective as consolidators, and at choosing the right time to move. Consolidators enter a market at the right time, segment the market, build brands, create buyer loyalty, and standardise services.

Markides and Geroski (2004, p. 30) propose that established firms: "Subcontract the creation of radical new products to the market, and for startup firms to subcontract the consolidation of these products to big established firms." For established firms to work through how they might do this, consideration of the diffusion and pre-diffusion literature is informative.

The invention of new technological principles, their application in new product categories, and the subsequent diffusion of products based on these principles generally results in an erratic process that takes decades to develop (Gopalakrishnan & Damanpour, 1997; Nieto, 2003). A wide range of companies, individuals and organizations are typically involved in the process of developing and diffusing high-tech product categories. While some of the trail-blazing companies that propel these processes forward end up being very successful, most of them fail before their products can reach a mass market.

Rogers (2003) focused on the diffusion of products, generally considering diffusion from the demand perspective and identifying patterns of adoption for what he saw as invariant product versions. In contrast, research shows that in a new industry, the focus is generally on major product innovations (Abernathy & Utterback, 1978; Utterback, 1994; Utterback & Abernathy, 1975). Later on, when a dominant product design has become widely accepted, the focus moves to process innovations that fundamentally change the production and distribution chain rather than the physical product. A dominant design, once established, is made up of a configuration of components that represents the standard in a market for an extended time, as it meets the requirements of a broad range of users.

Technological discontinuity comes in cycles (Tushman & Anderson, 1986; Murmann & Tushman, 1998), with a variation stage that emerges through a scientific advance or through a unique combination of existing technologies. The next stage, described as an era of ferment, sees parallel processes of substitution, competition and ongoing technical change. In the third stage, a dominant design is effectively selected by the market, with a dominant design emerging. Finally an era of incremental change sets in, with the dominant design remaining relatively unchanged. While Rogers' representation of the diffusion process is valid for many product categories, the position of Tushman and Utterback also applies in many contexts, particularly for complex technological products.

Different theories consider different factors and mechanisms to explain the variance in diffusion. Diffusion researchers such as Rogers (2003) typically explain the start and the speed of diffusion considering the characteristics of potential adopters and their perception of the innovation. Economists may focus more on legal and institutional characteristics. Ortt (2010) sought to unbundle the factors affecting the duration of the pre-diffusion phase, and developed a simple model of the environment within which the product is developed and adopted. He found that the most important categories of factors affecting the pre-diffusion phase in high-tech environments are:

1. The main (focal) organization(s) responsible for the development, production, supply and use of the new product
2. The technological system required to use the new high-tech product
3. The market environment, including all the other actors (than the main organizations) and factors involved (e.g. the availability of regulations and standards).

The pre-diffusion phases have significant consequences for companies working to commercialise new high-tech products:

1. The average length of pre-diffusion phases is long (about 17 years)
   Implication: Both managerial stamina and long-term financial resources are needed. High-tech product categories require tremendous investment over long periods of time. Relevant to this study, while Reed Elsevier's 2013 full year results showed that their Scientific, Technical and Medical division generated 72% of revenue from electronic services (Habgood & Engstrom, 2014), it was print based revenues that funded investment in electronic services during the mid-1990s
2. Dispersion around the average is significant (about 15 years)
   Implication: Companies can hope for shorter pre-diffusion periods, but their industry context will influence how long it takes. The more extensive the infrastructure that has to be built, the longer the adaptation phase is likely to be
3. A large number of factors can influence the length of pre-diffusion phases, with an average of seven factors decisive in each of Ortt's cases
   Implication: Managing the erratic patterns in the pre-diffusion phases, and the complex inter-actions that affect them, particularly in the adaptation phase, demands specialised innovation management skills.

The complexity of the pre-diffusion process, allied to the difficulties encountered in opportunity recognition and opportunity evaluation, confirms that established firms contemplating radical innovation have difficult decisions to make about the relationship between structure, performance and the business ecosystem. Entrepreneurial business approaches in smaller companies or corporate venture units can be allied to the power to consolidate opportunities possessed by established firms.

This review of the diffusion and adoption literature informs the book because offering development focused innovation search and select processes link with the wider offering development and market launch phases. The pre-diffusion stage is part of the exploration process within a business ecosystem. As the adoption of open innovation and agile MPV processes increases, search, select and the pre-diffusion stage are becoming increasingly interconnected. The pre-diffusion phase can be protracted and uncertain, and established "consolidator" organizations need to work out what mix of organizational approaches will work best to explore beyond the core.

The role of dynamic capabilities in responding to disrupting environments

The study of strategic management is primarily concerned with how companies develop and sustain competitive advantage. The RBV argues that resources which are simultaneously valuable, rare, inimitable and nonsubstitutable (VRIN) are a source of competitive advantage (Barney, 1991, 1996). Both practitioners and academics are concerned with how organizations change, sustain and develop competitive advantage, with Ambrosini and Bowman (2009) arguing that despite other fields being concerned with change-orientated themes (e.g. organizational learning, cognition), only the dynamic capability school specifically addresses how companies can change their resources persistently. While Teece and Pisano can be seen as the key early proponents of the dynamic capabilities perspective, their contributions built on Nelson and Winter's (1982) consideration of the role of routines and their influence on how companies adjust to changing environments while pursuing growth.

In the early stages of the development of the dynamic capabilities field, Teece and Pisano emphasised that strategic management is chiefly about: "Adapting, integrating and reconfiguring internal and external organizational skills, resources and functional competencies toward the changing environment" (Teece & Pisano, 1994, p. 537). The importance of changing environments, and the difficulties which organizations had in responding to them (Harreld, O'Reilly, & Tushman, 2007) influenced a change of the definition to: "The firm's ability to integrate, build, and reconfigure internal and external competences to address rapidly changing environments" (Teece, Pisano, & Shuen, 1997, p. 516). A somewhat more dramatic definition suggests that dynamic capabilities are: "The firm's processes that use resources – specifically the processes to integrate, reconfigure, gain and release resources – to match or even create market change. Dynamic capabilities thus are the organizational and strategic routines by which firms achieve new resources configurations as markets emerge, collide, split, evolve and die" (Eisenhardt & Martin, 2000, p. 1107), and this definition is particularly appropriate to the research project, seeing that the case companies operate in disrupting environments.

Teece summarises dynamic capabilities as: "A firm's dynamic capabilities rest on two pillars: (1) the vision and leadership skills of managers, and (2) the cohesion and flexibility of the organization as a whole." He continues: "One way to think about dynamic capabilities is to divide them into three groups of activities at which successful firms must excel:

- *sensing* needs, threats and opportunities in a timely fashion
- *seizing* attractive possibilities by mobilizing resources, and
- *transforming* the organization to maintain its effectiveness"

A debate exists regarding the blurry line between capabilities and dynamic capabilities. "Ordinary" capabilities enable the production and sale of an offering in a firm's core environment, enabling the supply and support of a range of software solutions. They underpin effective marketing, customer relationship management, reliable operational delivery and cost control. It is essential for firms to have access to these types of ordinary capabilities, even though they do not need to manage them in-house.

My own family connections with publishing and printing are deep, having personally worked in both the printing and publishing industries. Before this, my father worked for almost thirty years managing up to 800 internal staff as a production director at the Oxford University Press. However the production centred capabilities that he used to manage within the firm are secured in the 2020s through using external resources to print books, and manage key parts of the digital operation that are taking the place of printing and distribution. Ordinary capabilities and best practices are essential, but insufficient for success, and are increasingly outsourced. When the game changes, such as in the mobile phone industry 2007–10, while Nokia had the ordinary capabilities required for the first phase of development of the industry in abundance, having previously driven the growth of the mobile phone category, they lacked the dynamic capabilities to both look ahead (they were well informed), and respond (much harder) to a latent demand for a combined computer-touchscreen phone offering.

Contrasting with an ordinary capability, a dynamic capability enables a firm to alter how it makes its living. Dynamic capabilities enable organizations to explore and analyse their external environment, so that they can assess the long-term health of their business model and the value proposition at its centre. When change is needed, they can re-create and reconfigure internal and external competencies to respond to conditions in current and emerging markets. Dynamic capabilities control how ordinary capabilities should be altered. Schoemaker, Heaton and Teece (2018) argue that: "In short, dynamic capabilities serve as the bridge between the present and the future. Without them, an organization is stuck, and will likely be deeply disrupted by change."

Much of this chapter has centred on issues relating to strategy, and it is important to clarify the inter-relationship between strategy work, and the high impact realm of dynamic capabilities. Effective dynamic capabilities set up the organization of the skills and knowledge required to respond to near-future market opportunities, and the development of business models that explain and deliver value. Strategy work is the activity through which top management teams decide how their dynamic capabilities can best be used to beat the competition. Making decisions about segmentation, fresh dimensions of competition, eco-system partnerships, geographical priorities, pricing and critically – the development of talent – are all part of the strategy domain.

A firm's dynamic capabilities do not just reside in individual business units or disciplines, but enable organizations to sense and seize opportunities before competitors of all shapes and sizes. They underpin the growth of new businesses – sometimes cannibalizing historic revenues – and sometimes enhancing the overall business portfolio as proposed by Nagji and Tuff. Developing and deploying dynamic capabilities is hard to do, so once in place and working well they are tough to imitate. They are best seen as "signature" routines rooted in each organization's culture, history, investments, experience, stories, and problem-solving approaches (Gratton & Ghoshal, 2005).

But when dynamic capabilities don't keep up with fast moving technologies, stakeholders and ecosystems they become backward facing (non) dynamic capabilities that get in the way of sensing, seizing and transforming the organization. Dynamic capabilities enable a wide range of activities, including new offering development and its constant partner – business model innovation, along with alliance formation and M&A.

Dynamic capabilities play their role best when they are deeply infused into an organization's culture, with shared values guiding risk-taking, attitude to failure, learning, and the increasingly important work of running experiments to probe and learn (Schoemaker et al., 2018). Below the high level dynamic capabilities of sensing, seizing and transforming, firms need to focus on the sub-capabilities that they need to mobilize their intent to build new businesses, and adapt existing activities to changing circumstances. To sense effectively in often ambiguous digital environments, new research tools need to be adapted to make sense of emerging environments in the periphery of the organization's activities.

The next chapter is deeply concerned with the dynamic capabilities and sub-capabilities that need to be present in organizations to manage search and select in disrupting environments, so that they can sense needs and opportunities, seize possibilities and transform the organization to maintain and increase its effectiveness.

3 Search and select sub-capabilities that enable offering development

The book focuses on the high impact dynamic sub-capabilities that particularly influence the successful management of the search and select processes to develop new offerings in the STM publishing industry. An extensive literature review was undertaken considering 28 different areas of the innovation research literature relevant to the development of new offerings. The presence of these sub-capabilities was then explored through over 60 interviews, confirming their significance to developing new offerings. Before diving into the findings from the case companies in Chapters 4 and 5, it is helpful to establish what the dynamic sub-capabilities are that are most relevant to B2B focused publishers when it comes to searching for and selecting new offering opportunities.

Strategic clarity, through a clear and well communicated high level, portfolio driven strategic plan

"Strategy" is one of most elusive and often unhelpful management related words of our times, much like innovation, value proposition and business model. It is often used to sound important and clever. When working with managers in the innovation space, they often describe how they feel the expectation for radical innovation literally pushing down on their shoulders.

Richard Rumelt, author of "Good Strategy/Bad Strategy" (2011) helps us size up what strategy work is useful for: "Despite the roar of voices wanting to equate strategy with ambition, leadership, 'vision', planning, or the economic logic of competition, strategy is none of these. The core of strategy work is always the same: discovering the critical factors in a situation and designing a way of co-ordinating and focusing actions to deal with those factors." He continues: "A leader's most important responsibility is identifying the biggest challenges to forward progress and devising a coherent approach to overcoming them."

Strategy should be seen as a process for managing mature businesses to operational excellence in changing environments, while at the same time exploring new opportunities and markets. However, it is through the process of innovation that competitive advantage is actually developed and brought to market. "Whatever the dominant technological, social or market conditions, the key to creating – and sustaining competitive advantage is likely to lie with those organizations that continually innovate" (Tidd & Bessant, 2018 p. 12).

https://doi.org/10.1515/9783110657326-003

There are many definitions of strategy, considering political, military, business and other areas of endeavour. Freedman explains the essence of strategy as follows: "The realm of strategy is one of bargaining and persuasion as well as threats and pressure, psychological as well as physical effects, and words as well as deeds. This is why strategy is the central political art. It is about getting more out of a situation than the starting balance of power would suggest. It is the art of creating power" (Freedman, 2013, p. xii).

Strategy work enables organizations to understand and respond to market and environmental change, particularly considering how they can compete and outperform competitors large and small. A well thought through strategy will not make success inevitable, but it can provide protection from organizational failure. The work needed to put together a successful strategy is made more complex by the high velocity technological, societal and competitive change that faces businesses in the digital era, when platform based businesses can rapidly pivot and scale new business models. Strategy centres on creating competitive advantage that differentiates the firms' value proposition(s) from competitors, despite their attempts at replication or changing the rules of the game. Successful value propositions provide tangible benefits to customers and consumers, delivered through the integration of organizational components in ways that rival firms find hard to imitate.

RBV researchers identified three main categories of firm resources: physical capital resources, human capital resources, and organizational capital resources. The RBV challenged the positioning view directly, as it considered that it was internal resources, and how they are allocated, which yield competitive advantage.

During the uncertainties of the 1990s, as companies struggled with unclear and depressed economic conditions, thinking developed concerning building capabilities that support adaptability, flexibility, innovation and organizational learning to generate competitive advantage as a more secure route to growth. The aim of strategy moved on from Porter's positioning view (1985) which sought best fit with an existing environment, to the idea that organizations could seek uniqueness by creating their own internal environment, so that they could reshape themselves in revolutionary ways in the manner of Dell or Southwest airlines, with reconfigured value chains or alternative methods of value delivery.

Mintzberg recognized the highly reactive human forces at play in developing and implementing strategy (Mintzberg, 1987, 1990), with the process of running an organization offering few certainties, and little stability internally or in the external environment. As different perspectives came into the strategy process, different ideas and developments could be taken into account and diffused through the organization. As the importance of knowledge, and the integration of knowledge across functions became acknowledged as a pivotal element within the strategy toolkit, skills and expertise in "organizational knowledge creation" were recognized as being key to how companies innovate (Leonard & Barton, 2014; Nonaka & Takeuchi, 1995). The importance of current insights and stakeholder understanding started to become part of the oxygen fuelling decision making, planning, resource allocation and strategy execution within firms.

For established firms, strategic renewal is a set of practices that can guide leaders into new phases of innovation. Strategic renewal demands that changes and decisions are taken ahead of a crisis, but the strategic renewal process is hard to initiate, finance, lead and translate into value for internal and external stakeholders. The role of senior management is to design and lead strategy, experimentation and execution, embedding these capabilities through the culture and day-to-day routines of the organization. Many companies have tried to respond ahead of their respective crises, such as Xerox, Kodak and Firestone, but failed. To support strategic renewal, businesses need to be able to identify the "must win battles" in both their core and emerging market areas, so that they can channel resources to compete and innovate effectively (Killing, Malnight, & Keys, 2005).

Moving the strategy frame to developing a portfolio of opportunities

Around a hundred years ago Frank Knight of the University of Chicago explained to business and economic circles that there is a significant difference between uncertainty and risk: "Uncertainty must be taken in a sense radically distinct from the familiar nation of risk, from which it has never been properly separated." He continued: "The essential fact is that 'risk' means in some cases a quantity susceptible of measurement, while at other times it is something distinctly not of this character; and there are far-reaching and crucial differences in the bearings of the phenomena depending on which of the two is really present and operating" (Knight, 1921). In Knight's analysis, risk is measurable and manageable, and uncertainty is not. While the world is frequently summarized as being VUCA, particularly following the impact of the COVID-19 pandemic, I argue that while some things are becoming more uncertain, there are also activities and combinations that are moving from uncertainty to risk. While uncertainty is the order of the day when it comes to geopolitical instability (as compared to the previous 30 years), technology advances, and cybersecurity, there are also areas where increasing AI and associated data analytics are moving the unknowable into the knowable, e.g. firms can increasingly measure and monitor behaviour more accurately and at scale through sensor technology connecting the IoT (Tuff & Goldbach, 2018).

Set against this background of risk and uncertainty is the central issue that most firms attempt to use a single innovation management system to work across the whole innovation portfolio including core, adjacent and breakthrough environments. The task of managing in arenas where risk can be assessed is very different from the ongoing exploration of uncertain but high return opportunities in breakthrough arenas where risk cannot be assessed. The further that organizations operate from the core, the more that what existing customers say needs to be ignored, and the more that boundary spanners need to be exploring and running experiments with a wide spectrum of external innovators to sense and frame emerging opportunities.

Managing an offering development portfolio needs structure, and the allocation of resources across the portfolio to operationalize the different types of activities required in the core (rigorous market research and analytics) to working with lead users, ecosystem orchestrators and technologists of many types beyond the core. Different skills are needed in different arenas, at different points of their lifecycle (McGrath & Kim, 2014). An aspect of being effective in strategy work is the operation of a range of different approaches to strategy across the innovation portfolio (Reeves et al., 2015)

Connecting strategy with managing an innovation portfolio: The role of communication

The fields of strategy and innovation are inextricably entwined. But with both "strategy" and "innovation" often being seen as such elusive, power-based and ego-driven words there are high levels of scepticism about the impact that strategy plans, and the innovation projects that make them come to life, will actually make. Yet analysis demonstrates that established organizations with clear strategies and effective portfolio driven innovation plans grow faster and more reliably than incumbent firms that stay focused on their core markets.

We have established that while most companies strongly prioritise the offering development efforts in the core, and demonstrated that firms with a balanced innovation portfolio typically earn stronger returns than firms that do not develop an innovation portfolio. Research shows that a staggering 95% of a firm's employees are typically unaware of, or do not understand, its strategy. Unsurprisingly, firms that are poor at communicating their strategy are weak at managing innovation, and fail to execute their strategy plans (Collis & Rukstad, 2008; Kaplan, Norton, & Sher, 2005). Effective communication of a portfolio strategy enables core market staff to excel at "do better" offering development in the core, and gives staff developing adjacent and breakthrough "do different" opportunities the focus, flexibility, skills, resources and senior level backing they need to explore successfully beyond the core.

Following our consideration of the strategy and innovation portfolio management literature, I will use the rich data generated through the study to assess whether the interviewees from the case companies had strategic clarity as a result of a clear and well communicated high level, portfolio driven strategic plan, supported by appropriate structures considering core, adjacent and breakthrough environments.

Peripheral vision: Can searching the periphery for weak signals generate offering development opportunities?

A study of corporate strategists revealed that their organizations had been surprised by as many as three high-impact competitive events in the past five years (Fuld, 2003). In addition, 97% of respondents said that their firms lacked any early warning systems to prevent similar surprises in the future. Companies regularly run through red lights, and with hindsight, managers wonder how the signals could have been missed (Wissema, 2002). Widely known examples abound in both the corporate and public sectors, including the 9/11 terrorist attacks, Hurricane Katrina or corporate scandals seen too late such as Facebook's challenges in managing the Cambridge Analytica episode. Risk management researchers categorise potential disruptions on two dimensions: the likelihood of occurrence and the magnitude of impact, with the importance of early detection to increase organizational resilience also an important factor.

Day and Schoemaker (2006) identified that most organizations lack the capability for peripheral vision through a study of 300 global senior executives, with over 80% of them admitting a shortfall in this area, exposing their organizations to a "vigilance gap". They also recognized that the peripheral vision capability and routines of an organization must be designed for the firm's strategy, industry dynamics and overall volatility of its environment. Further research reveals that organizations are 50 percent more likely to be surprised by major events from outside the organization than from inside. Big firms with global operations reported that they are surprised by outside events more than twice every year. The results are an indication of frequency and not size or impact, but suggest that firms need to allocate the attention of leadership teams to both perceiving threats and opportunities. A lack of attention to threats can lead to short sightedness externally, and wilful blindness internally. When insufficient attention is given to internal opportunities, missed chances can occur, such as the famous Polaroid and Kodak cases. Without attention externally, tunnel vision is often the result, with resources and management time staying focused on the core business and the here and now (Day & Schoemaker, 2019).

A broad range of revolutionary products and services have been created through breakthrough innovations that have brought together seemingly irrelevant knowledge. Qualcomm created its revolutionary Mirasol colour display technology through analysing the microstructures of *Morpho* butterfly wings. Merrill Lynch transformed retail brokerage through connecting concepts from traditional banking with lessons from the supermarket sector. Design Continuum developed the revolutionary (at the time) Reebok Pump basketball shoe through combining sports shoe design approaches with medical bag technologies, including inflatable splints and intravenous bags. Breakthrough innovations in a company's offering can have far reaching effects, generating new growth opportunities, enabling them to reinvent themselves, change the balance of power in existing and nascent arenas, and even create new industry landscapes (Haas & Ham, 2015).

Researchers have made the case for many years that both breakthrough innovation and incremental innovation involve the recombination of existing ideas. The big difference is that breakthrough innovation is often sparked by the recombination of ideas from remote and previously unconnected knowledge domains such as display technologies and the wings of butterflies. A key theme in the book is understanding how established firms can manage organizational vigilance to access new and recombine new ideas so that they can develop their offerings beyond the core. We know that working with lead users, open innovation processes, ecosystem partners, and the introduction of individuals from outside a sector can introduce different thinking, and supports the recombination of ideas and mental maps to generate new offerings. So how can established firms cast their eyes to the periphery, and absorb ideas from distant domains? There are problems of attention within the firm, as ideas from the periphery seem irrelevant to the here and now. It is helpful to understand the development of research into peripheral vision, and how knowledge from the periphery can be introduced within firms to overcome inertia and enable "do different" breakthrough innovation.

The development of the concept of peripheral vision in business was driven forwards through a conference in May 2003 at Wharton Business School, with contributions considering the organizational periphery, and how to manage it more effectively (Day & Schoemaker, 2004b). Prahalad developed his insights in the area of organizational dominant logic: "The dominant logic of the company is, in essence, the DNA of the organization. It reflects how managers are socialised. It manifests itself often, in an implicit theory of competition and value creation. It is embedded in standard operating procedures, shaping not only how the members of the organization act but also how they think. Because it is the source of the company's past success, it becomes the lens through which managers see all emerging opportunities. This makes it hard for established companies to embrace a broader logic for competition and value creation" (Prahalad, 2004a, p. 172).

Day and Schoemaker developed their thinking further through the publication of Peripheral Vision (Day & Schoemaker, 2006, p. 4), where they proposed seven steps to bridging what they saw as the "vigilance gap":
1. Scoping: where to look
2. Scanning: how to look
3. Interpreting: what the data means
4. Probing: what to explore more closely
5. Acting: what to do with these insights
6. Organizing: how to develop vigilance
7. Leading: an agenda for action

The peripheral vision metaphor developed by Day and Schoemaker helps to highlight the complex process and dynamics supporting an organization's capacity to see what lies ahead, and how ideas from distant domains can support the development of new offerings. In human and animal vision, the periphery is the "fuzzy zone" outside the area of primary focus. For humans, focal vision helps us to concentrate on core tasks, and to be efficient in completing them. For individuals as well as organizations, weak signals from the periphery are typically hard to see, difficult to understand, and ambiguous in terms of how to respond. Peripheral vision demands an interplay between sensing, interpreting and probing. A major factor is that what *we think we see* is highly influenced by *what we expect to see* (Day & Schoemaker, 2019).

The individuals who make up project and leadership teams all have limits to their capacity to pay attention, and to absorb and make sense of information. All of us have limits to our mental resources, and consciously and unconsciously block signals that do not seem relevant. When signals appear unconnected and irrelevant in isolation, it is difficult to spot the underlying threads that connect them. The difficulties are not just cognitive, but also emotional. Collectively and individually there may be trends and facts that we don't want to notice, which leads to "wilful blindness" (Day & Schoemaker, 2019).

Researchers into attention have explained that teams and individuals have limits as to how much information they can process at any point in time, and different levels of control regarding what we notice. Our capacity for vigilance is influenced by motivation, or how our interest in something is directed. Day and Schoemaker emphasise four insights that point to how a team's processing capacity can be improved:

1. Attention is a filtering mechanism for balancing our internal capacity with external demands
2. What we see depends on what we expect to see
3. The ability to sense weak signals can be improved
4. Attention can be (re)directed (a key lever for organizations)

Distributing collective attention internally and externally, on the requirements for success in core operations and beyond the core, is exposed to two problems. Firstly, just as generals and politicians are often accused of preparing for the battles of the last conflict, the danger exists that recent shocks and failures will demand attention at the cost of other future focused challenges. For example, the VW group's "Dieselgate" scandal pulled attention from the strategically important development of activities to transform the firm into a transportation company with an offering stretching from traditional personal purchases to fractional ownership, electrification and autonomous vehicles. Navigating through shocks needs to be more ambitious than just seeking stability and parity with known competitors.

Secondly, leadership teams can fall into the trap of "looking busy" with wishful thinking, town hall meetings invoking current buzzwords, targets based on spreadsheet derived growth targets – or even accepting that the future is more about fate than engaging with the future.

Vigilant firms can get the jump on their competitors through mobilizing the ordinary capabilities needed for stability, and the dynamic capabilities required to create fresh businesses in new to the company and sometimes new to the world arenas. The economic returns from future preparedness come from capturing gains sooner, slowing down rivals, gaining first-mover advantage and turning threats into opportunities.

Organizations, just like individuals, find it difficult to see and comprehend the periphery, making it difficult to respond to che emerging threats and opportunities. Peripheral vision requires alternative strategies and capabilities to searching the focal (core) area of the firm's activities: "In areas such as scoping, scanning, interpreting, probing and acting. It entails much more than merely receiving a signal at the edge of vision. It is knowing where to look, how to look, what the signals mean, when to turn one's head to look in a new direction, and how to act on these ambiguous signals" (Day & Schoemaker, 2006, p. 20).

The periphery is identified as the by-product of what the organization sees as important. However, challenger companies: "Have no legacy systems and nothing to forget," blindsiding established firms (Day & Schoemaker, 2004b, p. 119). Considering the rapid growth of companies such as Facebook, Google, eBay, Amazon and Alibaba, it is clear that expertise in exploring the periphery is becoming increasingly important as a source of innovation signals. Thoughtful practitioners recognize the importance of both immersion in the periphery, and 'targeted hunting', as processes that supported the generation of breakthrough opportunities.

The study explores how established firms in the HE centred STM publishing sector manage this process. The importance of search and select to the overall innovation process has already been established. Searching for innovation signals is complex, requiring organizations to look both at their focal activities, and those at the periphery where disruptive innovation threats and opportunities are frequently developing. The rapid development of digitally enabled product usage in HE and other arenas e.g. scholarly journals, entertainment (Netflix) and online shopping (Amazon) means that to survive and grow, established firms have to develop their capabilities to search core (focal), adjacent and peripheral (breakthrough) arenas, so that they can size and respond to both short and long term developments affecting their future relevancy and growth.

Day and Schoemaker (2006, p. 140) identified five components of peripheral vision capability critical to organizations seeking to sense the periphery:

1. Vigilant leadership that encourages a broad focus on the periphery
2. An inquisitive approach to strategy development
3. A flexible and inquisitive culture
4. Knowledge systems for detecting and sharing weak signals
5. An organizational structure and processes that encourage the exploration of the periphery

Since the publication of Peripheral Vision, the business environment has changed considerably, and Day and Schoemaker significantly updated their thinking through the publication of "See Sooner, Act Faster" in 2019. A particular aspect of human and organizational change has been the increase in digital connectedness. Schmidt (former Executive Chairman of Google) and Cohen (Director, Google Ideas) wrote in 2013: "Soon everyone on earth will be connected. With five billion more people set to join the virtual world, the boom in digital connectivity will bring gains in productivity, health, education, quality of life and myriad other avenues in the physical world" (Schmidt & Cohen, 2013, p. 13). They also note "The internet is the largest experiment involving anarchy in history. Hundreds of millions of people are, each minute, creating and consuming an untold amount of digital content in an online world that is not truly bound by terrestrial law" (Schmidt & Cohen, 2013, p. 3).

Global smartphone shipments having risen from 173M in 2009 to around 1.5 billion annually in 2018. The number of mobile phone users worldwide is forecast to reach 6.95 billion in 2020, as compared to a global population of 7.7 billion (United Nations, 2019). Mobile internet traffic as a percentage of total web traffic was over 73% in 2019 in high population countries such as Nigeria and India. While the statistics can change fast, in 2019 WhatsApp (1.6 billion monthly users) and Facebook Messenger (1.3 billion users), both owned by Facebook, led the field in terms of global mobile messenger usage. WeChat (owned by Chinese tech giant Tencent) dominated mobile messenger usage in China with 1.1 billion users ("Statista," 2018). This increase in digital connectedness, and the attendant changes in social behaviour, expand and change the periphery that organizations need to sense and respond to. The dramatic growth of digitally based communication, along with increasing consumption of digital services, is a fundamental challenge to many businesses.

The processes and capabilities needed to develop peripheral vision are distinct from the capabilities that an organization typically has in place for effective focal vision in core business markets. Developing these new capabilities increases costs, and creates the need for senior management attention and skills to process weak, peripheral signals. This: "Leads to a fundamental challenge for the organization: What is the right balance between focal and peripheral vision?" (Day & Schoemaker, 2006, p. 22).

Multiple perspectives help to provide greater peripheral vision, as no single technique will reveal the whole picture, particularly when dealing with weak signals. The risk of weak signals being ignored or distorted due to "groupthink" are significant, with unexpected or hard to categorize information not fitting in with what the organization expects or wants to hear. In rapidly changing business landscapes, there is a need to explore options and ideas outside the mainstream, with teams needing to develop different modes of inquiry and the capacity to learn from setbacks. With greatly expanded connections with the world outside their firm, leaders can become overwhelmed with external information, and there is a need to integrate sources of data with knowledge systems and analytical support to prioritise signals and collective sense making.

Peripheral vision helps firms see emerging threats, and recognize opportunities at the edge of their environment, particularly in rapidly changing markets. Firms with good peripheral vision gain advantages over competitors, as they recognize and act on opportunities more quickly than rivals, and avoid being blindsided. To shift attention beyond the core market, organizations need to establish different cognitive frames, routines and skill sets to make sense of the periphery.

The book uses the STM publishing industry to explore how organizations search the digital periphery for breakthrough opportunities in turbulent environments. Research has not kept up to date with how major changes associated with the digital era affect established firms, and how offering development focused innovation search and select is structured and operationalized in peripheral environments regarding products and services that are principally consumed online.

Operationalizing structured search and select processes

Innovation opportunities, new markets, and threats to established firms particularly present themselves under discontinuous conditions. The danger for established firms is that innovation momentum builds up outside the "normal" search arena, and by the time that opportunities are visible to them they have limited or compromised reaction time.

Where there are stable markets, "do better" innovation is appropriate, and there are well established approaches for managing evolutionary product and service development. Strong connections with existing customers are developed, and the system delivers a regular flow of incremental product improvements.

The move to transient competitive advantage environments means that, in contrast to the planning processes described by Ansoff and Porter, the general manager or leader managing the strategy process has to balance both the strategy and innovation processes, acting as an orchestrator to develop a range of new product development options across core, adjacent and breakthrough environments.

In fast-moving environments, new products are far more likely to fail than to succeed. Nielsen, the market research group, found that only 18 out of 8,500 new product launches in the consumer goods industry could claim to be a breakthrough innovation (Daneshkhu, 2015). Despite the odds often being stacked against successful offering development, competitive pressure and the need for new profit streams demand that companies invest in product focused innovation, even though little is often known about the likely costs and commercial returns.

R&D groups, and even market sensitive new offering development teams, can have inflexible and slow design and development processes, and they are often poorly equipped to respond to the unexpected. Dynamic product portfolio management techniques supported by project portfolio management and agile design processes enable organizations to re-prioritise projects and re-allocate resources regularly, helping them to anticipate and respond to changes in their markets. Portfolio management tools enable R&D groups to identify and prioritise the product ideas that warrant the greatest funding and attention at different times.

There are four main goals for portfolio management: 1) To maximise the value of a given resource expenditure; 2) Balance the right mix of projects; 3) To achieve a strategically aligned portfolio; 4) To manage the right number of projects for the resources available (Cooper et al., 2001; Cooper, 2013). Central to all offering development is uncertainty about technological complexity, adoption, the actions of competitors and even partners. Innovation portfolio decisions are therefore taken under uncertainty, and organizations strive to reduce this uncertainty to increase success rates and limit costs and wider organizational waste.

Offering development projects are typically viewed as involving high levels of novelty, complexity and dynamism, and these factors lead to the characterisation of offering development as a high reward but high risk activity, with risk management an essential capability for the successful management of offering development. A wide range of portfolio management matrices exist to help organizations to develop a balance range of new offering development projects, including some developed and promoted by consultants including the GE McKinsey nine box matrix.

Different strategies for the allocation of resources to innovation projects enable organizations to manage this challenge (Klingebiel & Rammer, 2014). The allocation of resources is a key activity for managers building an product innovation portfolio, with a developing literature exploring how differences at the organizational level concerning the strategic management of innovation influence performance (Cassiman & Veugelers, 2006; Laursen & Salter, 2006; Leiponen & Helfat, 2010, 2011; Li & Atuahene-Gima, 2001).

The effective use of processes for screening and managing ideas is significantly related to the successful pursuit of radical innovation. Connecting ideation, selection, and project portfolio management increases the rate of return a firm can secure from its innovation resources, supporting the investment of money, time and intelligence in the earlier stages of innovation projects (Reid & de Brentani, 2004; Verworn, Herstatt, & Nagahira, 2008). Heising (2012) developed the concept of "ideation portfolio management", as there is typically a lack of integration between the search and select phases, and the management of a balanced offering portfolio.

Research has found that innovation performance increases the wider that firms search for opportunities. The assumption that a wider range of opportunities increases innovation performance is implicit in the conceptual models of the offering development process. The literature also identifies that there can be disadvantages for firms exploring a larger number of opportunities, including the reduction of attention given to individual projects, greater organizational complexity, loss of strategic focus, and reduced incentives at the individual project level (Baumann & Schmidt, 2019; Boudreau, Lacetera, & Lakhani, 2011; Sull, 2003).

Organizations with greater innovative intent within their offering development portfolio typically have a larger proportion of novel projects at a relatively long distance from the company's existing capability and knowledge base, posing a challenge for the allocation of limited resources. While the outcomes of incremental innovation are relatively predictable, organizations undertaking more radical offering development regularly experience limited sales on new launches, even if the returns on the infrequent successes are higher. The importance of the selection process to firms with higher innovative intent (i.e. those pursuing radical innovation) and their correspondingly broad innovation portfolios is clear, otherwise the commercialisation of products suffers. An additional factor when considering the breadth of innovation portfolios is that greater learning happens in uncertain environments (Eggers, 2012; Huchzermeier & Loch, 2001).

Innovation efforts are prone to failure, including well resourced initiatives. Klingebiel & Rammer (2014) found that increasing the quantity and quality of resources dedicated to the offering development process does not meet the challenge of lowering the uncertainty implicit in innovation activities beyond the core. A company's innovation performance also depends on the allocation of resources to projects. Breadth positively influences performance, independent of resourcing, with the effect greater for companies allocating resources selectively and for those projects with greater innovative intent. The breadth of resource allocation increases innovation performance more than the intensity of resource allocation, particularly with more novel products. The degree of ambition of an organization, as revealed in its innovation portfolio, boosts new product sales through adopting a broad approach to the product portfolio, if resources are allocated selectively.

Timing also has a major impact on outcomes, as there are major disadvantages of excessive breadth later in the offering development process, where resource commitments are more demanding, and concurrent learning capacity is limited. Effective innovation portfolio governance, including formality and explicitness, information support and the frequency of reviews all positively influence innovation outcomes (Eggers, 2012; Klingebiel & Rammer, 2014; Urhahn & Spieth, 2014).

The question: "How do organizations manage search and select in disrupting environments?" is at the heart of the book. Whether organizations manage their search and select activities guided by a high level, portfolio driven strategic plan supported by appropriate structures considering core, adjacent and breakthrough (or transformational) environments emerges as a key capability warranting further exploration in publishing firms through the research project.

The role of ambidexterity

Organizations competing in different categories in complex geographic and cultural contexts face similar contradictions which require ambidexterity, being the ability to explore new avenues and exploit existing capabilities and markets. Duncan (1976) first used the term "ambidextrous organization" to describe the "dual structures" that firms often put in place to manage activities requiring different time horizons and managerial approaches. The term was resurrected two decades later focused on understanding how companies can manage sustaining and revolutionary change processes simultaneously (O'Reilly & Tushman, 1997; Tushman & O'Reilly, 1996), and the emphasis was on structural separation between evolutionary and radical change. While some research progress was made in the area of organizational learning (Levinthal & March, 1993), and balancing efficiency and flexibility (Adler, Goldoftas, & Levine, 1999), ambidexterity did not fully catch the interest of academic researchers until Birkinshaw and Gibson (2004) used ambidexterity as a frame for the tension between alignment and adaptability, and introduced the notion of contextual ambidexterity, as distinct from Duncan (1976) and Tushman and O'Reilly's structure-orientated approach to ambidexterity.

March (1991) argued that sustained firm performance is associated with the organization's ability to balance exploitation with exploration, and this fundamental insight has been supported through the results of a substantial body of research. Innovation streams, which represent the capability of an organization to undertake radical and sustaining innovation, is one means to operationalize ambidexterity (Benner & Tushman, 2003; Gibson & Birkinshaw, 2004). Another route to ambidexterity is through alliances, joint ventures, acquisitions or venturing (Rothaermel & Alexandre, 2009; Van de Ven et al., 1999). The organizational structures best suited to manage the strategic challenges connected with the pursuit of a range of innovation types remain the focus of research and debate.

Mudambi and Swift (2014) found that the companies that make the step between exploitation and exploration perform better. However, Swift (2016) found that a significant proportion of firms fail to make the change, or die in the process. He was: "Able to observe firm performance as firms are making the attempt to transition between these opposing forms of R&D-based innovation, and observe organizational mortality rates as the process unfolds . . . (which) . . . shows that the magnitude of compact, significant changes in R&D spending, in either direction, is associated with a higher incidence of firm mortality. These results are found after controlling for organizational failure that is attributable to the firm's financial health, and whether the firm is currently practicing exploration, exploitation, or simultaneous ambidexterity" (Swift, 2016, p. 1689). The ability of the firm to manage both exploit and explore can be a matter of organizational life and death.

Tushman et al. (2010) identified four main approaches to the design of organizations regarding their capability to exploit and explore:
– Due to senior team and overall organizational inertia, established firms sustain current technologies and customers
– Successful innovation uses interdependencies across business units through explicit linking mechanisms, and is contingent on task interdependencies.

Exploratory innovation takes place in cross-functional teams led by project managers, reporting in to a senior team

– Ambidextrous designs consistent with the different requirements of exploit and explore, with integrated structures that are inconsistent with each other. Highly differentiated structures are linked though senior team integration

– Structures that temporally switch between looser designs for exploration and mechanistic designs for exploitation. This is a switching form of ambidexterity. Senior teams support these inconsistent structures to deal with the tensions experienced as structures change across explore and exploit

This identification of organizational design alternatives to support ambidexterity is helpful, but despite a significant literature on the benefits of successfully managing both exploration and exploitation, there is no one organizational approach that seems to offer a solution to the wide variety of ambidextrous challenges facing firms.

Following the conception of contextual ambidexterity (Gibson & Birkinshaw, 2004), academic research into ambidexterity intensified, with the concept applied to a range of phenomena e.g. venture units, alliances, individuals and teams. Birkinshaw and Gupta (2013) summarise ambidexterity as the ability to do two things equally well. The concept is regularly applied to the evaluation of the capability of an organization to manage the mutually complex – but not irreconcilable – imperatives to manage both exploitation and exploration. The theory of ambidexterity: "Says that managers are making choices and trade-offs among competing objectives, and when they do their job well they override the organization's tendency to go down the path of least resistance" (Birkinshaw & Gupta, 2013, p. 293). They see ambidexterity being achieved through managerial capability, in the face of self-reinforcing behavioural routines, the dominant logic of the firm, and how executives deal with paradox. Ambidexterity is a multi-level construct, with different forms of corporate venture unit being deployed (Hill & Birkinshaw, 2012) to enable organizations to develop a portfolio of commercial activities.

A tension always exists between focusing on alignment and exploitation, with the prospect of short term results, and adaptability and exploration to develop options for the future. BCG developed an Adaptive Advantage Index to measure how well companies adapt to turbulence in their environment, identifying the firms that outperform in their sector in both stable and turbulent periods (excluding financial firms due to government intervention) (Reeves, Love, & Mathur, 2012). On this measure of ambidexterity, i.e. having the capabilities to succeed in both stable and turbulent periods, the most ambidextrous firms outperformed the market by 10 to 15 percent of total shareholder return on average between 2006 and 2011. This outperformance required the combination of modes of thinking and acting that can be diametrically opposed (Reeves et al., 2015, p. 177), demonstrating that ambidexterity is a valuable dynamic sub-capability.

The structural and resource attributes of an organization significantly influence performance, with better results when the corporate venture unit is better resourced and empowered through a greater degree of decentralisation. Competing objectives can be managed in many different ways, with ambidexterity scholars seeking to understand how firms transit between exploration and exploitation, and how to deliver the highest level of achievement in terms of exploitation and exploration simultaneously. Major tensions continue to exist between exploitation and exploratory innovation routines, and there is still a lack of understanding of the micromechanisms that enable ambidexterity at both the individual and organizational level (Turner, Swart, & Maylor, 2012).

Birkinshaw & Ridderstråle (2017, p. ix) argue that: "The formulae for success that worked in prior decades offer only very limited insights into what might work in the future. This is because the business context keeps changing: not in the banal sense that we face increasing levels of technological change and higher levels of competition, but rather in the more fundamental sense that every source of competitive advantage carries with it the seeds of its own destruction. This is a version of the famous 'Icarus Paradox'; the attribute or capability that makes companies successful in one era makes them susceptible to failure in the next era." They continue that there is a newly emerging management model called *adhocracy* which sees firms coordinating activities based on external opportunities, or as Drucker would see it – *creating the customer* (Drucker, 1954).

The operationalization of structured processes across the offering development portfolio gives the firm the capability to manage vigilant innovation through search and select projects focused on opportunities outside the firm, particularly where ambiguity is high beyond the core. The effective operationalization of search and select across the portfolio typically requires different structures, metrics, mindsets, processes (e.g. different types of stage-gates and project controls), skills and management approaches in the core, and beyond the core. Structured search and select processes improve project management, and increase offering development success rates across complex core, adjacent and breakthrough environments.

Identifying and sharing deep contextual domain insights

Forecasting and scenario planning

Firms that invest in corporate foresight activities seek to support the renewal of a portfolio of strategic resources, with strategic resources being the basis of the competitive advantage of the firm. Innovation is central to the renewal of the firm, with different capacities required to innovate incrementally and radically. The RBV has shown that a firm's resources should be difficult to imitate, be scarce, and yield competitive advantage.

Dynamic capabilities lose their power to sustain competitive advantage over time. To regain competitive advantage, or build new advantage in new environments, firms need to develop new resources. The renewal of resources has been shown to take place inconsistently, spanning periods of slow, incremental change, and intense periods of radical change. When companies cannot change and develop new resources, their existence is challenged.

However many firms fail to detect discontinuous change due to ignorance, which can be due to an adherence to organizational planning cycles, and signals remaining undetected as they are outside the reach of the firm's sensors. Senior management can suffer from too much information, or lack the capacity to make sense of the signals, with the added complication that middle management can filter information to protect business unit interests.

To avoid being blindsided, organizations can decide to design and implement a strategic radar system to pick up signals and make sense of them. Scenario planning can be useful in seeking information, and making sense of it. A few scenarios usually help to establish a broad range of exogenous futures which might develop. What is important is that a broad range of alternatives are considered. Scenarios do not represent states of the future, but illustrate what might happen. The objective in developing scenarios is to frame the uncertainty range of the future, helping to provide frameworks for managerial discussions, both widening thinking, and helping to create focus when it comes to resource allocation.

There is now good evidence that firms can improve their future preparedness through applying the disciplines of corporate foresight. Through a longitudinal research design centred on 85 European multinationals, future preparedness was assessed in 2008, and its impact on firm performance was then evaluated in 2015. Using multiple metrics, the strength of foresight capability ranged from neurotic to vigilant, and focused to vulnerable. The researchers assessed that 36% of the firms were vigilant in 2008, and this group of future prepared firms was 33 percent more profitable in 2015 (as measured as earnings before tax, interest, depreciation, and amortization) than the rest of the sample. The vigilant organizations also saw their market capitalization increase by an average of 75 percent since 2008, as compared to the firms classified as vulnerable, who only gained an increase of 38% over the same period (Day & Schoemaker, 2019; Rohrbeck & Kum, 2018).

Schoemaker et al. (2013) suggest that an organization's strategic radar system is made up of three major activities:
1. Monitoring external signals to deliver regular updates about pre-specified trends and forces shaping the targeted business environments
2. Assessment of strategic actions informed by the monitoring of external signals
3. Scanning for additional weak signals that might shape the external environment. This step is different from (1) above, as it involves looking for unexpected signals

Shell has long been a leader in scenario planning, which it has used to explore options and drive forward innovation in a structured manner, and now uses the GameChanger programme to support scenario planning. "Transitional objects" are used in much the same way as prototypes, concept models and beta versions of software are used in product development, to generate reactions and shape a focus for strategy development and the allocation of innovation resources.

Projected demographic trends for the next 50 years will dramatically change markets. The aging population in Western economies will create particular needs including healthcare funding and needs for a range of low-cost products and services. Asia will see growing demand for education, with opportunities growing across the whole spectrum of the population. Companies that can accurately identify the needs of users and customers in developing markets will be at an advantage. Appropriate products and services may be low-tech and have fewer features than their Western equivalents.

Forecasting work and scenario planning considers regulation, which can both accelerate and dampen innovation, in different situations. Certain innovation pathways might be closed off, while other new ones may be mandated for exploration. Research considering the impact of EU regulation on innovation suggests that regulation is progressively slowing down the development of innovation (Amable, Demmou, & Ledezma, 2009). However, regulation also drives changes in behaviour, particularly in the area of safety (Dodgson et al., 2007).

Even with the rise in risk management procedures, including business analytics and the massive rise in access to data, businesses continue to be caught unawares, or are just unprepared for changes in their business environments. A survey highlighted the special challenges for decision- making arising from big data, with 85% of respondents indicating that the issue was not so much the volume of data, as the need to analyse and act on large data sets in real-time. Familiar challenges relating to data quality, governance and consistency also remain relevant, with 56% of respondents citing organizational silos as their biggest problem in making better use of big data. The respondents consider that: "Data is now the fourth factor of production, as essential as land, labour and capital" (The Deciding Factor: Big Data & Decision Making, 2012, p. 2).

Publishing as an industry is good at knowledge management. This is unsurprising, as publishers have played a key part in the flow of knowledge since the invention of printing ("From Papyrus to Pixels," 2014; Ware & Mabe, 2015). However, while incumbents are good at looking at their focal business using known techniques, they typically have greater difficulties understanding environments beyond the core.

Due to the importance of searching for signals to inform the longer term strategy of the firm, the research project looked for the presence of the capability in the case companies to both seek out and share contextual domain insights regarding the macro social and technology trends impacting on core and beyond the core environments.

Firms with deep domain understanding make better choices through reducing uncertainty. Strategic choices require understanding of broad market and technology trends and less visible undercurrents. Firms also find that deep domain insights into the workings of DMUs, budget holder incentives, industry standards, competitor activity, and the speed of adoption of new industry metrics etc. improve opportunity recognition and evaluation.

Insights into the core, and beyond the core, help companies back established markets appropriately, and place bets with improved odds in adjacent and breakthrough environments.

Firms will only benefit from these insights through establishing knowledge sharing routines.

Deployment of digital era market research techniques (e.g. netnography)

Market research in the digital era

Innovation is a process that involves moving ideas forward, improving and finetuning them over time, threading a complex mix of "knowledge spaghetti" together to deliver value to stakeholders through a product, process or increasingly a service based offering. Triggering the innovation process is not just concerned with "eureka" moments, but involves seeking out promising higher level problem areas and more detailed jobs-to-be-done. A wide range of stimuli exist, from knowledge push, when scientific breakthroughs and new technology create "new to the world" opportunities, to needs pull, with innovators using techniques such as ethnography or collaboration with lead-users to identify and figure out solutions to unmet needs, or better ways (cheaper, faster, easier) ways to deliver solutions. What is clear is that the digital era demands relevant research tools, and cross-functional development teams to plan where to look for high level problem areas, and detailed jobs-to-be-done.

Examples abound of occasional breakthroughs followed by longer periods of exploring and elaborating better ways to develop the original idea. Developing knowledge creates an "opportunity field", but opportunities are distinct from the actual delivery of value to stakeholders in a sustainable way. The major cause of failure for new products and services is that they cannot be differentiated. To understand root causes, Japanese quality philosophy demands that product developers ask "why" multiple times (Ohno, 1988). Research has shown that 98 percent of products that managers perceived to be "superior and differentiated" succeeded, whereas only 18 percent of "me-too" products survived (Cooper, 1998).

Companies tend to not use innovative approaches to market research because they do not have the resources, their organizations are not familiar with the new techniques, or they perceive data to be difficult to collect and analyse. Such perceptions act as a strong barrier to the adoption of new approaches, and potentially choke innovation activity and potential. Organizations have always used information to make decisions, but there is currently a radical change taking place, namely the dramatic rise in access to digitally generated data. Firms are moving from a constant shortage of data, to potentially having too much information. Organizations can at last harness greater quantities of information, drilling down into details that could never be seen before.

Traditional market research mainly uses surveys and focus groups. Typically, the questions asked are based on knowledge of existing products, markets and customers. Companies strive to identify representative groups of customers or users. Insight is also sought into the dynamics of the decision-making unit (DMU) in B2B markets, and for influences on the purchase of expensive consumer items such as cars and white goods. Surveys are becoming increasingly difficult to administer as response rates are frequently very low.

Focus groups have been widely used, with a mix of interview techniques and observation using two-way mirrors and video recording. The majority of market research managers report that the ideas generated by focus groups are unexciting and the new products based on them involve incremental innovations: "Customers often describe the solutions they want in endless focus groups and surveys . . . . How sad it is, then, that when the product or service is finally introduced – and the only reaction in the marketplace is a resounding ker-plop" (Ulwick, 2002). Focus groups do not serve offering development beyond the core well.

Cooper (2011) found that 96% of the poorest 20% of product innovation performers do a poor job of assessing the value of the product to the customer, with 93% doing market research poorly, if at all. These figures remain weak for average product innovation firms, with 83% doing a poor job of assessing the value of the product to the customer, with 82% doing market research poorly, if at all. The author advocates that the search for innovation triggers should focus on the real value that customers seek, and that the search process benefits from looking at the jobs-to-be-done by customers, users and non-customers.

Cooper and Edgett's study (2008) surveyed 160 US companies, looking at the various ideation methods and their perceived effectiveness. Interestingly, open innovation methods performed weakly. The results show that ethnography is perceived to be the most useful method, providing the greatest insight into user's unmet and unarticulated needs, but it is only used by about 13 per cent of organizations. Ethnography offers the opportunity to understand at a deep level what is important to the user "doing the job". Lead user techniques and focus groups are both widely used and regarded, while other methods such as disruptive technologies and peripheral vision are relatively often used, but their impact is not rated as highly. Limitations do exist with the study, as the impact of the methods is only measured by the manager's perceptions, and not through more systematic comparisons. In addition, how different methods were used in combination was not analysed.

Surveys and focus groups remain valid parts of the market research toolkit, provided that they are combined with a wider set of digital experience centred techniques enabling deeper insights and cross-validation of results. This is the philosophy behind hidden needs analysis, which uses a combination of techniques (Goffin, Lemke, & Koners, 2010). The importance of new approaches to understanding users and customers is equally important to the service sector. Research shows that: "Traditional market research and development approaches have proved to be particularly ill-suited to breakthrough products" (Deszca, Munro, & Noori, 1999, p. 613). Customer needs identified through market research will include:

1. Known needs: Common knowledge and addressed in the features of existing products and services (Core market – do better innovation)
2. Unmet needs: Needs that are known and articulated by customers, but are not currently addressed by current products and services (Adjacent environments: Do different innovation for the firms adjusting their value propositions)
3. Hidden (or latent) needs: Needs that have not previously been identified either by market research or the customers themselves (Breakthrough innovation, which is new to the market and the firms/ecosystems developing the offering)

Social science methods were initially used to understand the user-product interface, but they are now increasingly used to not only understand how products are used, but also to identify user's hidden needs. Particularly in B2B arenas the real value of a market offering can only be assessed through the lens of the customer or user. The innovation search process should not focus on the market offering *per se*, but on the customers value creation processes. The market research literature remains centred on decision making, focusing on what customers buy rather than what they actually do (Xie, Bagozzi, & Troye, 2008).

Digital technologies are strong arming companies into recreating their value propositions. New mobile applications, approaches to sharing experiences, IoT, AI, analytics, cloud and edge computing and other developments enable users and customers to experience value in ways that just were not possible previously. With all of this potential, how do companies work out which offerings are worth backing for future development and launch? Digital technologies are changing the game, providing instant access data and unlimited connectivity through new digital offerings. High impact digital offerings are born at the intersection of what customers want and will pay for (not always the same thing), and what technologies can deliver. To develop their offerings, firms must run ongoing experiments and co-create value with their customers. To be successful they need cross-functional development teams who explore externally, and share the findings internally to build minimum viable offerings for their most innovation hungry users (Ross, Beath, & Mocker, 2019).

Digital offerings respond well to minimum viable product (MVP) focused rapid test and learn iterations, consistent with the software enabled agile working movement kicked off by the Manifesto for Agile Software Development (Beck et al., 2001). Singapore based DBS bank has distributed digital innovation and idea evaluation across the firm. As the biggest bank in Southeast Asia in terms of assets under management, and serving nine million customers in 18 markets, the company's 22,000 employees ran 1,000 small experiments concurrently in 2015. While many of the experiments fizzled quickly, others were later launched as new digital offerings (Sia, Soh, & Weill, 2016).

Customer journey mapping has become a significant source of ideas worth evaluating at DBS, examining the full experience of customers as they interact with the firm. They move beyond functional value, and consider what the customer is thinking and feeling, and what their concerns are. This is consistent with ethnographic approaches, and takes account of the jobs-to-be-done methodology which recognizes that every job has a functional, a social and an emotional dimension. The insights generated set up experiments to test hypotheses with real users (Sia et al., 2016).

With considerable focus on emerging big data research techniques, a conflict might be expected between ethnography and digital data approaches to identifying innovation triggers, particularly as practitioners appear slower to take up ethnography than academic social scientists, but Cayla et al. (2014) argue that organizations will need to combine both big data and ethnography, and highlight researchers at IBM developing "ethno-mining". This involves ethnographic storytelling based on the huge amounts of sensor and behavioural tracking data now being generated.

The latest change in ethnographic research is that consumers and companies are increasingly interacting digitally, through user groups. Researchers are adapting the conventional techniques of ethnography for use on the in the online digital environment, with netnography first emerging early in the millennium and the approach developing terms to describe the observed communities such as "Crowds, Hives, Mobs and Swarms" (Kozinets, Hemetsberger, & Schau, 2008, p. 339). While a great deal of business activity in the digital social media era is focused on marketing promotion, webnography can provide access to leading and extreme users of digital services (Puri, 2009). A model for "Community Based Innovation" has been developed integrating input from online communities and more traditional lead user techniques (Füller, Bartl, Ernst, & Mühlbacher, 2006). Use of ethnography on the web, also known as web ethnography, is most appropriate when the relationship between a company and its' users is concerned with digital services, rather than communication about a physical product or service (Prior & Miller, 2012).

Due to rapid changes in how customers and users engage with the HE publishing products, research has been undertaken into how social media is used within the rapidly evolving research workflow (Rowlands, Nicholas, Russell, Canty, & Watkinson, 2011). In STM research communities, research workflows are an area of both development and research. A question emerging from the literature is whether HE publishers have the capabilities in place to undertake market research using digital era research techniques such as data analytics and netnography in current fast evolving HE research environment.

Interesting work has been undertaken in B2B environments by Bain, who have identified 40 building block "elements of value", which have been structured into the levels on a pyramid, with those providing more measurable value – e.g. product quality, meeting specifications or ethical standards at the bottom. Value is separated out into five categories: table stakes (essentials, e.g. regulatory compliance), functional value (e.g. cost reduction). Things get more interesting higher up the value pyramid, in areas including "ease of doing business" value (e.g. cultural fit), and "individual value" (e.g. expanding networks). The pyramid sees "inspirational value" at the top, where factors such as social responsibility and the alignment of the purpose of buying and selling organizations play their part (Almquist, Cleghorn, & Sherer, 2018). When value requirements need to be explored across such a wide spectrum, a full range of digital, ethnographic and cross-functional customer visit team based research methodologies are needed.

As organizations follow Drucker's advice to create customers, they are turning to the jobs-to-be-done approach to identify pain points through pain storms. Traditional surveys, focus groups, marketing studies and analyst reports do not provide the insights required, particularly beyond the core. While familiar tools may work in "do better" environments, they fail when development teams are operating in uncertain fields in far adjacent and breakthrough arenas. In the digital era, counter-intuitively, firms need super-savvy digital teams as well as enhanced qualitative research skills, usually mobilized in B2B spaces through multi-skilled teams engaged in discussion and observation.

Providers of digital solutions require a range of digital era market research techniques to understand fast evolving user needs, budgets, and changing/new decision making unit (DMU) structures and priorities in new markets. Practitioners with access to the research (particularly ethnography based) techniques and digital data collection capabilities to identify and validate workflows and the potential value capture models required to capitalise on solving problems for users will enhance their offering development success rates.

Seeking out and sharing deep domain insights into user workflows

User driven innovation

Users are often ahead of suppliers, with their ideas and frustrations leading to experimentation and prototypes of what can become mainstream innovations. Eric von Hippel pioneered the study of the opportunities presented by users, demonstrating that the approach enables both firms and individuals to innovate with both information based products, e.g. computer apps, and physical products, e.g. running shoes or toys. Crowdsourcing enables innovators to seek insights from both B2C and B2B users, creating insights which risk being buried in massive amounts of data.

Extreme users are an important place to look for innovation triggers, linking the idea of the lead user and needs on the periphery of existing markets. Looking for extreme environments or users stretches innovators, as they encounter challenges which provide new opportunity spaces. The thinking is that if firms can please the most demanding users in the toughest environments, then opportunities should follow. The "bottom of the pyramid" environment generates extreme opportunities that companies may, or may not have the capabilities to meet. Jugaad innovation (Radjou et al., 2012) has emerged as an approach to innovating with extreme users based on the Hindi word "Jugaad", which is translated as "an innovative fix, an improvised solution born from cleverness and ingenuity" (Radjou et al., 2012, p. 4). This approach can create solutions and indications of possibilities beyond extreme environments, setting up reverse (Govindarajan & Trimble, 2012) and frugal "do more with less" (Radjou & Prabhu, 2015) innovation opportunities through deep user understanding.

Users will often reveal their innovations openly, and this has been observed in sectors such as sporting equipment. The user innovators may give the innovation away to increase diffusion, or due to a community having a norm of sharing, or to enable a third party to produce the innovation at a cheaper cost than the innovator could. The pattern of freely revealing developments to the benefit of other users has been summarized as the "private-collective innovation model" (von Hippel & von Krogh, 2003), which is an approach consistent with the open-source-software (OSS) and open science movements. Three main methods have been identified for exploiting user innovativeness: (1) lead user methods; (2) toolkits for user design; (3) crowdsourcing. The approaches are not mutually exclusive (Franke, 2014). The field of user driven innovation is dynamic, and the summary below is not exhaustive.

The lead user method was developed as a managerial heuristic, helping organizations to search for user validated innovations, and encounter radically new business opportunities. It is useful to break down the lead user research process into a number of phases, being the identification of major needs and trends, and the identification of groups of lead users. A number of early detailed studies demonstrated that the lead user method can systematically generate and validate ideas for commercially attractive new products (Lilien, Morrison, Searls, Sonnack, & von Hippel, 2002; Lüthje & Herstatt, 2004; Urban & von Hippel, 1988).

Toolkits represent another method to outsource product design to users and customers. von Hippel developed the idea of: "Toolkits for user innovation and design" as sets of design tools enabling users to design their own products including their own preferences, sharing their designs with a supplier (von Hippel, 1998, 2001; von Hippel & Katz, 2002). An important feature of toolkits is that they give the supplier (or design orchestrator) feedback during the design process, while also enabling both the user and supplier to benefit from von Hippel (1998) called "trial-and-error" learning. Franke and Piller (2004) found that customers were ready to pay twice as much for a self-designed watch than for a similar watch with the same level of objective quality, and this preparedness to pay higher prices has been confirmed in a number of studies across a range of product areas including kitchens, t-shirts, and fountain pens.

A third means to access user creativity is to "crowdsource" the task, and this method is also referred to as "broadcast search" (Jeppesen & Lakhani, 2010) and "virtual co-creation" (Füller, 2010). Companies pose problems or questions to "crowds" through online calls for solutions, with the sponsor then evaluating the solutions, selecting what they view as the best solutions (Dahlander & Magnusson, 2008; Ogawa & Piller, 2006). The strength of the crowdsourcing concept is that "crowds" are typically made up of a wide range of contributors with a wider range of perspectives on the problem, skill sets, and solution options than are available within any single company. Crowdsourcing is being used in a wide range of industries including consumer electronics, pharmaceuticals, and high-tech R&D problems. Studies have demonstrated that crowdsourcing can outperform the internal professionals in identifying new product ideas in consumer markets such as baby products (Poetz & Schreier, 2012). However it is important to connect core business skills with crowd sourcing approaches, otherwise great ideas fail due to a lack of resources and project management capabilities, with the implementation of structured selection tools also being particularly important (Brauen, 2017; Brunneder, Acar, Deichmann, & Sarwal, 2020).

A strong theme running through the user driven innovation literature is how widespread distribution of the internet has opened up the innovation search process to engage and learn from users both in identified and analogous segments. The research project is focused on the STM publishing market which is dominated by digital products that are deployed by users virtually, as they integrate digital products into their own workflows, creating the opportunity to explore the role of user driven innovation.

The significance of workflows in design thinking

The concept of workflow grew out of business process management (BPM), and can be defined as: "Supporting business processes using methods, techniques and software to design, enact, control and analyse operational processes involving humans, organizations, applications, documents and other sources of information" (Aalst, Hofstede, & Weske, 2003, p. 4). A workflow consists of an orchestrated and repeatable pattern of personal and/or business activity enabled by the systematic organization of resources into processes that transform materials, provide services, or process information.

Productivity has slowed down in most "Global North" economies in the past decade, and organizations are looking to secure savings through the widespread implementation of digital workflows, while also making the work life of workers better. Back-office financial and technology activities, project management and human resource tasks are also targets for technology enabled workflow automation improvements. Recent research into the impact of digitizing workflows found that eight out of ten employees said that greater automation simplifies work processes, increases efficiency, and improves productivity. Importantly – when considering our hypercompetitive world – seven out of ten employees reported that greater automation boosted job satisfaction, as well as increasing time to focus on opportunities for advancement and creativity. In the most automated companies 56% of employees said that digital workflows had added new roles in their firms, instead of reducing employment (Davenport, 2019a).

The 21st century has seen the rapid growth to dominance of a series of digital platform firms such as Apple, Amazon, Tencent, Google, Apple and Samsung that provide compelling consumer experiences to consumers. It could be argued that services such as WeChat and Instagram operate within a "socialflow". Considering B2B activities, firms such as Salesforce, Alibaba, Amazon and a resurgent Microsoft have grown through understanding and serving the workflow needs of their suppliers, business partners and users. These organizations focus user experience designers to create rewarding human-computer interface experiences. Service designers radically re-shape the overall service experience and customer engagement. As users and customers get used to excellent service enabled through digital workflows in certain aspects of the lives e.g. Spotify, they become frustrated with other sectors that are lagging such as financial services. Organizations that supply digitally enabled services, such as STM journal publishers, are operating in the digital workflow space, as their offerings mesh with the increasingly digitally centred workflows of their primary users – students and researchers.

The idea of developing solutions to increase user effectiveness connects with design thinking, which can be seen as the: "Human-centred approach to innovation that puts the observation and discovery of often highly nuanced, even tacit, human needs right at the forefront of the innovation process. It considers not just the technological system constraints but also the sociocultural system context" (Gruber, de Leon, George, & Thompson, 2015, p. 1). The positive role of a more "designerly" approach, stretching beyond services and products to business processes and public service innovation has been led by IDEO and its high profile chairman Tim Brown and fellow founder, Stanford Professor David Kelley. Other standard bearers have included Roger Martin of Toronto University, and the UK's Design Council. The approach of a designer to a design challenge starts with a *discovery phase* involving the detailed observation of users, and of the constraints and context of the system within which the users function. The discovery phase often involves ethnography (watching people), visual anthropology, the use of design probes and co-creation workshops. The *define phase* comes next, which involves establishing insights, and framing the problem – with a continued focus on problem solving.

The *ideation phase* uses physical and increasingly digital visualizations of prototypes, providing a range of potential solutions, all with the aim of exploring how a spectrum of users and stakeholders interact with a number of solution concepts. The final *delivery phase* sees physical or digital prototypes being tested considering their effectiveness and technical resilience, and how they fit the users needs and the wider context of their lives. The four step process is iterative, and non-linear at times, with projects moving forwards and backwards through the phases. Importantly, the process is collaborative, involving stakeholders, users and DMU members in the framing of the problem, and in evaluating where design interventions will particularly add value.

Consistent with agile team approaches, understanding workflows and responding to them is multi-disciplinary including the design, commercial, operational and technical disciplines at each stage. Design thinking demands a highly disciplined approach to both observation and analysis in the discovery phase, followed by flipping to the area of imagination in the definition and design ideation stages. The process switches to the material space as concepts are prototyped and evaluated by users before the commercial development phase can be triggered. This approach works best when breakthrough creativity and disruptive innovation is needed, or where "wicked" problems involving unclear problems and complex – and emergent – contexts or ecosystems are involved (Gruber et al., 2015).

Other approaches to developing an offering typically start with defining a problem or market opportunity using structured market analysis and the personal insights of customers and users. Projects can then be advanced through assessing the problem definition and possible solutions using primary and secondary market research methodologies and more traditional market research and testing. The next step would then be the development of a commercial plan using estimates of market size, penetration, distribution, advertising and pricing. This approach is relatively risky, as it relies on entrepreneurial insights, faith in the definition of the problem, and operational agility to act on new market information. However, when it works, the approach can be very successful.

Sometimes an engineering or technology based approach is more suitable, analysing problems through breaking them down to components, followed by a systemic solution that answers the technical requirements highlighted in the problem-definition stage. This approach works well when problems are defined clearly, particularly when the limitations are more rooted to the technical rather than the human realm – especially when the goal is incremental rather than more radical innovation.

Design management and design thinking are regularly used as tools for both product and service innovation, as organizations seek to understand the pervasive problems facing individuals in their work. The importance of understanding the problems of stakeholders across the business customer from the decision making unit (DMU) to the user is particularly important in service marketing environments. A key issue for firms is to understand the different workflow of its users across core, adjacent and breakthrough environments, with the workflows of users changing fast in the HE publishing environment.

Identification and validation of "big enough" pervasive problems and detailed jobs-to-be-done requiring solutions

Harvard Professor Theodore Levitt (1980) proposed the concept of a company's product as: "A tool to solve their (customers) problems," also reminding us that: "People don't want to buy a quarter-inch drill. They want a quarter-inch hole!" (Levitt, 1975). The notion of problem solving as the focus for search and select activities outside the firm aligns well with the exhortation of Drucker that firms must create the customer. Through solving problems for customers – and in B2B contexts – users/and or DMU members – firms create value from ideas. Through adopting the "jobs-to-be-done" approach to problem solving, value proposition development becomes more focused on integrated product and service solutions (Yip et al., 2014) that deliver value-in-use to users (Grönroos, 2008; Macdonald, Wilson, Martinez, & Toossi, 2011).

To really get to the heart of solving problems for customers, it is therefore essential that organizations provide solutions that help users to get their jobs done. The importance of end-users as important actors in external innovation is now well established, and it is widely accepted that user inspired innovations can enrich the innovation ecosystem, and offer vital feedback and ideas for the organization. Studies of the medical device industry have revealed that innovations integrating user knowledge diffuse more broadly, with greater impact, than those that do not (Chatterji & Fabrizio, 2012; Franke, 2014; von Hippel, 1986, 2005; von Hippel, Thomke, & Sonnack, 1999).

Identification and validation of pervasive problems, considering jobs-to-be-done

The market segmentation processes that companies adopt have major consequences, as they determine what the firm decides to produce, how it takes products to market, who it competes against and the size of its commercial opportunities. Historically most companies have segmented their customers along criteria defined by product characteristics (price; performance; technology) or customers (age; income). In B2B sectors, size of customer, technology or industry have also shaped categorization. Recent research has shown significant benefits from segmenting markets and developing products considering the "job" that a customer finds that they need to get done, and they "hire" products or services to do the job (Bettencourt & Ulwick, 2008; Christensen, Anthony, Berstell, & Nitterhouse, 2007; Ulwick, 2002; Wunker, Wattman, & Farber, 2016). This means that innovators need to understand the jobs that customers encounter, so that they can develop offerings that can be "hired" to solve them. This is consistent with the service-dominant logic (SDL) perspective, which considers that a market offering is only attractive if it delivers value-in-use (Vargo & Lusch, 2004).

Aligned with service dominant logic, but largely developed through professional practice, the jobs-to-be-done approach to opportunity recognition and evaluation moves the innovation focus of the organization from what is being produced – a product or service – to enabling customers to get their jobs done effectively. The approach has gained recognition in both the academic and practitioner spheres.

The key points at the heart of the jobs-to-be-done approach are:
- People and organizations buy offerings (products and services) to get jobs done
- As jobs are completed, there are certain measurable outcomes that they are trying to achieve
- The approach prioritises the identification of important but poorly served jobs, rather than unimportant or over-served jobs
- A focus on segments defined by customer desired outcomes rather than demographic and product centred segmentation techniques
- Jobs-to-be-done approaches link a firm's value creation activities to customer and user-defined metrics

Organizations like Innosight (co-founded by Clay Christensen) have developed consultancy offerings focused on helping large firms to mobilize the jobs-to-be-done approach. A robust and helpful approach is offered by Wunker, Wattman and Farber (2016), who advise that jobs-to-be-done projects should move through the following stages:
1. Strategy: Establish objectives
2. Planning the approach: Selecting research methods
3. Customer research: To build a map or atlas of the jobs-to-be-done

4. Ideation: To generate ideas
5. Open innovation: To support the reframing of perspectives of project team members
6. Experiment and iterate: Testing prototypes using MVP techniques to maximise learning

The jobs-to-be-done approach is at the centre of the popular Business Model Canvas and Value Proposition Design approaches (Osterwalder & Pigneur, 2010; Osterwalder, Pigneur, Bernarda, & Smith, 2014; Osterwalder, Pigneur, Etiemble, & Smith, 2020). However, to really get the best results from focusing on jobs-to-be-done, it is critical to deliver solutions for precisely identified customers, users and occasions within deeply understood workflows. Through focusing on particular users and customers in highly specific contexts, richer and more useful detail emerges than considering high level problems "on average." Current approaches should be explored, and pain points identified, with organizations like Intuit undertaking "painstorming" sessions to examine where opportunities for offering development can be found.

Through mapping the success criteria associated with jobs in both B2C and B2B environments, the development of an offering is centred on the significant detail that customers and users value above all else. The critical importance of delivering an offering that covers the social, emotional and functional aspects of the job should not be underestimated. The current obstacles to achieving the job should also be mapped for current and future solutions. This detailed mapping activity should assess the value of the offering that the firm might offer, and consider how the offering beats the competition. This approach works best when applied to important but under satisfied jobs in the eyes of the user and customer through designing specific offerings for specific and "big enough" i.e. monetizable occasions.

There are drivers which affect each job, and how users and customers undertake them. Attitudes will need to be considered, including personality traits that affect behaviour and decision making including social pressures. Both the long and short-term contextual factors affecting the job require attention, such as family or organizational dynamics (e.g. in a B2B DMU or project team), as well as wider cultural dynamics and socioeconomic factors. Circumstances that regularly impact on a job, such as weather or seasonal factors, work schedules, the need for collaboration and tiredness also require attention.

The importance of understanding workflows, and the jobs-to-be-done within them, can be illustrated considering the steps that need to be taken by a group of students who want to celebrate a friend's birthday – while also being under pressure to deliver a number of study assignments at the end of term. The friends could order in, eat out – or effectively contract out the planning and ordering of food and drink items to a range of suppliers, including supermarkets. Many players in the convenience food category have already established the stakeholders involved, current approaches and pain points.

The planning stage would be influenced by the need to establish what supplies are already available. The shopping stage would consider the fact that shopping after classes is more tiring, and more expensive, than shopping with good advanced planning. The cooking stage has pain points such as the kitchen being a mess, and the need to organize help – while avoiding the distractions of social media. The serving stage requires co-ordination, the supply of drinks, and infrastructure such as pots, pans and other houseware items. The cleaning stage can involve loneliness and resentment – or engaged conversations and teamwork – depending on the workflow and socialflow after the meal. All the pain points provide jobs-to-be-done, and commercial opportunities to a wide range of players.

If we flipped this scenario to the workflow involved in providing a wedding dinner in a hotel – the language is the same, but the social, functional and emotional jobs are very different. The workflow to prepare a dinner for political leaders and civil servants around a G20 summit focused on climate change in Paris would require different elements. The jobs-to-be-done in preparing for a working dinner for a startup with a potential investor, or initial major client, would be different again. Moving from general areas of commercial opportunity, to specific occasions with precisely defined jobs is essential for firms developing a range of offerings that separate them from the competition (Kalbach, 2020).

Digital jobs-to-be-done

In providing digital solutions to jobs-to-be-done that will be experienced in the digital realm, companies must develop the capacity to capture data to validate what value is required, and to measure if the solution has helped the user to achieve their desired outcomes. Research by strategy& shows that a leading group of 1,000 companies increased investment in R&D by 11.4 percent in 2018 as compared to 2017. Investment in software and internet focused R&D increased by 20.6 percent (Jaruzelski, Chwalik, & Goehle, 2018). However a previous study also found that investors in R&D typically underinvest in the "fuzzy front end" of innovation (Jaruzelski, Staack, & Goehle, 2014). The same study estimates that a mere 8 percent of large R&D spending is allocated to digital tools that track changing customer needs. Despite the runaway success of organizations such as Facebook, Amazon and Alibaba that have invested heavily in understanding jobs-to-be-done in both the B2C and B2B digital spheres, greater attention is needed in most organizations in serving emerging jobs beyond the core in fast moving digital arenas.

The development of B2B solutions to support companies and managers in becoming more efficient and effective in operational terms has a long history, advanced by a literature that has moved beyond goods dominant logic to widespread acknowledgement of service dominant logic (Lindgreen, Hingley, Grant, & Morgan, 2012; Lusch & Vargo, 2011). The solutions that are being developed in the B2B space increasingly seek to solve the problems faced by individuals and work groups in their value creation processes, and companies focus on value creation as helping customers to get one or more jobs done (i.e. achieving a goal or solving a problem) (Bettencourt, Lusch, & Vargo, 2014).

Due to the speed with which user behaviours are changing, and new digitally enabled jobs are developing in the workflow of stakeholders, the research project evaluated the presence of the capability to identify and validate "big enough" pervasive problems (jobs) requiring solutions within the case companies in the HE publishing sector.

Validation and iteration of opportunities through MVP testing and learning

Kirzner's research concerning alertness to profit opportunities has had a major influence on the development of the field of entrepreneurship (Kirzner, 2009; Klein & Foss, 2010). Shane & Venkataraman (2000, p. 218) defined research into entrepreneurship as: "The scholarly examination of how, by whom, and with what effects opportunities to create future goods and services are discovered, evaluated and exploited." To achieve these goals: "The field involves the study of sources of opportunities; the processes of discovery, evaluation, and exploitation of opportunities; and the set of individuals who discover, evaluate, and exploit them" (Shane & Venkataram, 2000, p. 218). A particular characteristic of entrepreneurial opportunities is that they require vigilance to discover new means-ends relationships, whereas all other opportunities develop the efficiency of existing goods, raw materials, organizing methods and services.

Scholars have argued that entrepreneurship is principally concerned with newness, often related to new technologies, resulting in novel products, new markets and new processes (Ireland, Hitt, & Sirmon, 2003), with both discovering and exploiting opportunities the basis of wealth creation through entrepreneurship. To create additional wealth, companies and individuals with enhanced skills in sensing and seizing opportunities stand to benefit. Without doubt, opportunity recognition is at the centre of entrepreneurship.

The strategic management literature emphasises the importance of advantage seeking for wealth creation, as well as opportunity seeking (i.e. entrepreneurship). However opportunity seeking to develop competitive advantage in core, adjacent and breakthrough environments requires firms to develop both opportunity and advantage seeking capabilities at the same time to generate a set of real options for growth. Considering the research project, the requirement to develop both advantage (sustaining innovation) and opportunity (adjacent and breakthrough) seeking capabilities informs both the development of a portfolio of opportunities, and the organizational structure to manage these different processes.

Startups and small companies have typically been relatively effective in identifying entrepreneurial opportunities, but are less skilled in creating and maintaining the competitive advantages required to exploit and grow opportunities over a prolonged period. Established large organizations are typically adept in developing and sustaining competitive advantage, but often lack the capability to identify fresh opportunities suitable for exploitation through their capabilities and resources. However, some vigilant established firms are effective at introducing radical innovations into markets (Chandy & Tellis, 2000; Tellis, 2013), and are skilled in opportunity recognition. The challenge for established firms is how best to identify opportunities effectively. Should they be looking themselves, or should they be working through smaller organizations better suited to developing opportunities, but who lack the scale and skills to commercialise radical opportunities?

While the literature suggests that opportunity recognition demands different structures to operationalize the search process beyond the core business, recent research suggests that firms do not necessarily need to separate the processes of opportunity discovery and opportunity realisation. The decentralisation of opportunity discovery and realisation furthers performance, as long as it happens in the same corporate venture unit (Foss & Lyngsie, 2015; Hill & Birkinshaw, 2008).

A persistent and key question addressed in the entrepreneurship field concerns why some entrepreneurs recognize opportunities that others fail to see? Busenitz and Barney (1997, p. 11) found that: "After a great deal of research it is now often concluded that most of the psychological differences between entrepreneurs and managers in large organizations are small or non-existent." Research on cognition has indicated that entrepreneurs who recognize opportunities are strong at pattern recognition (Baron, 2006), but there is limited evidence to support this premise. Dyer, Gregersen and Christensen (2019) suggest that innovative entrepreneurs differ from executives who have never started an innovative venture on four behavioural patterns: (1) questioning, particularly challenging the status quo; (2) observing; (3) experimenting with a "hypothesis testing mindset"; and (4) idea networking, testing ideas across a diverse network.

Opportunity evaluation has suffered from a lack of attention as an area of research as compared to opportunity recognition (Wood & McKelvie, 2015). Research in this area has advanced since Shane & Venkataraman (2000) helped the academic entrepreneurship community to conceptualise the opportunity recognition task, which logically needs to be paired with an effective opportunity evaluation process. Recent research has served to increase the overall understanding of opportunity evaluation looking at the characteristics of both individuals and organizations. Amongst others, it has been established that factors such as emotions (Grichnik, Smeja, & Welpe, 2010), uncertainty (McKelvie, Haynie, & Gustavsson, 2011), values

(Shepherd, Patzelt, & Baron, 2013), and prior knowledge (Haynie, Shepherd, & McMullen, 2009) all influence opportunity evaluation.

As opportunity evaluation research develops, there is a need to establish how different factors, such as values (Shepherd et al., 2013) and worst-case scenarios (Wood & Williams, 2014) combine to influence evaluation and decision making (Drover, Wood, & Payne, 2014). The role of heuristics and rule-based reasoning in opportunity evaluation presents an opportunity to develop a theoretical framework to advance understanding in this key stage of the innovation and entrepreneurial processes (Sull & Eisenhardt, 2012; Williams & Wood, 2015).

Entrepreneurship is fundamentally about "doing" and "entrepreneuring" can be seen as how change makers deal with the situations that they encounter. The notion of entrepreneurship as a sequence of routinized solution finding fits well with the jobs-to-be-done approach. Entrepreneurs flex social, human and financial capital to solve problems, with their skills in mobilizing networks a key element within their toolkit. If entrepreneuring is a flow of "doing", then entrepreneurs, whether they are working in startup or corporate environments, need to manage a series of experiments to validate understanding – and establish options. Agile innovation techniques allied with MPVs enable change makers to solve problems and test solutions as they occur.

Agile innovation and minimum viable products (MVPs)

Thomke (1998, p. 743) observed that: "Experimentation, a form of problem-solving, is a fundamental innovation activity and accounts for a significant part of total innovation cost and time", and two decades of research into offering development and innovation has particularly focused on understanding how best companies can manage experiments to develop higher success rates at lower cost (Thomke, 1998; Thomke & Manzi, 2014; Thomke & Reinertsen, 2012). Early work with Toyota (Thomke & Fujimoto, 2000) emphasised the potential of rapid problem-solving to increase development performance. The positive impact of user engagement in shortening offering development cycles while increasing success supports experimentation activities that enable fast failure, as the best teams aim to fail fast, often and cheaply (Blank, 2013; McGrath, 2011).

The notion that companies will flourish if they learn to be nimble and good at product development is not new, with the term "agile" being: "Coined by a group of researchers at Iaccoca Institute at Lehigh University in 1991. The group involved many of the senior executives of US companies and the study culminated in a two-volume report conveying an industry-led vision for a fundamental shift in manufacturing paradigm" (Yusuf, Sarhadi, & Gunasekaran, 1999, p. 33). The most significant sector-wide adoption of internal agility has been in software development, following the creation of the "Agile Manifesto" in 2001 (Beck et al., 2001).

The aim of the Agile Manifesto was to place the goals and needs of the end-users of information and communications technology (ICT) at the centre of software development to deliver software that is both useful and usable. User-centred agile software development considers the process, practices, people/social and technology dimensions of delivering software (Brhel, Meth, Maedche, & Werder, 2015).

The agile process for developing software has been adopted widely and with significant effect in areas such as efficiency and stakeholder satisfaction, and positively influences project velocity and effort. The agility concept has been applied to supply chains, and has identified that: "No less than nine different Agile methods have been described, including Scrum, Crystal, Extreme Programming, Adaptive Software Development, Agile Modelling, Dynamic Systems Development Method, Feature Driven Development, Internet Speed Development, and Pragmatic Programming" (Sommer, Hedegaard, Dukovska-Popovska, & Steger-Jensen, 2015 p. 35).

Despite the rapid adoption of agile software development processes, companies still struggle with the offering development process, with many companies treating the development process as being similar to manufacturing (Thomke & Reinertsen, 2012). Some organizations are starting to mix their offering development methods, combining elements of the agile method with traditional stage-gate processes.

The publication of "The Lean Startup" (Ries, 2011) and "The Startup Way" (Ries, 2017) increased the crossover between the agile movement and the practice of innovation, particularly in the US. Ries emphasised the critical importance of validated learning to product development, particularly in startups, as he encouraged technology entrepreneurs to move their products through a six stage loop made up of: (1) Ideas; (2) Build; (3) Code; (4) Measure; (5) Data; (6) Learn, minimising time and maximising learning constantly. The approach was influenced by the continual organizational learning approaches central to Toyota's management system, inspired in turn by Deming, and Christensen's research into disruptive innovation (Christensen, 1997; Christensen & Raynor, 2003).

The argument is that multi-disciplined agile teams made up of 6–9 multi-disciplinary staff are well suited to driving innovation. They create value from ideas to develop products and services, processes, and the business models through which organizations structure their business activities with a range of stakeholders. When challenged with a significant and complex problem, agile teams break their work down into modules, creating solutions for each component through rapid prototyping and fast feedback loops. Many of the elements of the approach such as "probe and learn" have been studied for many years, with Rapid Prototyping Journal having been around since 1995. The notion of agility sees the teams being focused on solving problems outside the firm wherever possible, to increase impact and speed. As Rigby, Sutherland and Noble put it (2018, p. 90–91), agile teams: "Place more value on adapting to change than on sticking to a plan, and they hold themselves accountable for outcomes (such as growth, profitability, and customer loyalty), not outputs (such as lines of code or number of new products)."

Ries promoted the critical role of MVPs to entrepreneurs who need to start the learning process as quickly as possible, claiming that: "It is simply the fastest way to get through the Build-Measure-Learn feedback loop with the minimum amount of effort" (Ries, 2011, p. 93). The MVP term had been in use since at least 2000 as an element within a number of offering development approaches, with the MVP approach being very similar to Blank's concept of the "minimum feature set" (Blank & Dorf, 2012). Ries was also influenced by Moore (1998), who advocated that early adopters accept, or even prefer, an 80 percent solution. Experimentation enables managers to drop the components of an offering that have a low or negative ROI. There are also parallels in the highly iterative MVP process with design thinking.

The lean startup approach favours experimentation rather than elaborate planning, customer feedback rather than intuition, and iterative design instead of traditional "big design up front development". Although the methodology is just a few years old, its concepts and terminology, such as MVPs and "pivoting" – have quickly taken root in the startup world, and business schools have already begun adapting their curricula to teach these approaches, with a strong emphasis on experimentation. Agile innovation approaches, typified by the application of MVP experimentation, have been embraced by practitioners as a valid part of the innovator's toolkit in the digital era in technology enabled organizations and networks (Shepherd & Gruber, 2020).

Entrepreneurship in all types of organization, including startups, scaleups, and established firms, can be seen as a process of problem-finding and problem-solving under conditions of uncertainty. Entrepreneurs and firms create value as they frame, identify and solve problems. Sull (2004) envisioned the entrepreneurial process as one where entrepreneurs conduct experiments to test hypotheses focused on a hypothesized space in the market that could be satisfied profitably by a fresh combination of resources. Hypothesis testing is also a part of the foundations of the lean startup method. Up until recently academic research interest in the deployment of MVPs has been limited, despite the widespread use of agile approaches in IT technology dependent sectors, and the popularity of lean startup inspired practices (Brhel et al., 2015; Kupiainen, Mäntylä, & Itkonen, 2015; Serrador & Pinto, 2015).

Fortunately this gap has been explored by a research group from Bocconi Business school in Milan, who looked for insights into entrepreneurial decision making and new venture performance (Camuffo, Cordova, Gambardella, & Spina, 2019). They were interested in how the performance of hypothesis based MVPs which benefited from relatively high levels of planning might compare to less refined and more quickly assembled MVPs using search heuristics like trial and error processes, effectuation or confirmatory search. Based on findings from 116 Italian startups, they found that MVP based decisions based on hypotheses developed through a scientific testing approach performed better than decisions relying on non-hypothesis based and less developed MVPs. The more scientific approach increases firm performance, because those pursuing entrepreneurial activity (identifying and validating opportunities) can identify when their early-stage projects indicate low or high returns, or when it is better to pivot to different ideas.

In summary, startup and corporate entrepreneurs with carefully considered and validated theories of their business and hypotheses about what their users and customers require can test their ideas for future offerings through experiments. More scientific, hypothesis based MVPs generate objective results to better mitigate their own biases and lack of clarity regarding new offerings, as compared to less developed and more chaotic MVP testing, where less prepared entrepreneurs tend to test ideas with friends and those who feel less able to give objective feedback. MVP and agile approaches lower development costs, and shorten the time that firms take to move through the Build-Measure-Learn loop, helping firms to stop weak projects faster, and develop promising opportunities quickly and cheaply.

The measure phase secures data to determine whether the offering development effort is solving problems and creating value, supporting the design of value capture models.

Recruitment and connection with individuals outside the firm's core industry

We have established that to compete in today's rapidly changing world that vigilant external knowledge sourcing, and the capability to spot and exploit new technologies and ideas from beyond the firm's boundaries, are becoming ever more important. We know that the firms that are more open to external knowledge achieve higher levels of innovation performance. However, organizations find the acquisition of external knowledge complex, with complicated webs of geographical, organizational and technological boundaries. An added complication is that the skills needed for external search are not the same as those required for the internal transfer of knowledge (Hansen, 1999; Monteiro & Birkinshaw, 2016).

Research indicates that scientists and engineers with access to different domains of knowledge are better able to transfer solutions originally developed for one domain to another (Fleming, 2001; Gruber et al., 2013; Hargadon & Sutton, 1997; Singh & Fleming, 2010), increasing the efficiency of search activities. People who span heterogeneous communities access unique information which develops a "vision advantage" (Burt, 2004). The vision advantage is recognized by colleagues (Dahlander et al., 2014), with external sources of knowledge more highly valued by other organizational members, due to the perception that this information is rarer than internal knowledge sources (Menon & Pfeffer, 2003). Individuals with the potential to increase search breadth increase access to a variety of knowledge sources that increases the total number of ideas on offer to solve innovation problems within the firm.

The benefits flowing from linking a range of knowledge resources in new ways are restricted when individuals only search within their own firm. Innovation search that does not reach beyond the boundary of the firm has a lower likelihood of impacting on technological developments (Rosenkopf & Nerkar, 2001). Research into the inventor's search and discovery routines found that: "It is not always the depth of knowledge and experience of the searcher that results in discovery. Rather, it is the unique breadth of these components in addition to the ability to draw from seemingly different terrains and categories to arrive at solutions and discoveries" (Maggitti et al., 2013, p. 97). A study considering the innovation platform InnoCentive found that individuals distant from the knowledge domain where the innovation problem arose were more able to develop solutions to the challenges than people closest to the original knowledge domain (Jeppesen & Lakhani, 2010).

IDEO, the highly influential design agency with deep connections to Stanford University, is engaged by organizations to foster original thinking and stimulate creative solutions to user problems. A leader in design thinking, the firm highlights the importance of the cross-pollination of ideas. Cross-pollinators can see patterns where others don't, and spot key differences. They often think in metaphors, enabling them to see relationships and connections that others miss. IDEO describes cross-pollinators as T-shaped people, who typically have a depth of knowledge in at least one area of expertise. What makes them different – and highly impactful, is that they have a breadth of knowledge in many fields, and they are good at "joining the dots". Good cross-pollinators can send shock waves across an organization, as they bring in big ideas from the outside (Kelley, 2006). It is important for firms to bring in cross-pollinators from outside, with different knowledge sets and skills to more established staff. T-shaped thinkers can freshen up thinking, and connect ideas internally as well as exploiting pro-active linkages with external individuals and partner organizations. The importance of T-shaped thinkers is also emphasised by Dyer, Gregersen and Christensen as they consider what makes up "The Innovator's DNA" (2019).

Established firms often risk being limited in their search and select activities through a lack of collaboration both internally, and externally (Hansen, 2009), with boundary spanning an important capability both individually, and as an enterprise. Through recruiting and connecting with individuals with knowledge from outside core markets, firms gain access to the different skills, perspectives and networks that they need to search for and select a balanced portfolio of options beyond the core.

Identification and validation of external acquisition & investment opportunities

A number of key factors influence the degree of engagement, and the probability of activity in acquiring external organizations considering innovation contexts: the size and characteristics of the technological innovativeness of the organizations involved, their performance, and the nature of the environment (Ahuja & Novelli, 2014). Companies with declining levels of internal productivity have a need and greater likelihood of acquisition activity to increase their R&D options than those that are effective at developing opportunities through company centred activity (Higgins & Rodriguez, 2006). Alternatively, an acquirer's strong performance in innovation activities can also lead to acquisition activity (Kaul, 2012). This can be the case because M&A does not just concern access to new knowledge, but can also represent effective and efficient means to secure complementary capabilities for commercialisation in response to a new technological innovation with significant potential (Ahuja & Novelli, 2014; Markides & Geroski, 2005).

A technologically stronger acquisition target firm has the potential to increase focal company knowledge. The RBV argues that that the level of technology resources of the acquisition target can support the choice of M&A over alliance, to tighten secure access to the relevant capabilities and resources (Villalonga & McGahan, 2005). Firms with lower levels of specialised knowledge can see M&A as a route to diversification, and are more likely to pursue them. Additionally, aspects of the knowledge seen as valuable to the acquirer, such as its uniqueness, or inimitability, also leads to a greater incidence of acquisitions as compared to alliances and other governance options, due to greater concerns over the opportunism of other parties (Schilling & Steensma, 2002). A mix of acquisitions and alliances have been seen to grow faster than their competitors using a narrower set of options (Dyer, Kale, & Singh, 2004).

The performance of the firms involved in acquisition – both acquirer and target, influences the likelihood of acquisition (Ahuja & Novelli, 2014). Firms growing through acquisition have reduced levels of R&D intensity than matched competitors who develop innovation activity centred on the firm (Miller, 2004). The likelihood of acquisition increases when the focal firm's level of performance falls below expected levels, and when organizational slack is available (Iyer & Miller, 2008). Companies are susceptible to acquisition when they face major hurdles such as CEO search, a funding round, or failures of their own (Graebner & Eisenhardt, 2004).

The nature of the technological environment also affects the incidence of M&A. The acquisition of small technology centred firms is a common option to secure knowledge, capabilities and resources in rapid change technology environments. While many organizations undertaking M&A identify innovation as their prime goal, and some researchers have found a positive influence on the innovation outcomes of the acquirers (Capron, Dussauge, & Mitchell, 1998; Desyllas & Hughes, 2010), many studies have shown a negative relationship between acquisition intensity and the level of internal innovation caused by the demands of preparation, negotiations and integration activities (Hitt, Hoskisson, Johnson, & Moesel, 1996). A further limiting impact on innovation stems from managers over-estimating their capacity to manage an acquired firm (Hitt, Hoskisson, & Harrison, 1991). Acquisitions regularly lead to more limited innovation impacts than anticipated (Chaudhuri & Tabrizi, 1999). M&A can reduce the productivity of inventors (Kapoor & Lim, 2007), often leading to key inventors exiting the acquired company (Ernst & Vitt, 2000).

The acquisition of companies and development of alliances are key parts of the innovation search and select toolkit. As companies develop a portfolio of opportunities, they require the capability to identify and validate high potential opportunities.

Investing in, acquiring, and collaborating with external organizations

The importance of networks to innovation search was foreseen by Rothwell's pioneering work, which saw a transition from organizations managing a linear R&D push or demand pull process to a situation of growing inter-activity. Some of the first moves that organizations make are to establish cross-functional teams, and increase collaboration with suppliers. These initiatives are then typically developed towards connections with external actors. Rothwell's vision in the 1990s of a "fifth generation" of innovation with deep and far reaching connections supported by IT supported communication envisaged the context within which innovation takes place today (Gardiner & Rothwell, 1985; Rothwell, 1977, 1992).

The importance of networks to business growth is now well established, with Adner highlighting the crucial role of innovation ecosystems. Importantly, he identifies the role of major and supporting complementors to lead firms, with the attendant innovation risk inherent in innovation eco-systems as they get more complex (Adner, 2006, 2013; Adner & Feiler, 2019).

Visible relationships with high-profile and respected organizations lead to more positive perceptions of the company's innovation by other key actors in the organization's network (Podolny & Stuart, 1995; Stuart & Podolny, 1996), which then leads to more high-status partners joining the network of relationships (or ecosystem) surrounding the company. Consistent with this view, the involvement of multiple low status partners can reduce the attractiveness of an innovation if they suggest low quality to the rest of the ecosystem (McGrath & Kim, 2014).

While strategy scholars have typically looked at the comparative performance of particular companies, innovation scholars have long understood that breakthroughs are usually supported by networks (Adner, 2013; Hargadon, 2003). Successful innovation typically draws on a mix of companies, investors, universities, corporate and government research labs, suppliers and customers. In an era of fast moving digital platforms and transient advantage, the network of actors outside the boundaries of the organization has become even more important to the understanding of innovation and strategic performance. Contributors to innovation are not restricted to for-profit companies, with the bio-technology sector showing how universities and public research organizations are also essential for success (Powell, White, Koput, & Owen-Smith, 2005).

Networks have a major effect on the adoption and diffusion of innovation. A network can influence the actions of its members in two ways (Gulati, 1998). Firstly, through the flow and sharing of information within the network. Secondly, through the differences in the position of actors in the network, which cause control and power imbalances. The position an organization occupies in a network is of great strategic performance, and reflects their relative power and influence in the network. Sources of power include technology, trust, expertise, economic strength, and legitimacy (Garud & Kumaraswamy, 1993). Networks are useful where the benefits of co-specialisation, sharing of standards and joint infrastructure, and other network externalities outweigh the costs of maintaining and providing governance to the network. Where there are high transaction costs connected with buying technology, network approaches can be more appropriate than market models. Where there is uncertainty, a network approach can be superior to acquisition or full integration (Tidd, 2010).

Innovation networks offer more than just ways to bring together and deploy knowledge in complex environments. They can also have "emergent properties" – the potential for the wider network to deliver more than the sum of its parts. Organizations in effective knowledge networks benefit from collective knowledge efficiency, access to different and complementary knowledge sets, reducing risks through sharing experience, access to new markets and technologies, and the pooling of complementary skills and assets (Tidd, 2010).

Networks can be tight or loose, depending on the quantity (number), quality (intensity) and type (closeness to core activities) of the links or interactions. Links are more than individual transactions, requiring major investments in resources over time. Historically, networks have often evolved from long-standing business relationships. All organizations have a group of partners that they do business with regularly, e.g. suppliers, distributors, customers, competitors and universities. Over time, mutual knowledge and social bonds develop through repeated dealings, increasing trust and reducing transaction costs. Therefore, an organization is more likely to work with members of its network when it comes to buying or selling technology.

Tidd and Bessant (2018) have summarized how engineered networks can be configured, identifying nine network types: entrepreneur-based; internal project teams; communities of practice; spatial clusters; sectoral networks; new product or process development consortium; new technology development consortium; emerging standards and supply chain learning.

The formation processes of networks have been studied (Ring, Doz, & Olk, 2005), identifying different managerial activities at different stages of the development of the network. Research indicates that two main activities are involved for companies building connections in networks: identifying the relevant new partners, and learning how to work with them. The process is somewhat like the development of effective teams (forming, storming, norming and performing), but the process has three stages: finding, forming and performing (Birkinshaw, Bessant, & Delbridge, 2007). Barriers to success in the process are geographical; technological; institutional; ideological; demographic and ethnic. Managing activities within the firm is complex, but managing within networks multiplies the level of complexity greatly. As networks move through the set-up, operating and sustaining/closure stages, there are some generic challenges for organizations operating within networks:

1. How to manage something the organization does not own or control
2. How to see system-level effects, not narrow self-interests
3. How to build shared risk-taking and trust without over-complex documentation and legal frameworks
4. How to minimise unintended consequences and spillovers

Research into organizational learning suggests that it is not just the number of alliances that matters, and that a broader selection of partnerships is advantageous, even if the immediate economic returns are not obvious. Working with a broad selection of firms has been shown to bring even more relationships, increasing demands on the company's absorptive capacity and its capability to adapt to different environments. The ability to collaborate is critical, and involvement in networks is an "admission ticket" to increasingly diverse future collaborations (Powell et al., 1996).

Understanding social networks has long played a role in management research. The more diverse an individual's social network, the more likely that individual is going to be innovative. Parise et al. have researched into the use of social networks identifying the roles of "idea scouts" and "idea connectors" (Parise, Whelan, & Todd, 2015; Whelan, Parise, Valk, & Aalbers, 2011) in a digitally enabled era of social networks. This work builds on Burt's seminal research into structural holes (Burt, 2000, 2004). The importance of social networks to the innovation enterprise concerns both collaboration with a firm's internal networks (Hansen, 2009), and with external organizations and individuals (Dahlander & Wallin, 2006). Open innovation relies on the widening of networks, including social networks. The digital era increases access to data, increasing the ability to analyse the social networks in place in business ecosystems, and for organizations to build connections through the activities of their staff.

Acquisition and/or collaboration can bring in essential capabilities and new opportunities, but only if the firm can mobilize itself to acquire and integrate target organizations effectively, or manage collaborations for mutual benefit.

Summary of dynamic sub-capabilities

Exposure to the research and thinking of Teece and proponents of the significance of dynamic capabilities establishes the importance to organizations of being able to sense and seize opportunities, and transform themselves accordingly. This chapter has explored the sub-capabilities below the sensing, seizing and transforming level that actually enable them to regenerate themselves. Through this process, 11 dynamic sub-capabilities have been identified that support the management of innovation search and select processes in disrupting environments.

4 Vigilant innovation in the STM publishing sector

The book assesses the search and select innovation capabilities of publishers in the scientific, technical and medical (STM) publishing sector worth $26.2 billion annually. The scholarly journals market alone is worth $6.8 billion (Cookson, 2015), and is primarily focused on the publication of research undertaken at great expense globally in the world's leading universities, and their regular research partners in R&D orientated firms and government funded institutes. The sector is significant not only due to its size financially, but because governments, companies, NGOs, public sector organizations, philanthropists and society look to research that has been undertaken using sound methodologies and robust validation techniques to make the scientific and social progress that moves our complex planet forwards. Every day in both our private and professional lives we are bombarded with discussions and decisions that include the consideration of research that is published in peer-reviewed "scholarly" journals. The integrity of the research published in scholarly journals is based on the effective operation of the peer-review system managed by journal publishers, and the subject specialist editors and reviewers that serve each journal.

Access to high quality research remains important to teachers in universities and schools, who develop and teach qualification centred courses. The diffusion of research through traditional means such as textbooks and non-researcher targeted publications such as Harvard Business Review and New Scientist also continues to be important. An increasingly educated society is frustrated by the inability of governments and global institutions to respond effectively to a complex range of social, ethical, technological and inter-generational challenges. As society and its institutions struggle to work through the complexities of climate change and the widespread digitization of workflows and socialflows, the demand for optimal access to the world's valuable research base has increased. The coronavirus pandemic saw political leaders and senior civil servants standing shoulder to shoulder with scientists and health professionals who relied on research to make decisions like never before.

Henry Oldenberg of The Royal Society founded the world's first scientific publication in 1665, and from the start it was an international journal, drawing on new ideas from France, Hungary, Italy and Germany. Fast forward over 350 years, and science is a massive and global activity, with the dissemination of research increasingly an imperative for the funders of research. In 2015 it was estimated that there were 7.8 million researchers worldwide, an increase of 21% since 2007 (UNESCO, 2015) supported by a collective international R&D (research and development) spend of US$1.7 trillion (UNESCO, 2019).

The digital era – as compared to the paper based era – has transformed how academic journal articles are written and used. It has also changed the way that the utility and use of a journal article can be assessed, adding usage figures to the assessment of

https://doi.org/10.1515/9783110657326-004

citation as measures of impact. Digitalization has underpinned the development of Open Access as an alternative business model for academic publishing, through which research outputs are made available online, at no cost, with no access barriers. Barriers to reuse and copying are also removed or reduced. The development of Open Access journals has meant that university based researchers are offered alternative routes to distribute their research outputs (Johnson et al., 2018). The growth in Open Access publishing since the early 2000s has made journal publishing more diverse and competitive. A report shows that 37% of UK research outputs are freely available to the world through Open Access at publication, and after 24 months 53% of UK research is available for free. Open Access publishing certainly meets Leifer et al's measure of a "significant (30% or greater) reduction in cost for readers".

STM publishing is disrupting due to the impact of the digitization of the research and learning processes, globalization, and an increasing expectation that research should be freely available. The study considers the key search and select capabilities in 10 established publishers, including six out of 10 of the largest STM journal publishers by number of journals at the time of the study, as they map the innovation space to identify, create and commercialise a portfolio of innovation projects in core, adjacent and peripheral/transformative markets.

Scholarly publishing is a high margin industry. Elsevier, the market leader, publishes 16% of the journal articles published by leading publishers, and secures operating profit margins of 34%, almost four times the average profit margin of groups in the FTSE 100 at that time (Cookson, 2015). The sector includes Cambridge University Press, the world's oldest publisher, established in 1534. The first journal was published in 1665 by The Royal Society in London. The STM publishing industry is disrupting due to fast changing delivery mechanisms, i.e. digital content, changing business models (Atkins, 2014), and limited funding for scholarly content (Johnson et al., 2018).

Scientific and academic publisher sales and margins have stayed under the spotlight since the research phase, with the University of California, Berkeley cancelling its $11M subscription to Relx (formerly Reed Elsevier's) journals in 2019. The prestigious university said at the time that "depriving" people of access to publicly-funded research is "terrible for society." While HE customers might be pushing back at scholarly publishers, in 2018 Relx and Informa (incl. Taylor and Francis) sustained margins above 35%, John Wiley & Sons achieved around 30%, with SpringerNature in the high 20% range (Financial Times, 2019).

Publishing and research dissemination are changing, with Research Councils UK, a means through which the UK government directs funding to academic researchers, ruling that from 2013 the results of the research that it pays for have to be published in journals that make them free through Open Access (OA) – ideally straight away, but certainly within a year. In the US the White House Office of Science and Technology has followed a similar path, as has the European Union. An EU report showed that the tipping point (more than 50% of the papers available for free) for OA has been reached in several countries, including Brazil, Switzerland, the Netherlands, the US, as well as in biomedical research, biology, and mathematics and statistics (Archambault et al., 2013). Disruptive services such as SSRN, ResearchGate and Academia.edu now connect millions of researchers to tens of millions of articles.

OA is upending the funding model, with online tools and illicit pirate-sites such as Sci-Hub taking readers from the publisher's paid-for platforms. A study by Our Research, a proponent of OA, found that 31% of all journal articles published in 2019 were outside the traditional paywall. Springer Nature and Informa's Taylor and Francis moved faster in the realm of pay-to-publish models, with more than 75 percent of Springer Nature authors in Sweden, the Netherlands and the UK now publishing through free-to-read journals. Elsevier, the publisher of the world's oldest medical journal, The Lancet, is now developing new offerings that bundle publishing rights, analytics services and data tools for the first time, demonstrating a marked willingness to experiment. These new moves have created a new positioning for Elsevier, moving the sector's largest player from journal publisher to supporting academic research from idea generation and funding to the collection of data and publication (Barker & Nilsson, 2020).

HE is globalising, in terms of the growth of foreign students enrolled in tertiary education systems beyond their own countries. In 2005 there were 2.8M tertiary international HE students, and by 2013 the figure was 4.1M (UNESCO, 2015). Collaboration between researchers from different institutions and countries is increasing, but the position of the established science superpowers of the United States and Europe is declining (Adams, 2012). Research driven universities guide their researchers to collaborate widely, as highly cited articles – the nirvana for research scientists – increasingly benefit from the diversity of thought and experience inherent in international research projects.

The role of China in the HE environment, considering both education (teaching students) and research, has changed dramatically during the 21st century. China has increased spending on R&D tenfold between 2000 and 2016, and in terms of purchasing-power parity, the US, Europe and China each spend over $400 billion. The US and China now award similar numbers of engineering and natural science doctoral degrees at around 30,000 per year. However, when it comes to first degrees in natural sciences and engineering, China awards almost twice as many BScs as the EU and the US put together. Staying focused on STM subjects, China now publishes the same number of peer-reviewed science and engineering papers as the US. India has increased its share of the number of papers published to around a quarter of the level of China and the US during the same period. It is telling that the US, EU and Japan have all seen their total number of peer-reviewed science and engineering articles declining since 2014 (Economist, 2019).

With STM publishing disrupting due to digitalization, globalization, cost pressures and new business models including Open Access mandates connected to government research funding, the STM information market is unlikely to escape further change. For these reasons the HE focused scholarly publishing sector provides a dynamic and rapidly changing research context to explore how well equipped publishers are when it comes to the key search and select sub-capabilities identified in Chapter 3.

Findings from 10 case companies in the HE publishing industry

Considering offering development search and select, the study was designed to explore the seven steps that Day and Schoemaker (2006, p. 5) identified in "Peripheral Vision" as being essential to bridging what they described as the "vigilance gap":
- Step 1: Scoping: where to look
- Step 2: Scanning: how to look
- Step 3: Interpreting: what the data means
- Step 4: Probing: what to explore more closely
- Step 5: Acting: what to do with these insights
- Step 6: Organizing: how to develop vigilance
- Step 7: Leading: an agenda for action

Rationale for the selection of the case organizations

The author is well networked in the academic publishing industry, having worked at board level for 12 years at one of the case companies, Emerald Group Publishing, which helped in selecting and accessing the case companies. Based on this in depth knowledge of both the HE environment and the differing missions and scale of scholarly publishers operating in the HE market, 10 case companies operating at a global scale in highly globalised HE publishing markets were selected. Comparisons are made between the findings from four large commercial companies, two medium sized commercial companies, two university owned publishers, and two society publishers (Table 4.1).

The case companies are all established organizations, tracing back their publishing activities for an average of 178 years at the time of the research phase, making this set of case companies possibly one of the oldest on record. The average length of service of the interviewees at each publisher was over 10 years, and across all of the organizations interviewed individuals had worked in publishing for an average of over 17 years. The interviewees collectively had 650 years of experience in their current companies, and 1,074 years of experience in total in publishing. This data reflects significant knowledge of STM publishing, as well as a limited level of movement from one publisher to another.

Table 4.1: Case sample structure.

Type Of Publisher	Number of Publishers
Large commercial companies	4
Medium commercial companies	2
University owned publishers	2
Society publishers	2
Total	10

The 10 largest publishers, by number of journals

A table showing the relative size of the 10 largest publishers by number of journals at the time of the data gathering process is below (Table 4.2). The research project engaged with six of the 10 largest publishers at the time of the fieldwork, by number of journals (Ware & Mabe, 2015). The quality of the case sample positively influenced the quality of the findings. It should be noted that the number of journals published does not necessarily equate to financial turnover. Analysis of the Thomson-Reuters Journal Citation database indicates that the proportions of article output by type of publisher were: commercial publishers (including publishing for societies): 64%; society publishers: 30%; university presses: 4%; other publishers: 2% (Ware & Mabe, 2015, p. 45).

Table 4.2: The 10 largest STM publishers, by number of journals (Ware & Mabe, 2015 p. 45).

Publisher	Number of journals
Springer (before merger with Macmillan)	2,987
Elsevier	2,500
Wiley	2,388
Taylor & Francis	2,105
SAGE	750
Wolters Kluwer (inc Medknow)	672
Hindawi	438
Cambridge University Press (CUP)	350
OUP	362
Macmillan (NPG: Nature Publishing Group)	178

Anonymising the case companies

The case companies were assigned simple identifiers as Case A, Case B etc., as shown in Table 4.3.

Table 4.3: Case company identifiers.

Case	Type of Publisher
Case A	Large commercial
Case B	Large commercial
Case C	Large commercial
Case D	Large commercial
Case E	Medium commercial
Case F	Medium commercial
Case G	University owned
Case H	University owned
Case I	Society publisher
Case J	Society publisher

The author took the view that it was important to collect data from staff at different levels, and from a variety of disciplines, from a range of different types of HE publisher. Therefore a key objective in designing the study was to interview staff from senior level, e.g. CEO; MD; Vice President and their direct reports across a wide range of business disciplines so that a full picture could be established of how innovation activities are managed within HE publishers.

The data was collected through 61 mainly face to face semi-structured interviews with 63 senior staff at the level of CEO/Senior Vice President/Managing Director, and their direct reports, as well as a number of market insight specialists. The interviews were mainly with UK based staff (53), and 10 individuals based in the US. The field work was conducted between October 2014 and April 2015.

Context: What has changed most within HE publishers in recent times?

Academia, and the closely associated STM publishing industry, was one of the earliest markets and user communities to fully embrace digitally delivered services. This is partly connected with Tim Berners-Lee driving forward the development of the World Wide Web at the CERN research laboratory in the early 1990s as a means to connect researchers, and facilitate the sharing of knowledge. The building of communities around subject areas, academic departments, research institutes, research intensive companies and journals has always been at the centre of the activities of both researchers and the publishers who have supported the diffusion of knowledge for centuries. It is therefore no surprise that researchers and publishers rapidly grasped the opportunities offered by the World Wide Web for mass access – for researchers and students – to scholarly journals.

The STM publishing industry, working closely with university librarians and web technologists, started to develop one of the first major digitally enabled subscription based markets in the world from the mid-1990s, around the same time that Jeff Bezos founded Amazon. The digitally enabled subscription models that emerged from the move to online journal delivery were the forerunner to the adoption of subscription based business models for offerings as diverse as razors and Disney+.

The period 1995–2010 saw the widespread move online of scholarly books, journals and other learning materials e.g. case studies. During this period, publishers were particularly focused on digitizing content, moving processes online, changing business models from paper based products to multi-year agreements centred on digital collections, building relationships with authors and budget holders (librarians), and moving the publishing and sales emphasis from a strong North American and European focus to a significant connection with wider global (e.g. Asia Pacific) markets, where growth prospects were greater due to economic and demographic growth.

Historically, the specific subject knowledge of content focused publishing staff was at the heart of the growth of publishers, supported by efficient production and distribution processes complying with industry norms. The period 1995–2010 saw the development of extensive sales teams engaging directly with library customers, which largely replaced commercial processes enabled by intermediaries and agents. Other vectors of growth included the acquisition and rapid integration of acquired content into the content portfolios of the publishers buying out smaller players. Acquisition helped publishers move into "new to them" subject areas, as well as bulking up existing subject collections, with well funded STM subjects generating faster growth than the humanities and social sciences (HASS) subjects which receive lower levels of research funding.

The visibility of the consumption of the products and services of publishers has been transformed by digitization, with the value delivered by publishers increasingly calculated by the cost per download of content bought on multi-year deals. The interviews revealed the pressures on all of the case companies to keep up with the content delivery expectations of stakeholders such as researchers, teachers, students and librarians. The pressures came from the need to comply with formal industry standards, the performance of the digital platforms of the leading players, and the increased flexibility of mainstream digital systems, particularly pervasive social media platforms. An informant explained that the major publishers had been in a: "Functionality arms race", focused on the technical performance of their platforms.

The introduction of digital workflows to manage content items (e.g. journal articles) through the publishing process has been a major part of the transformation of the industry into a dynamic digital environment. Publishers moved from being primarily focused on content and logistics to, at the most progressive firms, being technology, content and workflow solution centred organizations with technologists inside. Their structures and processes experienced change, and they delivered content in flexible ways, as well as solving wider and deeper problems for users as they stretched for new opportunities beyond their core activities.

All the case organizations described how they had found it demanding to build the culture and processes to support digitally enabled innovation in organizations that had historically centred on content acquisition, sales and logistics above other factors. The change to a greater focus on innovation activities demanded different roles and capabilities than those needed previously in the "Core" publishing areas. They had to unlearn old routines, and learn new tricks.

The language in the interviews was about the ability to learn from failure, manage technology and innovation in agile ways, understand user workflows and create MVPs as prototypes with which to conduct experiments with users and customers. A recurring theme was that the intense focus on building innovation capability and processes was all relatively recent, nicely summarized by an interviewee at a large publisher observing: "If you had come to interview us three or four years ago about innovation, we wouldn't have had a lot to talk about, as the key issues for the previous decade, and even longer, were the digitization of content, geographic expansion, and acquisition."

What had changed most within the HE sector in the last five years?

The research process revealed that HE markets for scholarly content were growing much more slowly than previously, pushing publishers to identify and secure revenues from new markets. The greatest changes in the previous five years within the HE sector affecting publishers had included:

- The development of new business models, such as OA publishing, supported by major research funders such as governments, the Wellcome Trust etc. There was widespread acceptance of OA as an alternative business model by publishers. OA publishing was increasingly seen a mainstream activity, with publishers aiming to make it profitable in the medium to long term. Academics, librarians, and the wider public campaigned for greater access to research based content, with

the Public Library of Science (PLOS) launching its first OA journal in 2003 operating as a non-profit STM publisher
- The visibility of usage data had been facilitated by industry standards projects such as COUNTER (2015). Having a standardised methodology for measuring the downloading (usage) of digital content had enabled buyers (librarians) and publishers to establish metrics to evaluate the average cost per download of a publisher's product
- An expectation amongst funders, students and academics that research should be available digitally, and should be available for free wherever possible
- Greater use of digital resources across both teaching and research
- The globalization of HE, typified by an explosion in research and scholarly article consumption in countries like China, India and Brazil
- The growth of HE globally in terms of student numbers, including the growth of international student populations
- The stagnation of library budgets, meaning that if publishers were going to continue to grow strongly, they would have to identify, pursue and capture value from opportunities beyond the traditional library budget
- Increasing focus on rankings and measurable research performance at all levels within the research intensive academic community, considering both research impact measured by citations, and the impact of research beyond researcher communities e.g. government, society and business
- The development of students acting as customers in HE, increasing the focus on student employability

The greatest game-changer affecting publishers following the widespread shift to digital offerings was the acceptance of OA as a dissemination opportunity, conflicting with the ongoing role of traditional, high citation impact factor journals as a way of assessing the quality of the output of researchers. OA had introduced different business models to the sector, challenging the dominant logic of the publisher subscription model.

Defining the core business of different publishers

Core markets were defined by the publishers as being HE institutions, i.e. universities, and the principal users were researchers, teachers, and postgraduate students. Core product ranges were academic journals, scholarly books, textbooks and case studies. The pre-eminent buyers were librarians, influenced by academics. In very hierarchical markets dominated by international ranking indices, success with the leading 100 universities globally was seen to lead to sales and dissemination success with other research intensive universities.

Another core activity for publishers was securing contracts to publish the journals of prestigious societies, with the proceeds from sales being shared between the society and the publisher. To grow in both core and beyond the core markets, the case organizations identified that they needed to have insights in the areas indicated in Figure 4.1.

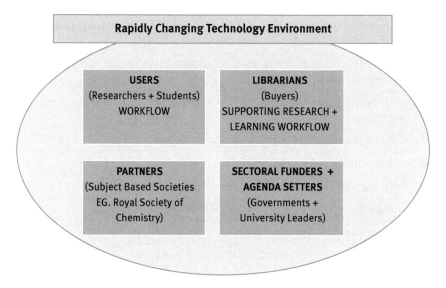

Figure 4.1: Critical stakeholders targeted by publishers through innovation search activities.

Operating "beyond the core" in uncertain but high potential adjacent markets

The innovation literature suggests that organizations need to be able to adapt to internal and external changes, and orchestrate and reconfigure their dynamic capabilities to compete successfully. More specifically, the literature suggests that organizations require the 11 sub-capabilities identified in Chapter 3 that support the management of search and select in disrupting environments, detailed in Table 4.4, to manage the search and select stages of the innovation process across core, adjacent and breakthrough environments.

Table 4.4: Innovation Search and Select sub-capabilities in Core, Adjacent & Breakthrough Environments.

Companies will manage search and select effectively if they can manage:
1) Strategic clarity, through a clear and well communicated high level, portfolio driven strategic plan supported by appropriate structures considering core, adjacent and breakthrough environments
2) Peripheral vision: Can search the periphery for weak signals to generate offering development opportunities (breakthrough environments only)
3) Operationalizing structured search and select processes across core, adjacent and breakthrough opportunities
4) Identifying and sharing deep contextual domain insights, e.g. macro social, industry and technology trends
5) Deployment of digital era market research techniques (e.g. netnography)
6) Seeking out and sharing deep domain insights into user workflows
7) Identification and validation of pervasive problems, considering jobs-to-be-done
8) Validation and iteration of opportunities through MVP testing and learning
9) Recruitment and connection with individuals outside the firm's core industry
10) Identification and validation of external acquisition & investment opportunities
11) Acting on strategic analysis, investing in, acquiring, and/or collaborating with external organizations

Evaluating the innovation search and select sub-capabilities of the case companies

While recognizing that the study is qualitative in nature, to draw meaning, and to enable comparisons, a simple rating system was developed to assess the presence of the 11 sub-capabilities in the case organizations, as shown in Table 4.5.

Table 4.5: Sub-capability rating system.

3	Sub-capability well established, with consistent and clear references to ongoing activities
2	Sub-capability present, with some references to ongoing activities
1	Sub-capability partially/patchily present, with limited supporting references to ongoing activities
0	No supporting reference s regarding current activities

Where did the respondents have the most to say?

As expected from the literature review, the research revealed that the case companies were engaged in a spectrum of activities, with their innovation projects ranging from targeting previously unserved users, e.g. undergraduates instead of academics and postgraduates, to opportunities further from the core such as video products and data informed workflow solutions for researchers. Six questions in particular engaged the interviewees, and it is informative to reflect on the weight of comments that certain questions generated. The interviews had much more to say about the core business, than beyond the core (BTC).

Cross case findings: Core markets

The research process established the presence of offering development search and select capabilities at the case company level, looking for patterns through:
- Analysing the similarities and the differences between the three large commercial publishers (Cases A, B and D) and single medium commercial publisher (Case E) with a sub-capability rating of more than 25 in the core market
- Analysing the similarities and the differences between the large commercial publisher (Case C), single medium commercial publisher (Case F), single university press (Case G) and two scholarly society publishers (Cases I and J), with a sub-capability rating of between 20 and 25 in the core market
- Considering the case of the single university press (Case H) with a sub-capability rating of below 20 in the core market

Core markets

- Cases A, B, D and E, all large or medium sized commercial publishers, were all highly effective across the 11 search and select sub-capabilities. The only ratings below a "3" (sub-capability well established, with consistent and clear references to ongoing activities) are identified in Table 4.6.

Similar sub-capability ratings do not signify that Cases A, B, D and E were all managing the 11 search and select sub-capabilities in the same way, or to the same standard, as the qualitative research techniques used for the project could only assess the presence of capabilities, not the quality of the management of the capabilities. Table 4.7 indicates which questions generated the most revealing insights from the interviews regarding core markets.

Learning from an outlier: The single university press (Case H) with a sub-capability rating of below 15 in the core market

Case H had a reputation for very high quality publications in core markets, but had struggled to keep up with competitors in the "rapid change core" (RCC), particularly in the area of technology. The organization was highly focused on content, and its connections with leading researchers, and it appeared that the editorial and content focus had crowded out the development of the operational processes to operate in increasingly digital markets and user environments in both core and adjacent markets.

Table 4.6: Core Markets: Innovation search and select sub-capability analysis.

Case	Overall Sub-capability Rating Core	Innovation Search and Select Sub-capability areas For Improvement	Sub-capability Rating	Researcher Comments
Case A	28	9) Recruit, connect with & learn from individuals outside core industry	1	Recruitment still seemed to target core industry professionals. The sample had the longest average experience any of the case companies, with an average of 21.3 years in publishing
Case B	30	Not applicable		All the sub-capabilities were well established, with consistent and clear references to ongoing activities. Repeated references to the recruitment of technology staff from outside the industry boosted their rating on sub-capability 9. The sample of 3 senior respondents averaged only 2.2 years with Case B, and an average of 5.2 in the industry, supporting fresh thinking
Case D	29	9) Recruit, connect with & learn from individuals outside core industry	2	Core industry professionals prominent in the core, based on the 5 interviews, with need for fresh thinking beyond the core
Case E	27	8) Validate and iterate opportunities through MVP testing & learning	2	MVP testing approach less prominent than with some other cases
Case E	27	9) Recruit, connect with & learn from individuals outside core industry	1	Core industry professionals prominent in the core, with need for fresh thinking beyond the core

Table 4.7: Core markets: Which questions generated the greatest volume of insightful comments?

Core: Which questions generated the greatest volume of insightful comments? Ranked in order of noteworthy comments	Researcher comments
In the core business, how does the organization identify opportunities for innovation?	All the interviewees had a lot to say about search in core markets, as this was a regular and significant activity for each organization. The reflections concerned strategic priorities, structure, technological change, and search activities including market research. The organizations with more limited exploration activities tended to be preoccupied by technology challenges and operational issues. The interviewees from organizations active BTC saw the identification of exploitation opportunities in the core as a demanding but routine process.
What particularly influences the innovation and offering development process?	The interviewees had almost as much to say about what influenced the innovation and offering development process, as they did about the search process itself. The organizations with more exploratory activities beyond the core were influenced by both the HE publishing industry and sectors outside the publishing industry. The interviewees also reflected on strategic priorities, structure, technological change, and the challenge of seeking data to support decision making in novel areas of opportunity.
What particularly influences which innovation projects are selected for further development?	The interviewees had strong opinions about what influenced decision making, including mission, the strengths and weaknesses of the innovation process overall (structure), the priorities of the firm which were influenced by strategy, structure, organizational attention, cognition, and technology capabilities.

Cross case findings: Is it clear who is responsible for searching for innovation and new offering development opportunities in the core business?

Even though the organizations were all well established, and had sustained themselves for an average of 178 years, a significant 15 out of 54 (28%) of those who responded to this question did not feel that it was clear who was responsible for searching for innovation and new offering development opportunities in the core business. Despite deep experience in the publishing industry, search and select processes in the core markets were not clear in all the case organizations.

Cross case findings: Effective knowledge management, or other systems, to support innovation and offering development processes in the core business

The management of knowledge lies at the heart of any innovation process. Even with the case organizations having extensive experience in core markets, the research found that only 28% of the interviewees were positive about there being effective knowledge management systems in place to support innovation and offering development processes in the core business. This exposes a weakness, or a lack of value placed on knowledge management, in the core business. Without clear and effective knowledge management, innovation projects are immediately limited in their prospects.

Why were certain organizations not active beyond the core

Unsurprisingly the interviewees from the case organizations that were not engaged in exploratory activities beyond the core had less to say about what they were doing in adjacent and breakthrough environments. However they had much to say about why their organizations were not active beyond the core, and suffered from inertia when it came to building an innovation portfolio. Table 4.8 indicates which questions generated the most revealing insights from the interviews regarding markets beyond the core.

Cross case findings: Adjacent markets

Figure 4.2 shows the distribution of search and select sub-capabilities across the 10 case companies. It is useful to look for patterns in the findings regarding adjacent markets through:
- Analysing the similarities and the differences between the three large commercial publishers (Cases A, B and D) and single medium commercial publisher (Case E) with a high sub-capability rating of more than 25 in adjacent markets
- Analysing the similarities and the differences between the large commercial publisher (Case C), single medium commercial publisher (Case F), single university press (Case G) and two scholarly society publishers (Cases I and J), with a sub-capability rating of between 20 and 10 in adjacent markets.

- Considering the case of the single university press (Case H) with a sub-capability rating of below 10 in adjacent markets

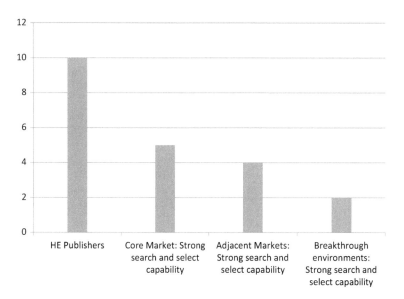

Figure 4.2: The distribution of search and select sub-capabilities across the 10 case companies.

Table 4.8: Beyond the core markets: Which questions generated the greatest volume of insightful comments?

Beyond the core: Which questions generated the greatest volume of insightful comment? Ranked in order of noteworthy comments	Researcher comments
How does the organization operate beyond the core business? What makes it successful beyond the core business?	**Organizations effective beyond the core:** The interviewees from organizations with exploratory strategies and structures supporting activities beyond the core had a great deal to report, particularly concerning the importance of insights from user workflows. These organizations had separate, portfolio driven structures designed to support business beyond the core, which had been well communicated across the firm. **Organizations less effective beyond the core:** The interviewees from less active organizations BTC reported that their organizations were more focused on exploitation activities focused on existing customers, keeping up with the industry technology race, and the demands of operational management challenges. The role of acquisition activity was a major theme for these firms.

Table 4.8 (continued)

Beyond the core: Which questions generated the greatest volume of insightful comment? Ranked in order of noteworthy comments	Researcher comments

What particularly influences the innovation and product development process beyond the core?	**Importance of trigger events:** The informants active beyond the core pointed to trigger events that had confirmed their organization's commitment to operate BTC.
	Importance of technology capabilities in the core: The interviewees from the organizations with more activities beyond the core were confident about managing technology in the core, enabling them to focus BTC. Activities to identify pervasive problems, supported by persuasive facts, were highlighted by those exploring BTC.
	    The interviewees active BTC commented on the need for an articulated strategy, strong technology, structure and processes, supported by senior team backing, to enable exploration activities BTC.
	    Activities in breakthrough/peripheral environments needed special understanding, and boundary spanning structures.

Beyond the core business, how does the organization identify opportunities for innovation?	The interviewees from firms active BTC tended to look for jobs-to-be-done in the user workflow. While interviewees with significant core industry experience were ready to explore adjacencies, individuals working on breakthrough opportunities in the periphery tended to have strong technology backgrounds, and significant experience outside STM publishing.

Comparing capabilities between core and adjacent markets: The leading organizations

An important finding from the research project was that the four companies with the strongest sub-capability ratings in core markets also demonstrated the strongest sub-capability ratings in adjacent markets. Case organizations A, B, D and E all had clear plans for adjacent markets that were repeatedly referred to throughout the interviews. In contrast, the other six case organizations did not have clear strategic plans for adjacent markets. A clear but not unexpected finding is that none of the 10 case organizations were more capable in adjacent markets than in their core markets.

Comparing capabilities between core and adjacent markets: The organizations with a marked difference in sub-capability levels

Case C demonstrated sub-capability levels at almost the same level as Cases A, B, D and E in core markets, and the organization had a strong history of growth. Recognizing that this is an exploratory study, Case C can be seen to demonstrate (almost) the same sub-capability levels as the leading four firms. The reason for categorising Case C alongside Cases F, G, I and J is based on the gap between Case C's search and select sub-capabilities in core markets (24), and its sub-capability rating in adjacent markets (14). Cases C, F, G, I and J, despite a collective average of 146 years of organizational experience, all had sub-capability scores between 14 and 17 when considering relatively unknown adjacent markets, as activities beyond the core were not given attention.

Cross case findings: Is it clear who is responsible for searching for innovation and offering development opportunities beyond the core business?

Half of the respondents felt that it was clear who was responsible for searching for innovation and offering development opportunities beyond the core business. It should be noted that there was no differentiation between adjacent and breakthrough markets in the way that this question was asked. The fact that 49% of the respondents did not feel that that it was clear who was responsible for searching for innovation and offering development opportunities beyond the core business indicates both a lack of attention to opportunities beyond the core. Directly connected to the lack of attention beyond the core is a lack of development in terms of organizational design to manage search activities beyond the core.

Cross case findings: Systematic searching of the periphery of the business environment for innovation and offering development opportunities

A significant finding is that of the 10 case companies, only two (Case B and Case D) were actively involved in breakthrough environments, with a maximum 30 out of

30 sub-capability rating regarding focus on uncertain opportunities at a significant distance from the core business. Case A had explored breakthrough opportunities in the past, but demonstrated a preference for adjacent opportunities. Case E secured a slightly higher sub-capability rating than the other case companies regarding breakthrough opportunities due to the strength of its six-box innovation matrix, which enabled the categorisation of opportunities as being breakthrough in nature, and therefore of no interest to this self-identifying fast follower organization which only considered core and adjacent opportunities. Apart from Cases B and D, none of the case companies were searching for or selecting opportunities in breakthrough environments.

While acknowledging the lower focus on markets beyond the core, the findings regarding the presence of effective knowledge management and other systems to support innovation and offering development processes beyond the core business demonstrate a lack of importance given to the sharing of information to support innovation and offering development processes beyond the core business. No respondents from five out of 10 companies gave positive answers concerning knowledge management beyond the core.

Of the 57 managers questioned on this topic, only 11 said that their organization was searching the periphery for innovation and offering development opportunities, and 46 said no. In five organizations, half the sample, no respondents replied positively. When it came to being vigilant in the periphery, half the organizations demonstrated no interest at all, despite the evidence from the literature that change starts in the periphery.

Summary of the key findings: How do publishers operate beyond the rapid change core?

The research project sought to identify the presence of the 11 dynamic sub-capabilities identified in Table 4.4 that organizations operating in disrupting environments require to manage offering development search and select processes in core, adjacent and breakthrough environments. The capabilities were distributed in different ways across the case companies. In disrupting environments, organizations need to explore adjacent and more peripheral opportunities, as they look beyond the core for growth. All the case companies understood the need to develop and manage a portfolio of opportunities, and recognized the demands of the rapid change core. Appropriate structures are required to identify, validate and develop the portfolio, supported by activities and processes within each part of the structure, and a range of people and skills to make each part of the structure successful. The challenge is that organizations have to look across a spectrum of opportunities at the same time.

As we would expect from the innovation portfolio literature, the research revealed that the sub-capabilities required to operate beyond the rapid change core were well established in certain organizations, and not present in others. Progressive innovation work ranged from scholarly publishers targeting previously unserved users, e.g. undergraduates instead of academics and postgraduates, to the pursuit of opportunities further from the core such as video products and workflow solutions for researchers. There was a marked divide between the organizations capable of developing their offering to include technology dependent workflow orientated solutions alongside more conventional products and services, and the organizations primarily focused on conventional publishing products targeting traditional HE budgets.

Discussion about offering development beyond the core saw informants repeatedly referring to the constraints limiting innovation in adjacent or breakthrough environments. The core business was often found to be demanding, particularly in terms of an organization's technology sub-capability, as competition to increase the visibility of online content was intense. The phrase "rapid change core" acknowledges that digitally enabled organizations can be stretched by operational demands in their core business. When organizations struggle to keep up in the rapid change core, they find it difficult to develop and operationalise a balanced innovation portfolio. The two most progressive large publishers were confident in building new propositions for emerging user problems exploiting data analytics, across core, adjacent and breakthrough environments.

5 Diving deeper: Learning from five rich case studies

A strength of qualitative research is that researchers get to know organizations in depth, and can sense the human aspects of organizations, beyond the "management speak" of modern business. Five of the case organizations revealed a relatively strong presence of the dynamic sub-capabilities needed to manage the early stages of the innovation process. However, while all five of them were well equipped to operate in core markets, only four were prepared to manage search and select activities in adjacent markets, and only two were pursuing activities in more peripheral, breakthrough environments.

The stories from the case studies will help the reader to move from a synthesized picture of the case organizations in Chapter 4 to a richer and more contextualized view of what is going on inside highly capable organizations grappling with the demands of being vigilant in fast moving and complex environments. The firms that were looking more widely had experienced trigger events, which jolted them out of their comfort zones to push against organizational inertia to find fresh opportunities. All organizations are influenced by their internal and external contexts, and this chapter aims to bring them to life case by case, with the reader brought face to face with what influences the choices that can move a firm from a more limited perspective leading to vulnerability, to a broader and long term perspective consistent with managing innovation vigilantly.

Case A: Large commercial publisher

Case A had taken the decision to look beyond the core, setting up a division to take this work forwards. The firm was numbers driven, slightly risk averse, and accustomed to incremental innovation. The impulse to invest in and progress innovation activities in adjacent areas, enabled through search and select routines, had only gained momentum as sales slowed in the core. The overall search and select sub-capability ratings were 28 out of 30 in core markets, 26 out of 30 in adjacent markets, and 9 out of 33 in breakthrough environments.

Even though Case A was connected with HE stakeholders, and understood the slowdown in the growth of key budgets, it took slowing sales to trigger initiatives focused on adjacent markets. As Christensen (1997) found, organizations challenged with managing their response to disruption frequently do not have problems developing the right technology to respond, but: "Sustaining projects addressing the needs of the firm's most powerful customers almost always pre-empted resources from disruptive technologies with small markets and poorly defined customer needs" (Christensen, 1997, p. 41–42). While a perception of threat can overcome inertia,

https://doi.org/10.1515/9783110657326-005

threats in existing markets can also limit the range of alternatives leaders are willing to consider, and the degree of experimentation can be reduced as a result.

There was a tension at Case A between the core business, which was evaluated internally using well recognized measures and favoured predictable outcomes, and projects in more uncertain environments. However companies need substantial innovations to boost profits, with one research study showing that while only 14% of new product launches were substantial innovations, they made up 61% of all the profits from innovations among the companies examined (Kim & Mauborgne, 1999).

Companies with the strongest innovation track records manage a balance of innovation activities across core, adjacent and breakthrough (or transformational) initiatives. A range of discontinuities exist which cause organizations to move "beyond the steady state" of core markets, to look for and validate new opportunities (Phillips, Noke, & Bessant, 2006). Case A had recently developed the capabilities required to search for opportunities in adjacent markets, as the firm had recognized that its financial growth objectives could not be met from core markets, and that it needed to identify, select and follow through on a range of opportunities.

The recognition of the need to develop significant businesses beyond the core is an essential precursor to firms engaging with innovation search activity outside well established markets. The importance of this recognition step needs to be taken into account when developing a model summarising how organizations can best manage search and select in disrupting environments. However, the capability had only started to develop at Case A in the 12–15 months before the interviews, through the creation of a new division actively considering opportunities in adjacent markets. The stage-gate process to manage search and select in adjacent areas had only been developed at the firm in the 12–18 month period before the interviews. The development of relationships with the funders of research had increased in the previous three years.

Day and Schoemaker (2004b, p. 117) wrote: "In a world in which changes come from many different directions, the ability to balance organizational focus with the wide-angle view may be the most important ability for long-term survival and success." Growth had slowed in the core, and Case A had responded in accordance with Day and Schoemaker's observations above, initiating search activities by internal staff in breakthrough environments, but concluding that the research workflow opportunities being pursued by other organizations were "nascent". After an initial foray into searching the periphery, Case A's preference for adjacent environments for internally driven exploration was evident, consistent with the slightly risk averse culture of the organization and the literature on organizational inertia.

The executive leadership team had supported the exploration of adjacent sectors through acquisition, with an interviewee observing: "There was the recognition that we weren't going to be able to innovate internally across the full set of options and organically, which is why (Case A) actively went out there and started acquiring companies, so actually I think the executive leadership thought that the fastest way to a successful outcome was not to try and do this internally, but to actually buy in that expertise, and have it bought in with associated revenues and customers, because there was also the recognition that building this stuff from the ground up is actually very difficult, very time consuming and that we may not have all of the requisite skills."

Organizations have to develop their core operations, otherwise they will lose their competitive position and profit streams. Case A had the capabilities and routines to make the right choices to sustain performance in core markets that were changing fast, through product development and acquisition activity, and they were not in the grip of the rapid change core. The interviewees recognized the need to assess what opportunities stay with the core (e.g. OA), and which ones should be developed by the group responsible for adjacent markets.

We have seen how some leading firms seek a market focused, agile R&D model. Case A sought pervasive problems following the "jobs-to-be-done" approach to market segmentation, and used MVPs to generate data to evaluate whether their emerging offerings provided solutions to them. With activity beyond the core still relatively new in some divisions, the technical and cognitive capability to interpret the data from unfamiliar markets and stakeholders needed to be developed further. The culture was driven by numbers, and the organization was slightly risk averse, making agile product development processes more difficult to embed. There was a tension between the core business, which was typically evaluated using well recognized measures and predictable outcomes, and projects in more uncertain environments.

Innovation activities targeting educational opportunities in adjacent markets appeared relatively well developed. Educational products were focused on supporting the learning workflow, and this content and technology mix displayed more of a solutions approach than products targeting Company A's research driven stakeholders. A solutions rather product centred approach helped to blur the lines between offerings targeting core and adjacent markets.

A recent exploration phase had considered adjacent and peripheral opportunities, but the organization had found that these market sizing activities were difficult, as they could not identify tangible and achievable opportunities in more peripheral areas. Case A appeared to have decided to focus exploratory search and select activity on adjacent areas, adopting a "make-and-sell" approach where searching the periphery could be added to the list of "unnatural acts", rather than acting as a "sense-and-respond" organization (Haeckel, 2004, 2008, p. 16).

Established firms face the dual challenges of resource rigidity and routine rigidity when it comes to overcoming the organizational inertia that so often sustains the focus on the core business. To overcome organizational inertia the executive leadership of Case A established a division to look beyond the core, designing the organization to develop a portfolio of options across core and adjacent markets.

The influence of context on the operationalisation of search and select at Case A?

Innovation portfolio management
Case A did not have a clear matrix or device to communicate priorities and structured approaches to adjacent markets, or breakthrough environments. The organization used acquisition to buy in new capabilities, as well as market position, in new sectors identified as offering growth potential. The use of company acquisition to increase revenues, and bring new skills, knowledge and processes into the firm gave the board significant options when it came to developing a portfolio of innovation options: "We tend to evolve through M&A activity, almost exclusively so. When we bring a new product on board or we add major technology capability that's not in the core, it's almost always through a partnership or acquisition." The alignment of market focused strategy processes with technology strategy was identified as having a particularly large influence on exploiting emerging opportunities, supporting the literature arguing that innovation strategy and technology strategy are intertwined.

Cognition
Case A's respondents were highly experienced, with the longest average length of service with their employer as compared to the other large companies. With such long service in the core business, which had grown through acquisition and incremental change, the interviewees faced learning challenges in equipping themselves to become effective at innovation beyond the core. The informants commented on the need to transform their own cognitive frames, to support the identification and pursuit of different types of problems and solutions.

Ambidexterity
The development of ambidextrous management approaches to run both the core and adjacent search and select processes, and the developing, portfolio business, was a work in progress. At the operational level, Case A had capabilities in place to identify and validate opportunities using stage-gate processes in both core and adjacent markets, despite only embarking on activity beyond the core 18 months or so before the interviews. Challenges existed in managing technology for both the core and emerging opportunities at the same time.

Peripheral vision
Case A had advanced market research capabilities, and was attuned to picking up signals through strategic partners, particularly the scholarly societies. However, the organization was in the early stages of making sense of signals from peripheral markets, and the organization did not appear proactive in recruiting different

thinking staff from different backgrounds to make sense of weak signals from unfamiliar environments.

Rapid change core

Case A had up to date technology in place in the core market. However, balancing the technical requirements across the portfolio was a new challenge which was still in need of attention at the time of the research.

Case B: A large commercial publisher

The informants from Case B were conscious of the need to manage the innovation process across core, adjacent and breakthrough environments, and the 11 search and select sub-capabilities identified in Table 4.4 were established across their innovation portfolio. They had identified three "zones of opportunity" corresponding with core, adjacent and breakthrough environments, and had created the language and maps to aid decision making. Their organized approach to innovation management had a major and positive influence on the firm's ability to manage a portfolio of opportunities, and the innovation search and select processes that underpin success. The "three zones of opportunity" strategy approach was followed through across the company's structure, processes, M&A and knowledge acquisition routines, ensuring that strategy was executed.

The overall search and select sub-capability ratings were 30 out of 30 in core markets, 30 out of 30 in adjacent markets, and 33 out of 33 in breakthrough environments. Success in the "old core markets" was built on selling to defined decision making units (DMUs) such as libraries. Success in core, adjacent and breakthrough markets was driven by a user driven, problem solving approach. Case B managed core and adjacent markets together, with a high technology, workflow solution focus, with an interviewee commenting: "It's difficult to know where 'beyond the core' starts and finishes." The firm had stopped managing the core market in isolation a number of years previously, recognizing that user focused opportunities in adjacent areas were extensions of many of the content and user workflow related problems found in the core. The company had recognized that content and user workflow were deeply interconnected. In adopting this joined up approach to core and adjacent markets, staff benefited from a clear strategic and tactical approach to managing innovation in core and adjacent areas. The organization's market research capability equipped it for search activities across the portfolio.

An important element in Case B's search for opportunities was the data centricity of its search approach, supported by user observation. An important objective of innovation in services is to deliver a positive user experience that is frequently highly personalised. The personalisation of services marks a major shift in focus in decision-making from producers to users – even if value capture occurs at the organizational level. This shift creates advantages for innovators who are able to use technologies that integrate user demands and requirements into the design, delivery, and positive valuation of services by both users, and the DMU who select and pay for the service on behalf of an organization.

Case B managed new offering development using a technology intensive approach, with relatively blurred lines between core and adjacent sectors. An interviewee with a technology background explained: "The separation of business and technology is something that we're consciously disrupting. It still exists but we're bringing the two halves closer together. Greater tech focus blurs lines."

The organization had a managed process to explore adjacent opportunities both geographically, and in terms of identifying adjacent problems and pain points. Market opportunities were being identified and validated. The process was established, rather than being in the early stages of development, giving Case B important operational advantages in managing new offering development targeting adjacent opportunities.

Case B had a distinct approach to the search process for breakthrough opportunities, as compared to core and adjacent markets: "It tends to fall to the likes of our senior strategy team to look at the blue sky area, and also our research and development group." The interviewees knew who was responsible for looking for breakthrough opportunities, and sensed that the company was managing its innovation portfolio proactively, increasing their trust in the firm's innovation process. Importantly, financial and human resources were being allocated across units to support the strategy.

The company assessed potential "problems to be solved" or "jobs-to-be-done", and abstracted away from the problems being considered to other sectors, seeking ideas and options. The faith that the interviewees had in the organization's technical capabilities gave them the confidence to select opportunities requiring advanced technical solutions. The alignment of market focused strategy processes with technology strategy was identified as having a particularly large influence on exploiting emerging opportunities. This supports the argument that in digitally enabled markets, innovation capability and technology capability are intertwined.

The organization deployed agile innovation techniques to secure the rapid and ongoing evaluation of MVPs, influenced by the practitioner literature. Case B's effectiveness in managing a structured, stage-gate driven innovation process in both core and adjacent markets delivered financial returns, allowing the company to focus on breakthrough opportunities beyond core and adjacent environments.

Acquisition was used as a part of the toolkit for managing the innovation portfolio by senior management to secure innovation options. The company had a proactive and structured search and selection process in place considering peripheral environments, with more peripheral opportunities considered through a central strategic group, as well as the ongoing work of recently acquired organizations operating in peripheral environments. The company was hungry for growth, and was seeking and validating opportunities across the innovation portfolio. The organization looked to learn from other sectors, applying new approaches to existing and emerging opportunities, constantly watching Google, Amazon, Apple et al. and startups for new ideas. Case B used analogies during discussion to help transfer insights from similar settings that they have experienced in the past to new environments.

In an intriguing observation, a respondent stated: "Technology people build 'facts' in different ways. The winner will be the person that actually creates the fact." Innovation is concerned with future products, technologies and customers, and radical innovations conceive of a future that is hard to envisage. The creation of facts to support decisions about future products is an essential part of the innovation selection process.

Established firms have often built strong positions based on the mastery of a particular technology. Organizational knowledge and memory about previous or current technologies can hamper innovation. Leonardi (2011) found that individuals who use a particular technology develop aligned cognitive frames through which they view current problems and design alternatives. He also found that different people, from different parts of an organization, who are used to working with different technologies, are often confused as to why they find it difficult to work together, creating complexity when it comes to exploiting useful technologies found in other parts of the organization, or within acquisitions.

The influence of context on the operationalisation of search and select at Case B?

Innovation portfolio management
The recognition of "three zones of opportunity", and the creation of a language and maps to aid decision making, had a major and positive influence on the organization's ability to manage a portfolio of opportunities, and manage the innovation search and select processes.

Cognition
Case B was open to change. The firm acquired different types of business at holding company level, and these had proved to be trigger points that changed the group's business and product portfolio. Individuals learned from other solution orientated divisions within the group, which kept thinking flexible and opportunity orientated.

The interviewees were highly experienced in businesses beyond Case B, having the lowest average number of years at the company (2.2) and the fewest years in publishing as compared to the overall sample of interviewees. Case B recruits non-industry staff to look at problems and opportunities with different lenses, and employs thousands of technology staff, and the three interviewees wanted to learn from the technology experiences of new staff, and technology colleagues in other parts of the business. The fact that the organization's HR probation routines were designed to capture relevant ideas and potential solutions from experiences in other organizations and industries demonstrated an intense interest in ideas from beyond the industry, recognizing that individuals can become blinkered by their own organizations and industries.

Once acquisitions had been made in breakthrough areas, bringing in new knowledge and solutions, the management of these businesses was kept independent, to ensure that the newly acquired business unit kept thinking differently, providing solutions to the "jobs-to-be-done" beyond Case B's core and adjacent environments. Maintaining a distance from the core business was recognized as being important to avoid the high failure rate of corporate venture units.

Case B identified, validated and acquired companies, bringing new knowledge into the organization. As a technology intensive firm active in providing information solutions to a wide range of markets, the company was able to draw on significant technology insight and capacity across the business. The main technology approach had moved from outsourcing to insourcing, increasing the internal skills and knowledge that could be applied to innovation projects across the offering development portfolio.

Ambidexterity

The firm appeared to be organized to support ambidexterity across the innovation portfolio, through its clear three "zones of opportunity" structure. The business was experienced at managing different types of high technology dependent businesses across multiple sectors.

Peripheral vision: Being vigilant to weak signals

The organization was prepared to use open ended questions that draw imprecise but valuable lessons from the periphery. This was demonstrated through a data centric approach on one side, and the discipline of learning from new recruits on the other.

Rapid change core

Case B managed the rapid change core effectively, and was therefore able to turn its attention to the development of its innovation portfolio beyond the core.

Case C: Large commercial publisher

Case C had grown strongly and profitably in recent years in core markets, and the respondents explained that the organization had not had the financial need to trigger the exploration of adjacent or breakthrough markets. The organization was heavily engaged in acquiring and integrating other publishers, with the content sold to traditional DMUs. This activity had left little time for projects beyond the core. The core market had consistently delivered strong financial growth, so the organizational view was that there was little need to embrace innovation activities beyond acquisition and sustaining innovation, and the development of OA publishing capabilities. The company's overall sub-capability "rating" in adjacent markets was boosted by the OA division. The organization had deep contextual understanding, and collaborated effectively with external organizations such as long-term commercial partners e.g. scholarly societies.

The overall search and select sub-capability ratings were a healthy 24 out of 30 in core markets. However, this dropped to 14 out of 30 in adjacent markets, and 3 out of 33 in breakthrough environments. The firm's innovation activities were sustaining in nature, focused on incremental innovation, working with existing partners and customers in the core market. Geographic expansion had been prioritised. The decision had not been made to look beyond the core in a systematic way.

Case C consciously avoided opportunities beyond the core, apart from the new business models connected to OA, as there was little senior level interest in exploring wider opportunities, supporting the literature on the influence of senior level cognitive frames on strategy development (Eggers & Kaplan, 2009), with career gain and reward in prospect from success in the core business, rather than through exploring beyond the core.

The OA division was focused on developing new business models, and solving the problems faced by authors and users, and the responses from this division boosted the capability ranking of the overall publisher significantly when considering the sub-capabilities needed to search for and select innovation opportunities in adjacent markets. The existence of the OA division demonstrated that senior management recognized that different skills and routines were needed to succeed in the changing publishing industry in the core and adjacent markets, although it was not clear if the creation of the division was to defend the core, or to create new opportunities. The division used multiple methods to scan beyond the core, watching competitors, and learning from other technology enabled sectors. The organization had no activities to explore peripheral environments, as it had no interest in exploring breakthrough environments.

Excepting the OA division, the organization's great success in the core market and the resultant lack of priority given to activity beyond the core limited the firm's capability to search for and validate innovation opportunities in adjacent and breakthrough environments, with core strengths having become core rigidities. The organization had no activities to explore breakthrough environments, as it had no interest in exploring them. The selection of opportunities for sustaining innovation was driven by the need to acquire, integrate and sell content, while building customer loyalty at the same time. Resource allocation was prioritised towards existing customers. Financial performance was strong.

Case C was well informed about customer needs in the core market, but the focus was primarily on the customer's DMU, rather than on the users of their products. The planning processes focused on traditional content priorities, rather than interpreting data concerning user behaviour.

The influence of context on the operationalisation of search and select at Case C?

What disrupts established firms in Christensen's story (1997) is not the inability of organizations to conceive of disruptive technology. Like Amit and Zott (2012), he identified the root of the tension in disruptive innovation as the conflict between the business model already established for existing technology, and the business model(s) required to exploit emerging technologies. The "dominant logic" of an organization guides the information that it seeks. An organization seeks data which fits with its dominant logic, and avoids information which conflicts with it. The dominant logic of Case C was the highly profitable acquisition policy, which had limited the search for other business opportunities, and negated the need to probe and learn regarding alternative opportunities.

The disruptive impact of acquisition on the acquirer is well established. The findings from Case C were consistent with the evidence that acquisition reduced the internal financial and human resources that could be dedicated to innovation activities. Without these resources it was difficult for Case C to develop a structured innovation portfolio, balanced resource allocation, and effective project management across the portfolio.

Innovation portfolio management
Case C had adopted a "Wait and see" approach to adjacent and breakthrough environments. With growth having come reliably from the core market, there had been little impulse to design or operationalize an innovation portfolio driven organization, and no trigger event had taken place to change this approach.

Cognition
The attention of Case C had primarily been on acquisition, integration, keeping up with technology in the rapid change core and sales activities in core markets. The organization was particularly strong in the HASS (humanities and social sciences) subject areas, which had been less disrupted than some other firms by the new publishing and dissemination models supported by advocates of open access to research information, and the funders of STM research. It was likely that this relatively late exposure to the practical threat of different business models slowed the

organization's response to OA business models either defensively, or in terms of developing new options. The organization had responded through setting up an OA division. However, the cognitive frames of the organization at both the strategy and operational level were limited by the demands of the rapid change core. The quotes were telling: "We're quite conservative. We like the core business", and "There are certainly opportunities that come up that are outside the core business, but people get very uncomfortable very quickly."

Ambidexterity

Beyond the new OA division, there were no signs of strategic ambidexterity, such as creating separate structures for different types of activity in the core and beyond the core. In fast moving high technology environments the tensions between exploration and exploitation occur within core markets, as well as across a portfolio of uncertainty further from the core. Case C encountered challenges within the core business between established and newly acquired businesses requiring integration, and the demands of keeping up with the technology requirements of a rapidly evolving sector. The demands of these challenges, and the strategic approach of the firm (grow in the core) limited the development of an innovation portfolio, and removed any emphasis on ambidexterity beyond the core.

Peripheral vision: Being vigilant to weak signals

Case C was not looking beyond core markets, influenced by the dominant logic of the core business, and the acquisition, integration and commercialisation routines that had delivered profitability in the core over many years.

Rapid change core

The meetings with Case C respondents intensified the researcher's reflections on the rapid change core. Publishing firms had to keep up with the "technology arms race." They also had to keep up with the operational demands of integrating new acquisitions across the value chain. A respondent noted: "The innovation side of development takes second place to the project work around acquisition, so large acquisitions have quite an impact on our ability to take forward new projects," reflecting the disruptive internal impact of acquisition on the capacity of the organization to innovate. The organization was heavily engaged in acquiring and integrating traditional, content driven publishers, with the content sold to traditional DMUs. This activity left little time and gave a low priority to projects beyond the core.

Case D: Large commercial publisher

The 11 innovation search and select sub-capabilities identified in Table 4.4 were well established across the core, adjacent and breakthrough divisions of Case D. A three colour coded matrix was central to how the organization designed and operationalized its opportunity portfolio, influencing the skills most valued in different divisions. The organization displayed an exploratory mindset, which freed up staff operating in adjacent and breakthrough environments to explore widely, with a respondent explaining: "The organization is built around innovation, and particularly our approach to technological innovation." The respondent continued: "We don't think publishing is about publications primarily, we think it's about information, and when you see things that way your view switches. You see many more opportunities afforded by new digital and network technologies."

The overall search and select sub-capability ratings were 29 out of 30 in core markets, 29 out of 30 in adjacent markets, and 33 out of 33 in breakthrough environments. Case D had started to explore the periphery systematically a number of years before the data collection phase, and had established a highly structured approach to innovation portfolio management across core, adjacent and breakthrough opportunities. The company used up to date search techniques to ensure that their core market product range maintained the brand's reputation as a leading platform. With incremental product development managed successfully in the core, supported by strong technology skills across the organization, the firm had maintained growth in the core. The sense of control and confidence in the rapid change core enabled the organization to turn its attention to opportunities in both adjacent and breakthrough areas.

The organization had processes in place to explore adjacent opportunities in terms of identifying both adjacent problems and pain points: "We solve problems within the workflow, so we do very detailed workflow analysis." The firm exploited close connections with the market place through digital usage based data analysis, ethnographic analysis of researcher (user) workflows, and strong connections to the evolving HE publishing and research environment. Market opportunities had been identified and validated. The process was well established, rather than being in the early stages of development, giving Case D important operational advantages.

Hill and Birkinshaw (2008) identified a range of corporate venture unit approaches to explore opportunities, and Case D had adopted the "internal explorer" approach for adjacent markets. The firm had experimented with both "internal explorer" and "external explorer" units in peripheral environments, and had found that the "external explorer" approach was more effective for breakthrough opportunities. Case D had found that the entrepreneurial routines, disciplines and lean startup approaches advocated by Ries (2011), and the instincts of smaller, stakeholder immersed organizations, were effective in identifying opportunities in the periphery. Analysis of Case D raised the question as to whether effective innovation in breakthrough environments is best served by "internal explorer" units, acquisition, or solution development through "external explorer" incubator type organizations.

The company had a very "fact based" approach, seeking the insights upon which they could make informed decisions, and this approach was enabled by the deployment of agile ideation processes supported by the discipline of MVP validation routines. Through making the right decisions in the rapid change core, the organization was able to turn its attention to adjacent and breakthrough opportunities. The firm had established an effective, data driven, problem focused approach to identifying and validating opportunities in adjacent areas. The adjacent focused division looked for ways to support researchers (users) in their work, with an interviewee observing: "Workflow solutions are a huge part of it, but it's also about extending the space in which we operate." While content mattered, the interview commentary often focused on problem solving: "It's all about making sure that we understand and deliver the need. What else is important?"

Case D could articulate internally and externally the problems that they aimed to solve for users and the research community, which the informants believed put them ahead of their competitors: "You really require deep domain expertise to access this area, and if you lack dedicated domain expertise which is being put behind a particular project, it will usually fail." The "probe and learn" validation process involved working with users on constantly evolving "beta" versions of products, generating data that helps with both concept validation and the improvement of the product offering. Case D was very focused on securing data from users: "One of the important things to us is not just that we have lots of products to generate revenue and it's used by lots of users, but that we gather lots of useful or potentially useful information," underlining the importance of digitally centred and data informed offering development.

Case D had become an expert in developing, testing and validating new business models, particularly concerning value capture, because their network of incubator companies were developing new solutions for newly identified jobs-to-be-done, and they were targeting unfamiliar, or newly emerging budgets. They aimed to be expert in capturing data from users, and the stakeholders engaged with the problems or jobs-to-be done where they sought to offer solutions.

An interviewee connected with the breakthrough business explained that when selecting future partner organizations for investment: "We are looking for people with deep domain expertise. We are not interested in people who are trying to make a quick buck. We look for people who have a similar value system to us, who are in it for the research not the money. We look at people who add something distinctive to the collection: a different approach, a different style of doing business." The focus on different types of people, with different skills appropriate for developing breakthrough opportunities, supports the literature considering the structures and capabilities required to explore "beyond the steady state" (Bessant, Lamming, Noke, & Phillips, 2005).

The influence of context on the operationalisation of search and select at Case D?

Innovation portfolio management
The organization had a clear strategic imperative and structure to enable the exploration of a portfolio of options beyond the core, across adjacent and breakthrough environments. This was communicated through a simply structured three colour coded portfolio matrix, reinforcing the positive influence of a clearly communicated approach to innovation portfolio management. Case D supported the importance of creating "real options", and emphasised the critical role of decision making to take advantage of the options being developed through the search and select phases.

Cognition
The greater the strategic focus on technology, the less an organization is bound by industry perspectives, and Case D's confident approach to technology management influenced the search and validation processes: "If you are going to be in the information business, and we live in the information age and the information technology driven age, you need to get really good with software and data, which redefines what it means to be a publisher, in terms of information and in terms of information technology."

There was little that was tentative about the engagement of the interviewees in their markets: "It is important to us to be a part of the research ecosystem and to support it positively." The strategy emphasised purposeful exploration, which affected the cognitive frames of staff, confirming the influence of cognition on managerial activity. Case D took a long term view when building for success in adjacent and breakthrough environments, particularly when operating in more peripheral spaces.

Ambidexterity
Reeves et al. (2015, p. 175) define ambidexterity as: "The ability to apply multiple approaches to strategy at any given time or successively," and in embracing the innovation portfolio approach, Case D had taken on the demands of managing a more complex set of activities than if it had chosen to stay in the core (like Case C), or had restricted its plans to operating only in core and adjacent markets (like Case E). The organization's approach to simplifying its ambidexterity challenge was through the clear structural separation of responsibilities across the innovation portfolio, communicated through the three colour coded portfolio matrix approach.

Peripheral vision: Being vigilant to weak signals
Case D understood the importance of searching the periphery, as well as the need to make sense of weak signals. However, even though they had operationalized search

and select in peripheral environments, only three out of the five respondents felt that the publisher had a systematic way of searching the periphery of the business environment for innovation and new offering opportunities. The wider the search process, the greater the volume of knowledge that needs to be managed within the firm, and the view of the respondents was that knowledge management systems were stronger beyond the core than in the core. This presented a challenge to the organization, as it needed to harvest innovation insights in core, adjacent and breakthrough (peripheral) environments.

Rapid change core
The interviewees all had great confidence in the management of the core business, so concerns over the rapid change core did not limit the management of search and select in adjacent and breakthrough environments.

Case E: Medium sized commercial publisher

The 11 innovation search and select sub-capabilities were consistently well established across the core and adjacent activities of Case E. However, having considered the potential rewards in breakthrough environments, the firm had decided not to pursue options in highly uncertain spaces, and had chosen to reduce their search and select activity to core and adjacent opportunities. The firm had a clear innovation portfolio management structure, with a six-box matrix referred to throughout the interviews. Case E followed a "Fast Second" strategy, relying on operational excellence to beat competitors in the core and adjacent sectors.

Case E was accustomed to strong growth. However, the board had decided that future growth must come from both the core, and beyond the core, as they were concerned about: "Disintermediation, and systemic displacement by a change in models."

The overall search and select sub-capability ratings were 27 out of 30 in core markets, 26 out of 30 in adjacent markets, and 6 out of 33 in breakthrough environments. The core business was supported by strong technology management, which facilitated continued acquisition and success in the core market, allowing the organization to explore adjacent opportunities.

The six-box matrix innovation portfolio guided the innovation search and select processes of the firm, defining the scope of where Case E looked for opportunities, i.e. in core and adjacent markets, but not in more peripheral breakthrough environments. The organization had also taken the view that it was a content focused publisher: "Ultimately there is a difference between a content based product, where the content is the play, versus selling a service" as: "Service provision is more easily displaceable."

The managers responsible for new and emerging opportunities deployed advanced market research processes to understand the "jobs-to-be-done" in the workflow of the teachers, researchers and students that they were serving. Case E recognized that their content based problem solving solutions had to work logically within the workflow of stakeholders, but they did not seek to provide end-to-end, software enabled workflow solutions. The firm had a strong market research culture, and had established search and select processes. The organization had strong knowledge management systems, and the robust planning cycle was supported by the availability of senior "vigilant" leaders, enabling balanced data interpretation.

In HE markets, the adoption of new technology such as social media and publisher databases is more advanced in STM subjects than in HASS. Case E had grown from a primary focus on the social sciences to a wider subject mix, and had been successful in transferring lessons from successful moves made by STM publishers, and had applied learning from the STM market segment to the social sciences. Through being watchful of developments by competitors, and with extensive connections with scholarly societies and HE stakeholders, they had confidence in their Fast Second approach, and in their strategic and operational capabilities to do so.

The decision not to pursue opportunities in breakthrough environments was felt to liberate the organization from distractions. The firm could identify and pursue emerging opportunities once they were gaining traction in the wider HE publishing sector, taking away the need to plan for breakthrough opportunities. The high quality of structured innovation portfolio governance enabled higher levels of portfolio innovativeness across both market performance and technological aspects. Effective innovation portfolio management is not just driven by the breadth of the options being pursued, but through the selectivity of resource allocation at the later stages of the innovation process.

A key step in Case E's probe and learn process was to consider whether the best way of delivering a solution to an opportunity was to build, buy, or partner? These terms were regularly referred to by the interviewees, as a part of an effective ambidextrous approach to core and adjacent product development. The firm had established search and select capabilities, and had carefully designed the organization to develop a portfolio of options. The firm was operationalizing the portfolio organization through structured planning, with autonomy given to the individuals developing new products in core and adjacent markets.

The influence of context on the operationalisation of search and select at Case E?

Innovation portfolio management
The publisher had set up a highly structured six-box matrix to manage their innovation portfolio, covering core, adjacent and breakthrough opportunities. They had

chosen to explore only four of the six boxes, placing uncertain opportunities in breakthrough environments in the two peripheral boxes where they did not want to operate. The firm was actively managing its innovation portfolio.

Cognition

The attention of the firm had moved from the core, to include adjacent markets, and a clear communication plan had ensured that the cognitive frames of the managers at the operational level included both core and adjacent opportunities. The organization's success here confirmed how firms can actively direct attention across a range of opportunities, consistent with research into the attention-based theory of the firm.

Ambidexterity

The growth of the organization had demanded ambidexterity to enable the acquisition and integration of other companies in new subject areas, while sustaining commercial momentum in core markets. The firm demonstrated the ambidexterity to select different strategies for different markets and opportunities at the strategic and operational level. Acquisition was a key tool deployed in the development of the firm's offering portfolio in the core, and beyond the core, the management of which demanded ambidexterity and appropriate resource allocation.

Peripheral vision: Being vigilant to weak signals

The firm was a vigilant organization, sensing and acting on early warning signs of new opportunities in core and adjacent markets. Even though the organization's innovation portfolio excluded high risk peripheral opportunities, the firm was focused externally, applying strategic foresight and encouraging exploration.

Rapid change core

The firm had robust processes in the core, and was keeping up with the platform technology arms race. Systematic planning routines sustained the performance of the core, enabling the organization to drive search and select processes in adjacent markets.

Five contextual factors influencing the operationalization of search and select

Following this deeper analysis of the best performing case organizations, and reflecting on many of the revealing quotes generated through the interview process, Table 5.1 seeks to highlight the contextual influences that most affect the operationalization of search and select sub-capabilities in the publishing companies at the centre of the book.

Table 5.1: Implications for practice: Five contextual factors influencing the operationalization of search and select.

Contextual influences	Implications for practice
Innovation portfolio management: Structured across core, adjacent and breakthrough opportunities	Firms benefit from the development of a portfolio driven strategic plan. Companies need to develop and operationalize a portfolio designed organization to mobilize the portfolio driven strategy. The effective communication of the portfolio strategy and structure needs to be supported through the visualisation and communication of the strategy and supporting organizational structure.
Cognition	The attention of the firm is strongly influenced by the visible priorities of leaders. If the firm wants to develop a portfolio driven business, the behaviours of leaders need to support this. Organizations need to recruit and develop leaders and managers with wide cognitive frames and the capacity to make sense of unfamiliar or disruptive discoveries across the opportunity portfolio. Different cognitive frames need to be matched to different parts of the opportunity portfolio, which is best achieved through appropriate structures, and human resources with the diverse skills needed across the innovation portfolio.
Ambidexterity	A firm needs to be able to answer the question: "How are we going to be able to exploit the core business, and explore and seize opportunities beyond the core?" Managing the tensions implicit in doing different things in the core and beyond the core involves trade-offs between short- and long-term demands. An effective structural approach is needed for core, adjacent and breakthrough opportunities, and in all likelihood, one size does not fit all. Different skills and experience are needed for do-better and do-different activities. Senior level leaders have to be able to manage the ambiguity implicit in managing a portfolio firm and corresponding networks.

Table 5.1 (continued)

Contextual influences	Implications for practice
Peripheral vision: Being vigilant to weak signals	Practitioners need to look at the periphery in terms of opportunity identification, as well as risk management. Opportunities beyond the core need to be framed as the "next business", rather than a worrying source of uncertainty and cost. Digital era research and decision making capabilities are needed to make sense of the periphery.
Rapid Change Core: Avoid being pulled back into the core business	The phrase "core business" can suggest "unchanging and routine business", but this is generally not the case in the digital era in disrupting core markets. The language chosen to communicate the notion of the "rapid change core" will help practitioners acknowledge the demands of keeping up in core markets. Use of the phrase "rapid change core" will motivate practitioners to spread their bets and adopt portfolio approaches, breaking out of the "rapid change core" to seek new opportunities in adjacent environments, even if breakthrough opportunities are more the preserve of entrepreneurs and appropriately organized corporate venture units.

Lessons from the case studies

Arie de Geus made his name as head of Shell's Strategic Planning Group, and was one of the key players in the development of scenario planning. He emphasised the importance of learning from diverse sources, arguing that: "The ability to learn faster than competitors may be the only sustainable competitive advantage", adding: "Success depends on the ability of its people to learn together and produce new ideas"(de Geus, 1988).

The stories from the case organizations provide many opportunities to learn from companies that were amongst the first to see centuries old subscription models disrupted by the same types of digital technology and business models that are now upending the global media and entertainment industries, e.g. Netflix and Amazon. It is important to not just reflect on the power of technology to disrupt markets, workflows and business models connecting organizations and individuals. The stories in this chapter show how organizations, and most importantly their leaders, have choices to make about how they structure their firms, and how they move on from hierarchical decision making to empowering the more agile approaches that connect project teams with the jobs-to-be-done that are most important within the workflows of their external stakeholders.

Competence and confidence in applying technology to solve the problems of customers and users is key for organizations in the digital era. It is only when firms can manage the "rapid change core" affecting how they earn their living now that they can turn their attention to a portfolio of their "next" market arenas. When analysing the innovation fitness of organizations, the development and communication of an innovation strategy that mobilizes the firm's overall strategy is often lacking. The best managed firms in the study had recognized the importance of this step, and their managers were clear and purposeful in the way that they played their part in building and operationalizing the sub-capabilities required to make the higher order sensing, seizing and transforming dynamic capabilities a reality. The organizations that were most advanced in managing the 11 sub-capabilities critical to managing the search and select processes were the most vigilant, and best prepared for success now and in the future. The firms with weaker search and select sub-capabilities had shorter planning horizons, and were more vulnerable to change.

6 Looking for and validating opportunities: Future practice

The book has focused on understanding the nature and dynamics of offering development focused innovation, and the contextual influences on the early stages of the innovation process. Innovation takes place in disrupting environments in the digital era, with organizations challenged to develop a validated range of opportunities in core markets, and beyond the core. As companies operationalize the "fuzzy front end" of innovation, the search funnel can be too narrow, so there is a need for vigilance and peripheral vision, with selection filters set accordingly. This chapter proposes a number of tools to help practitioners manage key stages of the early stages of the innovation process.

The 11 search and select sub-capabilities that need to be in place to manage offering development effectively

The literature review identified 11 key sub-capabilities that organizations need to have in place to manage the fuzzy front end of NPD search and select effectively in HE publishing, within the wider innovation process, particularly considering opportunity identification, and idea selection tasks.

The empirical research process confirmed the significance of these sub-capabilities, all of which support Teece's three central dynamic capability priorities of sensing and seizing opportunities, and transforming the organization to respond better to endlessly changing market environments. Table 6.1 below synthesizes the findings from the research project with the relevant research literature, and identifies the implications for practice when considering these capability areas

Nine steps to bridge the vigilance gap

Day & Schoemaker (2006, p. 3) set out to establish: "How can managers and their organizations build a superior capacity to recognize and act on weak signals from the periphery before it is too late?" To help improve peripheral vision, they explored underlying organizational processes and capabilities, and developed a seven-step process (Day & Schoemaker, 2006, p. 5) for understanding and enhancing peripheral vision:
- Step 1: Scoping: where to look
- Step 2: Scanning: how to look
- Step 3: Interpreting: what the data means

https://doi.org/10.1515/9783110657326-006

- Step 4: Probing: what to explore more closely
- Step 5: Acting: what to do with these insights
- Step 6: Organizing: how to develop vigilance
- Step 7: Leading: an agenda for action

Table 6.1: The 11 search and select **sub-**capabilities that need to be in place to manage NPD effectively.

Sub-capability required for innovation managed on a Core / Adjacent/ Breakthrough basis	Implications for practice
1) **Strategic clarity, through a clear and well communicated high level, portfolio driven strategic plan supported by appropriate structures considering core, adjacent and breakthrough environments**	Firms need to structure their business on a portfolio basis to develop and resource a mix of offering development opportunities, spreading their risk across core, adjacent and breakthrough environments. While most companies strongly prioritise offering development efforts in the core, research demonstrates that firms with a balanced innovation portfolio typically earn stronger returns than firms that do not develop an innovation portfolio. Effective communication of a portfolio strategy enables core market staff to excel at "do better" offering development, and gives staff developing adjacent and breakthrough "do different" opportunities the focus, flexibility, skills, resources and senior level backing they need to explore successfully beyond the core.
2) **Peripheral vision: Search the periphery for innovation & offering development opportunities (breakthrough environments only)**	Peripheral vision helps firms see emerging threats, and recognize opportunities at the edge of their environment, particularly in rapidly changing markets. To shift attention beyond the core market, organizations need to establish different cognitive frames, routines and skill sets to make sense of adjacent arenas and the periphery. Firms with good peripheral vision gain advantages over competitors, as they recognize and act on opportunities more quickly than rivals, and avoid being blindsided.
3) **Operationalization of structured search and select processes across core, adjacent and breakthrough opportunities**	The operationalization of structured processes across the portfolio gives the firm the capacity to execute search and select, particularly where ambiguity is high beyond the core. Structured search and select processes improve project management, and increase offering development success rates across complex core, adjacent and breakthrough environments.

Table 6.1 (continued)

Sub-capability required for innovation managed on a Core / Adjacent/ Breakthrough basis	Implications for practice
	The effective operationalization of search and select across the portfolio typically requires different structures, metrics, mindsets, processes (e.g. different types of stage-gates), skills and management approaches in the core, and beyond the core.
4) Identifying and sharing deep contextual domain insights, e.g. macro social, industry and technology trends	Firms with deep domain understanding make better choices through reducing uncertainty. Strategic choices require understanding of broad market and technology trends and less visible undercurrents. Firms also find that deep domain insights into the workings of DMUs, budget holder incentives, industry standards, competitor activity, and the speed of adoption of new industry metrics etc. improve opportunity recognition and validation. Insights into the core, and beyond the core, help companies support established markets appropriately, and place bets with improved odds in riskier adjacent and breakthrough environments. Firms will only benefit from these insights through establishing knowledge sharing routines.
5) Seeking out and sharing deep domain insights into user workflows	Providers of digital services need to understand the workflow of their users, otherwise they are likely to segment opportunities poorly, and experience low offering development success rates. Through breaking down the tasks that the user wants to get done, a company understands the points at which a user would benefit from more help from a service, and the metrics users use to evaluate success. Through understanding digital user workflows, companies can identify and validate relevant user jobs-to-be-done, and the value capture models to monetize them.
6) Deployment of digital era market research techniques (e.g. netnography)	Providers of digital solutions require a range of digital era market research techniques to understand fast evolving user needs, budgets, and changing/new DMU structures and priorities in new markets.

Table 6.1 (continued)

Sub-capability required for innovation managed on a Core / Adjacent/ Breakthrough basis	Implications for practice
	Practitioners with access to the research (particularly ethnography based) techniques and data collection capabilities to identify and validate workflows and the potential value capture models required to capitalise on solving problems for users will enhance their offering development success rates.
7) Identification and validation of "big enough" pervasive problems and detailed jobs-to-be-done requiring solutions	Pervasive problems offer greater opportunities to generate value and revenues than isolated jobs-to-be-done. The identification of "big enough" problems focuses attention on opportunities where value can be captured, and which are large enough to be monetized for long enough to be profitable.
8) Validation and iteration of opportunities through MVP testing and learning	MVP and agile approaches lower development costs, and shorten the time that firms take to move through the Build-Measure-Learn loop, helping firms to stop weak projects faster, and develop promising opportunities quickly and cheaply. The measure phase secures data to determine whether the offering development effort is solving problems and creating value, which also enables the design of value capture models.
9) Recruitment and connection with individuals outside the firm's core industry	Through recruiting and connecting with individuals with knowledge from outside core markets, firms gain access to the different skills, perspectives and networks that they need to search for and select a balanced portfolio of options beyond the core.
10) Identification and validation of external acquisition & investment opportunities	The acquisition of companies and development of alliances are key parts of the innovation search and select toolkit. As companies develop a portfolio of opportunities, they require the capability to identify and validate high potential acquisition opportunities.
11) Acting on strategic analysis, investing in, acquiring, and/or collaborating with external organizations	Acquisition and/or collaboration can bring in essential capabilities and new opportunities, but only if the firm can mobilize itself to acquire and integrate target organizations effectively, or manage collaborations for mutual benefit.

Day and Schoemaker's first five steps focused on improving the process of receiving, interpreting and acting on weak signals from the periphery. The last two steps were concerned with building the broader organizational capabilities and leadership to support organizations in the deployment of peripheral vision routines to improve decision making. Their aim was to make peripheral vision an integral part of the organization's processes, leadership priorities and culture, connecting the management of the seven steps to bridge the vigilance gap to the management of the wider organization.

The study has considered a broader question highly relevant to organizations in the 2020s: "How do organizations manage innovation search and select in disrupting environments?" In contrast to Day and Schoemaker's earlier model, the book focuses on the wider search and select process including peripheral vision, across the full portfolio of core, adjacent, and breakthrough environments. The study took place in a specific industry (STM publishing), in a sector disrupting at the time of the research interviews.

Leaders and managers require a process to organize their search and select activities covering core markets (essential), adjacent markets (recommended) and breakthrough environments (for the far sighted and operationally excellent). Building on Day and Schoemaker's seven-step process, I propose a nine step operational process to enable the effective management of the search and select processes in turbulent digital environments. The proposed model adds two steps, and recommends extensions to four of the seven steps in the original model.

While Day and Schoemaker's 2006 model recommended that organizations take the decision to look for uncertainties, risks and opportunities in the periphery, the findings from the study and the literature indicate that organizations only establish offering development portfolio driven strategic plans considering core, adjacent and breakthrough opportunities once they have formally decided to look beyond the core. A trigger event inside or outside the organization, such as declining sales, an acquisition, a strategic review or the emergence of new business models such as Open Access publishing is required to kick start the search for opportunities beyond the core. The proposed model therefore includes a "Deciding to look beyond the core" step at the start of the process. The difficulty that organizations have in moving from making a commitment to change to actually transforming their firm and managing a portfolio of innovation projects is profound, with the need for this step confirmed by the literature on strategic renewal and organizational inertia.

The proposed model also recommends an additional step four: "What to look for?" to guide search and select activities. As B2B organizations seek to identify the opportunities with the greatest potential for offering development they focus on both on DMU members and users. However, each market or arena requires offering providers to identify specific and relevant user and customer jobs-to-be-done and measures of value in the "What to look for" step, which is explained more fully in Table 6.2.

Table 6.2: Nine steps to bridge the vigilance gap.

The nine step cycle	Key features
1. Deciding to look beyond the core	Organizations need to decide to look beyond the core to develop opportunities for the future, before they can mobilize search and select beyond the core.
2. Scoping: Where to look	The need to scope "where to look" at a high level is fundamentally the same as the original process. However, to map core, adjacent and breakthrough environments for opportunities to develop new offerings, B2B organizations need to scope their search and select activities considering issues such as user workflows, jobs-to-be-done and DMU maturity. The author proposes a scoping framework guiding where to look for offering development opportunities in Figure 6.2. This is best used alongside other frameworks used in the early stages of the innovation search and select processes for mapping the innovation space, e.g. Tidd and Bessant's 4Ps (2018, p. 22).
3. Scanning: How to look	The essence of this step is the same as before. What has changed is the range of digital era market research techniques now available. Research techniques rooted in ethnography (e.g. netnography) and AI are particularly effective when building up detailed profiles of users and their jobs-to-be-done.
4. What to look for	This step is new. Identifying the customer and user opportunities with the greatest potential for "offering providers" is increasingly important and complex, particularly when it comes to digital products. There is little point in commissioning research to understand customer and user needs without giving the individuals and team involved appropriate guidance on the types of information that they are looking for. See Table 6.3 below.
5. Interpreting: What the data means	In the digital, AI informed era, there is more information to make sense of than before, and firms and business ecosystems are juggling increasingly complex deadlines, priorities and uncertainties. The cognitive frames of an organization influence how they interpret data.

Table 6.2 (continued)

The nine step cycle	Key features
6. Probing: What to explore more closely	Organizations need to decide what to probe further. The development and widespread adoption of agile development techniques and MVP processes supports the probe and learn step. Working through unclear opportunities in adjacent and breakthrough environments takes more turns around the MVP build-measure-learn feedback loop than better understood core market product evolution projects.
7. Acting: What to do with these insights	Cognition influences how organizations respond to opportunities, as do the organization's knowledge management and learning processes. There is growing recognition that different types of insight, e.g. from the periphery, require different responses than those in core markets.
8. Designing The Portfolio Organization	This step encourages firms to design portfolio organizations and allocate resources appropriately to develop a range of offerings for the future across at least core and adjacent markets, and possibly breakthrough environments as well. Portfolio organizations are designed for ambidexterity, with different skills and mindsets needed in the core, and beyond the core.
9. Operationalizing The Portfolio Organization	Firms need to be strategically flexible to solve new problems for users and customers through new offerings, and operationally efficient, particularly in their core markets. They need to be operationally ambidextrous as they drive forwards a range of projects across their offering portfolio.

Figure 6.1 brings the nine steps together in visual form. A critical decision affecting the innovation management capabilities of all of the case companies in the study was whether their Executive Committee (ExCo) had decided to look for opportunities beyond the core business. Once organizations have made this decision (step 1), they have effectively committed themselves to manage ongoing cycles of scoping where to look for opportunities (step 2), figuring out how to look for them (research tools – step 3), as well as what data and knowledge they need to inform the development of their offerings (step 4).

Once they have generated data, they need to interpret their new knowledge to create the insights (or facts) to inform decisions regarding the next steps of the offering development process (step 5). Great strides have been made in recent times in terms of firms using iterative probe and learn steps – typically through MVPs – to validate what they need to explore more closely (step 6). Once the insights stand up to scrutiny, organizations have to decide how best to act to progress (or stop) projects targeting opportunities, which typically involves confirming how the next stage of the offering development project will be resourced and evaluated (step 7).

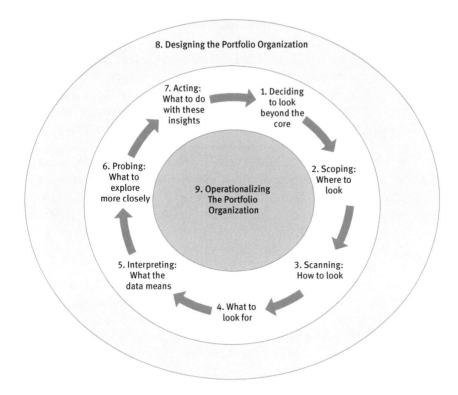

Figure 6.1: Managing search and select across the innovation portfolio.

The rings of the figure prioritize two further steps in managing search and select across the innovation portfolio. Step 8 demands that ExCos must design, drive and facilitate the development of their organization's capabilities (individuals, structures, decision making and routines) to absorb the knowledge generated through external search activity. They must support the development of large and diverse networks of external parties through boundary-spanning activity (Monteiro & Birkinshaw, 2016). In addition, ExCos must ensure that their search and select processes are designed to identify and validate new offering development projects across a portfolio of core (important for profitability), adjacent (essential for growth) and breakthrough (high risk – high reward) opportunities.

Step 9 recognizes that organizations increasingly manage a portfolio of projects with different levels of innovativeness. Operational managers are instrumental in developing and mobilizing the ambidextrous capabilities and processes needed to run innovation portfolios.

Organizations that strive to manage a portfolio of innovation opportunities without a sufficient mix of operational and innovation management practices in place will not overcome the high levels of organizational inertia typically in place in established firms.

Managing a successful innovation driven portfolio organization is very different from just sustaining the core business.

Four of the case companies (A, B, D and E) were found to conduct research into the jobs-to-be-done by users and work groups, and they also sought to understand the measures used by customers to assess if the jobs have been completed successfully. The further that the product development process is from the core market, the more that the value proposition development process moves from goods dominant logic (GDL) to service dominant logic (SDL) (Anderson, Narus, & Wouters, 2006; Payne & Frow, 2013, 2014; Vargo & Lusch, 2004, 2010). Products targeting adjacent markets see service as an integral part of what is sold and researchers exploring product-service systems (PSS) define them as consisting of a collection of products and/or services that fulfil a customer's needs (Yip et al., 2014). When considering integrated product-service systems, stakeholder engagement is the key process for securing information from individuals and organizations who may use the PSS, or may be impacted by it (Kohli & Jaworski, 1990; Yip et al., 2014).

The development of new offerings involves the coordination of novel and older technologies, new and established firm capabilities, and the re-configuration of business model components to solve problems that range from simple to complex. The ecosystem dimension of business is also becoming more complex, with very few organizations able to succeed through their own efforts, without support and co-operation from others within an ecosystem (Adner, 2017; Birkinshaw, 2019; Ihrig & Macmillan, 2017). Solving problems for users and customers involves the actors (the innovators) to make a large number of interdependent choices. Boundedly rational managers are challenged by the need to: "Develop high-performing combinations of interdependent choices" (Baumann & Schmidt, 2019 p. 285). When offering development is targeting adjacent or breakthrough opportunities in areas peripheral to a firm's knowledge base, the level of uncertainty is greater, and the choices are even tougher.

The research study involved the author conducting over 60 interviews. As readers will know from their own research activities, or through their professional discussions, at times conversations are sustained using general terms, and often there is a need to move to the "significant detail" that helps to break down a problem into relevantly structured themes or components. Sometimes it is easier to look at a problem close up, and sometimes from afar. As the interviews progressed, it became clear that the firms with the greatest levels of innovation capability were far more structured in framing the types of insights that they were seeking than the less capable organizations. They also knew that they were looking for the "facts" that decision makers could rely upon. However, none of the interviewees articulated clearly what categories of data they were looking for through the search and select process.

The publishers in the study who had undertaken effective strategy work were able to explain the high level problems that their organizations were seeking to solve for their B2B customers and end users, and had clear strategy plans that were referenced in the interviews. They were able to do this as the most advanced firms had developed

and communicated their strategy to their staff, often using highly visual or colour-coded communication techniques. Strategy development typically involves consideration of the following generic business environment areas (Strategyzer, 2019):
- Foresight: Regulatory, technology, societal and cultural and socioeconomic trends
- Market analysis (market forces): Market segments, needs and demands (high level), market issues, switching costs and revenue attractiveness
- Macro-economic forces: Global market conditions, capital markets, commodities and other resources, and economic infrastructure
- Competitive analysis (industry forces): Suppliers and other value chain actors, stakeholders, competitors (incumbents), new entrants (insurgents), substitute products and services

In terms of product and service (offering) development, and the management of more detailed search and select activities in disrupting environments, the best prepared organizations benefitted from well executed and communicated strategy plans. Leaders and staff were clear about which high-level problem areas they were targeting. One of the high-level problem areas where the 10 HE publisher case companies were seeking to develop solutions were the digitally enabled workflows associated with academic researchers reading and publishing articles.

However, traditional market research tools such as focus groups do not dive deep enough to observe and confirm tangible, detailed problems-to-be-solved that can be monetized. As Gianfranco Zaccai, the P&G designer behind the billion-dollar Swiffer product said: "In my 40 years working in design and innovation, alongside some of the most brilliant minds in the business, I have never seen innovation come out of a focus group. Let me put it more strongly: Focus groups kill innovation. That's both because of what they do and what they don't do" (Zaccai, 2012). Identifying high level problem areas such as workflows is an essential first activity when identifying "what to look for" on the innovation search and select journey. However project teams developing monetizable new offerings need to move from scoping high level problems to exploring detailed jobs-to-be-done, identifying major pain points and undertaking root-cause analysis. It is often helpful to deploy a "five whys" questioning process, as developed by Taiichi Ohno, the creator of the Toyota production system (Furr & Dyer, 2014, p. 95), to identify and confirm jobs-to-be-done.

What to look for: 10 market insight areas that inform offering development in STM publishing

To help guide HE publishers structure their external knowledge search activities, the author proposes 10 areas to be explored, below the strategic insight level that includes foresight (key trends), market analysis (market forces), macro-economic forces and competitive analysis (industry forces). The model identifies the key market insight areas where firms in the STM publishing sector need to focus during the "What to look for" (step 4) in the "Managing search and select across the innovation portfolio" process. The market insight areas have been developed to help practitioners identify the information that will help them to build their value propositions across a portfolio of business opportunities. The further from core markets a company explores, the more diverse and less understood the problems, workflows and jobs-to-be-done will be that they aim to resolve. Practitioners will need to explore and validate a range of jobs-to-be-done to identify where they are best placed to deliver value, whether the opportunity is big enough, and how they can develop a selection of business models to capture value and generate profits.

Table 6.3: What to look for framework.

	What to look for
10 market insight areas that inform offering development in STM Publishing	**Implications for practice**
1) High level problems to solve	The development of a successful offering (product and/or service) requires a firm to solve problems for customers and users. Before focusing in on detailed jobs-to-be-done, it is important to identify and segment the high level problems that customers and users are seeking to solve, to help provide a compass for search and select activity. For STM publishers, customer and user workflows are often the high-level problems areas within which more detailed jobs-to-be-done can be identified. After identifying high level problems to solve, more detailed offering development search and select activities across established (core), emergent, and frontier jobs-to-be-done need to take place.
2) Established jobs-to-be-done	Organizations are generally highly capable at understanding established jobs-to-be-done in core markets, keeping up with standard industry technologies and business models. Problem focused activities to identify jobs-to-be-done will be less resource demanding in well understood core markets than beyond the core, as practitioners will have a good idea of what users and DMUs value the most, and are ready to pay for Through understanding the jobs-to-be-done of digital users and work groups, and the measures used by users and customers to assess if the jobs have been completed successfully, firms can identify multiple innovation opportunities for making jobs simpler, cheaper, easier or faster to complete.

Table 6.3 (continued)

What to look for	
10 market insight areas that inform offering development in STM Publishing	**Implications for practice**
3) Emergent jobs-to-be-done	To understand emergent jobs-to-be-done, organizations must be ready to deal with inconsistent, fragmented and changing knowledge sets. Opportunities will be found:
	– Where established jobs-to-be-done are being changed by new technology, changing human behaviours or other factors
	– In environments which are new to firms, in adjacent and consolidating markets.
	Without a deep understanding of emergent jobs-to-be-done, resource allocation decisions will sub-optimal, as decision-makers will lack detailed knowledge of the outcomes that users and DMUs value the most, and are ready to pay for.
4) Frontier jobs-to-be-done	Frontier jobs-to-be-done are found at the leading edge of core, adjacent and breakthrough environments.
	To understand frontier jobs-to-be-done, organizations need to be prepared to acquire new knowledge in uncertain environments, as understanding emergent, "hard to pin down" jobs-to-be-done is time and resource demanding.
	Frontier jobs-to-be-done are elusive and hard to define due to the need for the different learning modes, temporal dynamics, cognitive limitations and problem decomposition challenges of operating the periphery. However, the potential rewards for getting into a job-to-be-done early (think Facebook) can be very high. Peripheral vision techniques are particularly useful in identifying these opportunities.
5) Pervasive jobs-to-be-done	Having worked through steps 1–4, firms need to rank the pervasive jobs-to-be-done that are big enough to justify resource allocation, as compared to alternative opportunities.
	Managers will also need to assess the time window of the job, i.e. is there enough time to make money out of solving the problem, before a technology changes or competitors make their moves?

Table 6.3 (continued)

	What to look for
10 market insight areas that inform offering development in STM Publishing	**Implications for practice**
6) DMU structure, and the influences on the buying decision	Firms need to identify established, emergent and frontier B2B DMU structures, which are likely to be different. It is important to understand how different DMU members interact, and what influences them internally, and within the external ecosystem (see ecosystem influences below).
7) B2B budgets to target	Firms need to identify where the budgets are located connected to pervasive jobs-to-be-done, to ensure that customers will pay for their new offerings, making opportunities monetizable. They also need to assess if the budgets and financial opportunity are big enough to warrant resource allocation, as compared to alternative opportunities? Where organizations are prepared to pay for offerings supporting emerging or frontier jobs-to-be-done, the budgets available to pay for these services will often be located in unfamiliar parts of buying organizations. Firms need to establish how expensive it will be to access these unfamiliar budgets, and how quickly customers will pay for new offerings.
8) Value metrics (facts)	In data driven B2B markets, firms need to identify the value metrics (data) that B2B customers use to assess the value that a company is delivering to them in providing a solution to a job-to-be-done. This enables the development of targeted value propositions and value capture mechanisms.
9) Value capture	The most significant value capture challenges facing firms concerning emergent and frontier workflow based opportunities are connected with the question: "What quantifiable service can we invoice for, and how do we capture value?" This information then informs the development of suitable value propositions and business models.

Table 6.3 (continued)

	What to look for
10 market insight areas that inform offering development in STM Publishing	**Implications for practice**
10) Ecosystem inter-relationships and power	Before allocating significant resources to projects focused on providing solutions to pervasive jobs-to-be-done, organizations need to map and understand the ecosystem surrounding the job-to-be-done considering: – "Who else in the B2B ecosystem needs to innovate for my innovation to matter" – "Who else needs to adopt my innovation before the end customer can assess the full value proposition?" – "What does it take to deliver the right innovation on time, to specification, to beat the competition?" (Adner, 2006).

What are the benefits of working through the "What to look for" steps?

The issue of developing new business models to capture value from solving new jobs-to-be-done in complex business ecosystems in digital environments is challenging, and requires key insights from stakeholders. The "What to look for" step is proposed as a tool to clarify how organizations operating in digital environments can identify the key market information and value metrics needed to inform "new offering development", and the development of appropriate value capture models across a portfolio of opportunities. Through working through the "What to look for" steps, firms will be properly informed when it comes to developing persuasive value propositions.

Identifying high level problems AND specific jobs-to-be-done

The study highlighted the attention given by STM publishers to understanding the workflow of key stakeholders. While the importance of workflow is well established in the automation literature, innovation researchers have not yet focused extensively on how the understanding of user workflows may offer valuable insights into hidden needs, and the outcomes sought by customers and users.

The author proposes that practitioners would benefit from routinely connecting outcome driven innovation focusing on jobs-to-be-done to the broader context of the user and customer's workflow. While the word "automation" has been in use for almost 75 years, the term "digital workflows" is useful in describing how digitally supported automation enables the movement of human workers from standardized, repetitive tasks to more creative and analytical work (Davenport, 2019a) in both service and manufacturing firms. B2B organizations increasingly target the integration of their offering within the developing digital workflows of their target customers and users.

Firms need to pinpoint detailed jobs-to-be-done within the higher level problem spaces that workflow processes help us to scope and understand. For example, Salesforce grew strongly as it helped firms to automate the management of their relationships (a critical high level workflow) with their clients. Salesforce continues to grow due to its success in identifying and resolving more detailed jobs-to-be-done such as improving real-time feedback to sales staff through its Work.com service, or providing personalised experiences to customers through its Marketing Cloud platform.

Influenced by Utterback and Abernathy's innovation life cycle (1975), and their three stages of fluid, transitional and specific (standardised) product and process design, the author has developed a scoping framework, shown in Figure 6.2, that guides B2B companies to map their search and select projects considering, on the vertical axis:

- Established jobs-to-be-done within a workflow, where keeping up with industry technology and business models is required to sustain innovation
- Emergent jobs-to-be-done within a workflow, where there is inconsistent knowledge and a range of user routines are in play. They include the phases where processes are consolidating, where the workflow is evolving from being fluid in breakthrough environments, to a state where a set of emergent workflows are starting to form. These jobs-to-be-done are regularly targeted by consolidating, fast second organizations. Due to the lack of clarity of emergent jobs-to-be-done, analysing them to identify which jobs are pervasive and solvable is particularly resource demanding
- Frontier (think fluid or "rapid change") jobs-to-be-done are "hard to pin down," and the organizations developing early stage offerings are typically challenged in trying out new ways to frame and provide solutions for new jobs-to-be-done. The requirement is for new knowledge in uncertain environments. This activity is time and resource demanding, with high levels of uncertainty, and requires peripheral vision

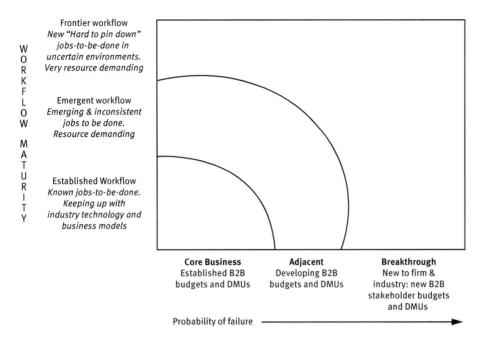

W
O
R
K
F
L
O
W

M
A
T
U
R
I
T
Y

Frontier workflow
*New "Hard to pin down"
jobs-to-be-done in
uncertain environments.
Very resource demanding*

Emergent workflow
*Emerging & inconsistent
jobs to be done.
Resource demanding*

Established Workflow
*Known jobs-to-be-done.
Keeping up with
industry technology and
business models*

Core Business
Established B2B
budgets and DMUs

Adjacent
Developing B2B
budgets and DMUs

Breakthrough
New to firm &
industry: new B2B
stakeholder budgets
and DMUs

Probability of failure ⟶

Figure 6.2: Jobs-to-be-done scoping framework.

The horizontal axis uses a typical core-adjacent-breakthrough approach to indicate how organizations face the challenge of managing the search and select process across a spectrum of environments, from core markets where knowledge is high and relatively easy to access and prioritise, to breakthrough areas with few reference points and significant uncertainty. The research project has been conducted in a B2B context, and so the horizontal axis emphasises the level of stability and clarity of understanding regarding the budgets and related DMUs targeted through new offerings.

While the probability of failure increases in Figure 6.3, the further that projects are from the core business, or from standardised workflows, the cumulative return on innovation investments allocated in adjacent and/or breakthrough environments also increases the further that activities are located from the core.

The framework is developed further in Figure 6.3 through using different sizes of bubble proportional to a project's estimated revenue, or profitability, building on previous research into options (McGrath, 1997; McGrath & Nerkar, 2004) and portfolio risk management (Day, 2007; McGrath & MacMillan, 2009). Through using appropriate financial measures, the framework can be used to map individual projects within a wider NPD portfolio, integrating a range of opportunities such as internally developed projects, collaborative initiatives across a network or organizations, and M&A activity.

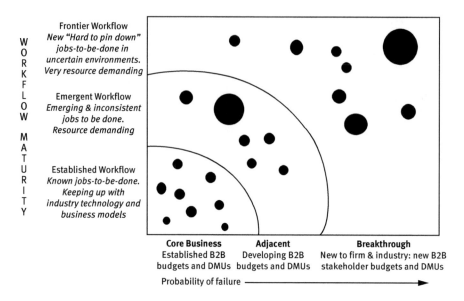

Figure 6.3: Scoping where to look for NPD opportunities across the innovation portfolio considering jobs-to-be-done and project potential.

Where to look for innovation opportunities: A new Business Model Evaluation Matrix

Managing innovation is becoming more complex, as organizations seek to deliver value and manage customer relationships across technologically enabled ecosystems. Making sense of the innovation search space is complicated. A wide range of tools have been developed over many years to map innovation options, helping firms to make important decisions considering a range of opportunities. To manage new offering development effectively, the use of visual portfolio maps helps to achieve a balance between high-risk/high-reward projects, and more limited sustaining innovation projects focused on exploitation markets.

Business models integrate value propositions, value chains and value capture. The simple Business Model Evaluation Matrix below (Figure 6.4) helps practitioners to create and evaluate high level/early stage maps of the innovation opportunity space, with a particular focus on business models, and the value propositions that are central to their operation. Kaplan and Norton (2001) have argued that the value proposition is: "The essence of strategy," as it is the point where the relevance and quality of strategy work and detailed market exploration comes together, and customers can very simply say yes – or no – to the offering. While the term "value proposition" is used a great deal, only one in 10 B2B organizations formally develop, communicate and use value propositions (Frow & Payne, 2008). If only one in 10 B2B firms are effective in developing and deploying value propositions, then it is safe to say that only one in 10 organizations or less are effective in mobilizing B2B business models.

However, the strong execution of B2B value propositions leads to competitive advantage and growth, and will reward the painstaking work recommended in this chapter. A value proposition is a firm's offering to a B2B decision making unit, summarising the benefits (value) that the customer and users will receive during and after the usage experience. It specifies the service (experiential) and product (physical) benefits and costs involved. To win: "A superior value proposition represents an offering to customers that adds more value or solves a problem better than other or similar competitive offerings" (Payne & Frow, 2013, p. 240). Persuasive value propositions bring together five key elements:

- The target customer
- The key problem faced
- How the firm can resolve the problem
- The product and/or service offering
- Why the offering is differentiated from the competition

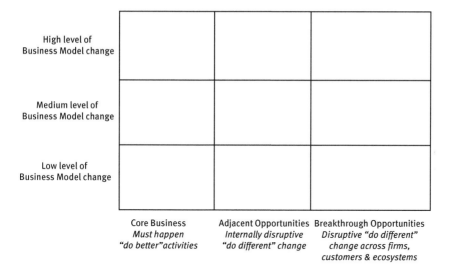

Figure 6.4: Business Model Evaluation Matrix.

Triggered by the widespread take up of the Business Model Canvas and Value Proposition Canvas by practitioners, and the associated increase in focus amongst researchers on business models and the value propositions, it is useful to map business models considering innovation portfolios. The matrix in Figure 6.4 helps to assess the level of business model change associated with an opportunity on the vertical axis, while considering whether the opportunity fits in as a core market activity where organizational knowledge is high, or whether it sits as an adjacent or breakthrough/peripheral market opportunity where organizational knowledge and preparedness in terms of structure, capabilities and staff numbers is lower, with fewer staff, established activities and routines in place. The further the opportunity is from the core, the greater the level of disruption for the firm.

By scoping – at a high level – a range of business model options considering the degree of business model change, established firms can start assessing "what's different" (technology, service delivery etc.) about a new B2B offering targeting beyond the core opportunities from incremental innovation work in established markets. Through connecting the degree of business model change with the impact of that change at the firm/customer/ecosystem level, organizations and ecosystem partners will need to work through the impact of changing value propositions on their wider business model. The matrix helps firms segue from the development of new offerings, and the value propositions that summarise their benefits, into considering how the development of new business models can be built and distributed. A firm has to master new processes and activities to create and operate new business models. To be successful they must manage the required resources and capabilities, orchestrating the focal organization's internal value chain. The matrix helps individuals and organizations to not only understand the potential level of change and associated risk involved in mobilizing a business model on the vertical axis, but also assesses the initial question of: "How equipped is our firm to explore an opportunity further?"

Managing the "Rapid change core" is becoming key to progressing more radical innovation projects

The importance of developing an established language around a management theme, so that practitioners, consultants, researchers, teachers and students can develop their thinking and manage projects, is well established. One of the most helpful outcomes of the research project was the identification of the challenges that many organizations have in keeping up with technology change in their core markets, hence the introduction and use of the term "Rapid Change Core" throughout the book. The automotive sector sees firms like Volkswagen and Toyota maintaining their focus in core markets on the design and selling of cars for personal use. However much of their core market now falls into the "Rapid Change Core" space due to the switch to electrification and the development of self-driving technologies. Major digital transformation projects designed to support core operations as well as enhancing the development of new offerings and business models report high failure rates, and this affects the ability of incumbent firms to manage innovation projects across the portfolio (Davenport & Spanyi, 2019; Ross et al., 2019).

	Core Business *Must happen* *"do better"activities*	Adjacent Opportunities *Internally disruptive* *"do different" activities*	Breakthrough Opportunities *Disruptive "do different"* *activities across firms,* *customers & ecosystems*
High level of Business Model change	*Rapid Change core* *Business Model* *devlopment* *High uncertainty*	*Rapid Change* *New Business Models* *Very high uncertainty*	*Rapid Change* *New "everything"* *Extreme uncertainty*
Medium level of Business Model change	*Business Model* *evolution*	*New to firm knowledge* *Business Model* *development*	*New to firm knowledge,* *customers, partners &* *Business Model* *Extreme uncertainty*
Low level of Business Model change	*Customer Learning* *Business models* *sustained*	*Ecosystem Learning* *Business Model* *development*	*Breakthrough opportunities* *with low levels of* *Value Proposition change are* *rare*

Figure 6.5: Business Model Evaluation Matrix: Impact on firms and ecosystems.

The more detailed version of the Business Model Evaluation Matrix (Figure 6.5) informs firms mapping potential opportunity spaces, who want to consider what impact different opportunities might have on their organization.

Deploying the new tools

We have seen how the pressure to keep up with technology developments in known markets, with established but vulnerable budgets to target, can increase "lock in" to familiar core market focused activity. The digitization of core business processes in established markets has built the phenomenon of the rapid change core, where less prepared organizations struggle to keep up with the technology arms race.

When it comes to managing search and select in adjacent markets, the environment is less certain. With less tacit knowledge of customer journeys, jobs-to-be-done, budgets, competitors and contextual factors, the requirement to understand the unfamiliar and make decisions beyond the core is challenging for many firms. While the language describing key market information might stay the same for core markets, exploring adjacent markets typically requires different roles and people, possibly with different cognitive frames, skills and experience, to operationalize search and select successfully beyond the core. These "beyond the core" thinking people need to be managed in different ways from the staff in established firms pursuing incremental (sustaining) innovation opportunities. An organization structured and resourced with an appropriate portfolio of corporate venture units linking organizational design, strategy, dynamic capabilities and operational excellence is well positioned to develop a portfolio of new offering development options.

The level of complexity progressively increases when organizations decide to develop a portfolio of options including breakthrough environments. Not only do organizations need to choose which strategies to use across the portfolio, they also need to adopt appropriate operational approaches across the corporate venture units attempting to manage and provide governance across rapid change core, adjacent and breakthrough environments. The case companies were all seeking at least some of the key market insights shown detailed in Table 6.3 (the "What to look for framework") which displays evidence from the interview process supporting the identification of the 10 key market insights that inform new offering development in STM publishing.

The purpose of this chapter has been to synthesise the most salient themes and details from the literature review in Chapter 1 (Creating customers in the digital era) and Chapter 2 (The innovation process in disrupting environments) with what we learned through the data collection phase. The in depth reflections in Chapter 4 (Vigilant innovation in the STM publishing sector) and Chapter 5 (Diving deeper: Learning from five rich case studies) triggered the development of the tools found in this chapter which aim to help firms to:

- Bridge the vigilance gap *through* developing the 11 dynamic sub-capabilities needed to manage the offering development process
- Manage and operationalize the overall search and select process across core, adjacent and breakthrough portfolio *using the* "Managing search and select across the innovation portfolio" model
- Plan where and how to search for opportunities *using the* "What to look for" framework
- Map a spectrum of workflow situated jobs-to-be-done *using the* Jobs-to-be-done scoping framework
- Map opportunities considering different levels of business model change *using the* Business Model Evaluation Framework

The main recommendations from the book are that firms develop and operationalize portfolio driven structures and processes to identify and evaluate the jobs-to-be-done that they aim to solve for unfamiliar users, targeting a variety of emerging budgets in adjacent and breakthrough environments. This can only happen if the demons of the rapid change core are under control, enabling firms to pursue vigilant innovation through looking forwards into the frontier workflows of existing and new users.

7 Final reflections on vigilant search and select

The highly influential educational theorist David Kolb is famous for developing his four stage experiential learning cycle. The model (shown in Figure 7.1) works well for both full-time learners, and managers who are squeezing in their personal learning in scarce moments between their roles and further responsibilities, supported by on-line materials in the shape of videos, podcasts, and a range of written materials.

Learning is generally enhanced when **experiential** events are part of the learning cycle. As I reflected on the research and writing project that has created this book, I realised that as a self-confessed boundary spanner and aspiring T-shaped thinker, that I had actually been moving through Kolb's learning cycle for 20 years, from the time I became a publisher in 2000 to the publication of this book in 2020.

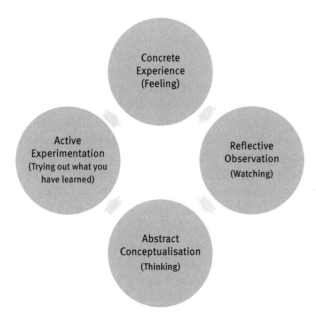

Figure 7.1: Kolb's experiential learning cycle.

Concrete experience

I worked in scholarly publishing for 12 years as a Board Director during the period that the industry moved from the early flowering of online delivery and digitally enabled business models in 2000, to the time when scholarly publishing was one of the first arenas that could claim that the majority of revenues and service delivery came from digital activity in 2012. This experience grounded the research project

https://doi.org/10.1515/9783110657326-007

that I undertook as part of my PhD in Innovation Management at the University of Exeter in the UK.

Reflective observation

Guided and refreshed with new lenses and perspectives from over 100 years of research into innovation management, I have been able to reflect on my concrete experience as a publisher. That reflection was boosted through over 60 interviews with scholarly publishers, which introduced fresh perspectives from some truly inspirational and thoughtful individuals. There was just so much to reflect on! As I regularly say to the students and managers that I work with in the innovation space: "As a manager and leader, I wish that I had known what I know now as a researcher about the key themes of innovation management."

Abstract conceptualisation

With the opportunity to reflect on 12 years in publishing and a further three and half years working on my PhD, the reader might think that the conceptualisation of new frameworks and models regarding innovation search and select in disrupting environments was completed a few years ago. The writing process for the book took place in 2019 and the first half of 2020, which have been momentous years for digital business and society more generally through the shocks flowing from the coronavirus pandemic. I was working with managers at Disney the day that the first plans for the new Disney+ service were released. We are witnessing a remarkable investment boom of $100 billion a year in digital entertainment. This is a rare level of investment frenzy, with comparisons appropriate with the investments made in the railways in the 1860s and the automobile industry in the 1940s. The recommendations for future practice in Chapter 6 have moved on considerably from my initial thoughts in 2016, based on reflection and the ongoing development of research concerning innovation search and select in the ecosystem orientated digital era.

Active experimentation

The recommendations for future practice continue to be worked through with managers and students, to evaluate their usefulness. The ideas in the book have benefitted from active experimentation as a part of a unique 20 year personal learning cycle. I am grateful to everyone who has supported my own reflection process. I have learned a huge amount from a great many people who have been very kind with their time.

Last word

The grip of the "rapid change core" remains strong in many efficiency orientated organizations. The need to develop innovation portfolios is reinforced with almost every discussion with a business or individual managers. To be successful, current research confirms that the requirement has never been greater for ExCos and their (hopefully) agile teams to manage the digitization of processes in the "rapid change core" effectively. Once activities in core arenas are under control, attention – that rare asset – can be turned to adjacent and breakthrough opportunities, where the "game changes" and the opportunities for new value creation and reward are greater. I encourage all organizations, be they startups, scaleups, established firms, NGOs or public sector bodies to build vigilant search and select capabilities to look beyond the core to the periphery where change and opportunities typically start to emerge from non-obvious locations.

Bibliography

Aalst, W. M. P. Van Der, Hofstede, A. H. M., & Weske, M. (2003). Business Process Management: A Survey. In *Business process management* (pp. 1–12). Heidelberg: Springer.

Abernathy, W. J., & Utterback, J. M. (1978). Patterns of Industrial Innovation. *Technology Review, 80*(7).

Adams, J. (2012). Collaborations: The rise of research networks. *Nature, 490*(7420), 335–336. https://doi.org/10.1038/490335a.

Adler, P. S., Goldoftas, B., & Levine, D. I. (1999). Flexibility versus Efficiency? A Case Study of Model Changeovers in the Toyota Production System. *Organization Science, 10*(1), 43–68.

Adner, R. (2006). Match your innovation strategy to your innovation ecosystem. *Harvard Business Review, 84*(4), 98–107.

Adner, R. (2013). *The Wide Lens* (2nd ed.). New York: Penguin.

Adner, R. (2017). Ecosystem as Structure: An Actionable Construct for Strategy. *Journal of Management, 43*(1), 39–58. https://doi.org/10.1177/0149206316678451.

Adner, R., & Feiler, D. (2019). Interdependence, Perception, and Investment Choices: An Experimental Approach to Decision Making in Innovation Ecosystems. *Organization Science, 30*(1), 109–125.

Adner, R., & Kapoor, R. (2010). Value Creation in Innovation Ecosystems: How the Structure of Technological Interdependence Affects Firm Performance in New Technology Generations. *S*

Adner, R., & Levinthal, D. A. (2004). What is Not a Real Option: Identifying Boundaries for the Application of Real Option to Business Strategy. *Academy of Management Review, 29*(1), 74–85.

Ahuja, G., & Novelli, E. (2014). Mergers and Acquisitions and Innovation. In *The Oxford Handbook of Innovation Management* (pp. 579–599). https://doi.org/10.1093/oxfordhb/9780199694945.013.026.

Almquist, E., Cleghorn, J., & Sherer, L. (2018). The B2B Elements of Value. *Harvard Business Review, 96*(2), 72–81.

Amable, B., Demmou, L., & Ledezma, I. (2009). Product market regulation, innovation, and distance to frontier. *Industrial and Corporate Change, 19*(1), 117–159. https://doi.org/10.1093/icc/dtp037.

Ambrosini, V., & Bowman, C. (2009). What are dynamic capabilities and are they a useful construct in strategic management? *International Journal of Management Reviews, 11*, 29–49. https://doi.org/10.1111/j.1468-2370.2008.00251.x.

Amit, R., & Zott, C. (2012). Creating Value Through Business Model Innovation. *Sloan Management Review, 53*(3), 41–49.

Anderson, J. C., Narus, J. A., & Wouters, M. (2006). Customer Value Propositions in Business Markets. *Harvard Business Review, 84*(3), 90–99.

Anthony, S. D., Patrick Viguerie, S., Schwartz, E. I., & Landeghem, J. Van. (2018). *2018 Corporate Longevity Forecast: Creative Destruction is Accelerating S&P 500 lifespans*. Retrieved from https://www.innosight.com/insight/creative-destruction/.

Ansari, S. (Shaz), Garud, R., & Kumaraswamy, A. (2016). The disruptor's dilemma: TiVo and the U.S. television ecosystem. *Strategic Management Journal, 37*(9), 1829–1853. https://doi.org/10.1002/smj.

Anthony, S. D., Trotter, A., Bell, R., & Schwartz, E. I. (2019). *The Transformation 20*. Boston, MA.

Archambault, E., Amyot, D., Deschamps, P., Aurore, N., Rebout, L., & Roberge, G. (2013). *Proportion of Open Access Peer-Reviewed Papers at the European and World Levels—2004–2011*.

Ashton, K. (2009). That' Internet of Things ' Thing. *RFID Journal, 22*(7), 97–114. https://doi.org/10.1038/nature03475.

Atkins, M. (2014). *Higher Education Funding Council for England Open Access in the post-2014 Research Excellence Framework*. Retrieved from http://www.hefce.ac.uk/media/hefce/content/pubs/2014/cl072014/Print-friendly.

https://doi.org/10.1515/9783110657326-008

Barker, A., & Nilsson, P. (2020, February 12). Mutinous librarians help drive change at Elsevier. *Financial Times*. Retrieved from https://www.ft.com/content/c846c756-49ac-11ea-aee2-9ddbdc86190d.

Barney, J. B. (1991). Firm Resources and Sustained Competitive Advantage. *Journal of Management*, Vol. 17, pp. 99–120. https://doi.org/10.1177/014920639101700108.

Barney, J. B. (1996). The Resource-Based Theory of the Firm. *Organization Science*, Vol. 7, pp. 469–469. https://doi.org/10.1287/orsc.7.5.469.

Baron, R. A. (2006). Opportunity Recognition as Pattern Recognition: How Entrepreneurs "Connect the Dots" to Identify New Business Opportunities. *Academy of Management Perspectives*, *20*(1), 104–119.

Baumann, O., & Schmidt, J. (2019). Effective Search in Rugged Performance Landscapes: A Review and Outlook. *Journal of Management*, *45*(1), 285–318. https://doi.org/10.1177/0149206318808594.

Beck, K., Beedle, M., Bennekum, A. van, Cockburn, A., Cunningham, W., Fowler, M., . . . Thomas, D. (2001). Manifesto for Agile Software Development. Retrieved December 9, 2015, from http://agilemanifesto.org/.

Benner, M. J., & Tripsas, M. (2012). The Influence of Prior Industry Affiliation on Framing in Nascent Industries: The Evolution of Digital Cameras. *Strategic Management Journal*, *33*, 277–302. https://doi.org/10.1002/smj.

Benner, M. J., & Tushman, M. L. (2003). Exploitation, Exploration, and Process Management: The Productivity Dilemma Revisited. *Academy of Management Review*, *28*(2), 238–256.

Bessant, J., Lamming, R., Noke, H., & Phillips, W. (2005). Managing innovation beyond the steady state. *Technovation*, *25*(12), 1366–1376. https://doi.org/10.1016/j.technovation.2005.04.007.

Bettencourt, L. A., Lusch, R. F., & Vargo, S. L. (2014). A Service Lens on Value Creation: Marketing"s Role in Achieving Strategic Advantage. *California Management Review*, *57*(1), 44–67.

Bettencourt, L. A., & Ulwick, A. W. (2008). The Customer-Centered Innovation Map. *Harvard Business Review*, *86*(5), 109–115.

Bingham, C. B., & Eisenhardt, K. M. (2011). Rational Heuristics: The "Simple Rules" that Strategists Learn from Process Experience. *Strategic Management Journal*, *1464* (June2010), 1437–1464. https://doi.org/10.1002/smj.

Binns, A., Harreld, J. B., O'Reilly, C. A., & Tushman, M. L. (2014). The Art of Strategic Renewal: What does it take to transform an organization before a crisis hits? *Sloan Management Review*, *55*(2), 21–23.

Birkinshaw, J. (2018). How is technological change affecting the nature of the corporation? *Journal of the British Academy*, *6*(October), 185–214.

Birkinshaw, J. (2019, August 8). Ecosystem Businesses Are Changing the Rules of Strategy. *Harvard Business Review Digital Articles*.

Birkinshaw, J., Bessant, J., & Delbridge, R. (2007). Finding, Forming, and Performing: Creating Networks for Discontinuous Innovation. *California Management Review*, *49*(3), 67–84.

Birkinshaw, J., & Gupta, K. (2013). Clarifying the Distinctive Contribution Of Ambidexterity To The Field of Organization Studies. *Academy of Management Perspectives*, *27*(4), 287–298.

Birkinshaw, J., & Ridderstråle, J. (2017). *Fast/Forward*. Stanford: Stanford University Press.

Blank, S. (2013). Why the Lean Start-Up Changes Everything. *Harvard Business Review*, *91*(5), 63–72.

Blank, S., & Dorf, B. (2012). *The Startup Owner's Manual Vol. 1*. Pescadero: K&S Ranch Press.

Block, F., & Keller, M. R. (2009). Where do innovations come from? Transformations in the US economy, 1970–2006. *Socio-Economic Review*, *7*(3), 459–483. https://doi.org/10.1093/ser/mwp013.

Boudreau, K. J., Lacetera, N., & Lakhani, K. R. (2011). Incentives and Problem Uncertainty in Innovation Contests : An Empirical Analysis Incentives and Problem Uncertainty in Innovation

Contests : An Empirical Analysis. *Management Science, 57*(5), 843–863. https://doi.org/
10.1287/mnsc.1110.1322.

Bower, J. L., & Christensen, C. M. (1995). Disruptive Technologies : Catching the Wave. *Harvard Business Review, 73*(1), 43–54.

Brauen, S. (2017). Rethinking Crowdsourcing. *Harvard Business Review, 95*(6), 20–23.

Brhel, M., Meth, H., Maedche, A., & Werder, K. (2015). Exploring principles of user-centered agile software development : A literature review. *Information and Software Technology, 61*, 163–181. https://doi.org/10.1016/j.infsof.2015.01.004.

Brown, S. L., & Eisenhardt, K. M. (1998). *Competing on the Edge*. Boston, MA: Harvard Business School Press.

Brunneder, J., Acar, O., Deichmann, D., & Sarwal, T. (2020). A New Model for Crowdsourcing Innovation. *Harvard Business Review Digital Articles, 31/1*.

Brynjolfsson, E., Hitt, L. M., & Kim, H. H. (2011). Strength in Numbers: How Does Data-Driven Decisionmaking Affect Firm Performance? *SSRN Electronic Journal*. https://doi.org/10.2139/ssrn.1819486.

Brynjolfsson, E., & McAfee, A. (2014). *The Second Machine Age*. New York: Norton.

Brynjolfsson, E., & McAfee, A. (2015). The Great Decoupling. *Harvard Business Review, 93*(6), 66–75.

Burt, R. S. (2000). The network structure of social capital. In *Research in Organizational Behavior* (Vol. 22). https://doi.org/10.1016/S0191-3085(00)22009-1.

Burt, R. S. (2004). Structural Holes and Good Ideas. *American Journal of Sociology, 110*(2), 349–399.

Busenitz, L. W., & Barney, J. B. (1997). Differences between entrepreneurs and managers in large organizations: Biases and heuristics in strategic decision-making. *Journal of Business Venturing, 12*(1), 9–30. https://doi.org/10.1016/S0883-9026(96)00003-1.

Camuffo, A., Cordova, A., Gambardella, A., & Spina, C. (2019). A Scientific Approach to Entrepreneurial Decision Making: Evidence from a Randomized Control Trial. *Management Science*, (October). https://doi.org/10.1287/mnsc.2018.3249.

Capron, L., Dussauge, P., & Mitchell, W. (1998). Resource redeployment following horizontal acquisitions in Europe and North America, 1988–1992. *Strategic Management Journal, 19*(7), 631–661.

Cassiman, B., & Veugelers, R. (2006). In Search of Complementarity in Innovation Strategy: Internal R & D and External Knowledge Acquisition. *Management Science, 52*(1), 68–82. https://doi.org/10.1287/mnsc.l050.0470.

Cayla, J., & Arnould, E. J. (2013). Ethnographic Stories for Market Learning. *Journal of Marketing, 77*(4), 1–16. https://doi.org/10.1509/jm.12.0471.

Cayla, J., Beers, R., & Arnould, E. J. (2014). Stories That Deliver Business Insights. *Sloan Management Review, 55*(2), 55–62.

Chandler, A. D. (1990). *Scale and Scope: The Dynamics of Industrial Competition*. Cambridge, MA: Harvard Business School Press.

Chandy, R. K., & Tellis, G. J. (2000). The Incumbent's Curse? Incumbency, Size, and Radical Product Innovation. *Journal of Marketing, 64*(July), 1–17.

Chatterji, A. K., & Fabrizio, K. (2012). How Do Product Users Influence Corporate Invention? *Organization Science, 23*(4), 971–987.

Chaudhuri, B. Y. S., & Tabrizi, B. (1999). Capturing the Real Value in High-Tech Acquisitions. *Harvard Business Review, 77*(5), 123–130.

Christensen, C. M. (1997). The Innovator's Dilemma. In *Business* (Vol. 1). Retrieved from https://www.opac.uni-erlangen.de/webOPACClient/search.do?methodToCall=quickSearch&Kateg=0&Content=2324510&fbt=7955401-2836663.

Christensen, C. M., Anthony, S. D., Berstell, G., & Nitterhouse, D. (2007). Finding the right job for your product. *MIT Sloan Management Review, 48*(3), 38–47.

Christensen, C. M., & Dillon, K. (2020). Disruption 2020: An Interview With Clayton M. Christensen. *MIT Sloan Management Review, 61*(3), 21–26. Retrieved from https://sloanreview.mit.edu/article/an-interview-with-clayton-m-christensen/.

Christensen, C. M., Hall, T., Dillon, K., & Duncan, D. S. (2016). Know You Customers' "Jobs to Be Done". *Harvard Business Review, 94*(9), 54–62.

Christensen, C. M., McDonald, R., Altman, E. J., & Palmer, J. E. (2018). Disruptive Innovation: An Intellectual History and Directions for Future Research. *Journal of Management Studies, 55*(7), 1043–1078. https://doi.org/10.1111/joms.12349.

Christensen, C. M., & Raynor, M. E. (2003). Innovators Solution. In *Director*.

Christensen, C. M., Raynor, M., & McDonald, R. (2015). What is Disruptive Innovation? *Harvard Business Review, 93*(12), 44–53.

Cohen, W. M., & Levinthal, D. A. (1990). Absorptive Capacity: A New Perspective on Learning and Innovation. *Administrative Science Quarterly, 35*(1), 128–152. https://doi.org/10.2307/2393553.

Collis, D. J., & Rukstad, M. G. (2008). Can You say What Your Strategy Is? *Harvard Business Review, 86*(4), 82–90.

Cookson, R. (2015, November 15). Elsevier leads the business the internet could not kill. *Financial Times*. Retrieved from http://www.ft.com/cms/s/0/93138f3e-87d6-11e5-90de-f44762bf9896.html?ftcamp=crm/email/20151116/nbe/CompaniesBySector/product#axzz3re7kx7pL

Cooper, R. G. (1985). Selecting Winning New Product Projects: Using the NewProd System. *Journal of Product Innovation Management, 2*(1), 34–44.

Cooper, R. G. (1998). *Product Leadership: Creating and Launching Superior New Products*. Reading, MA: Perseus.

Cooper, R. G. (2011). *Winning at New Products* (4th ed.). New York: Perseus.

Cooper, R. G. (2013). Where Are All the Breakthrough New Products?: Using Portfolio Management to Boost Innovation. *Research-Technology Management, 56*(5), 25–33. https://doi.org/10.5437/08956308X5605123.

Cooper, R. G., & Edgett, S. J. (2008). Ideation for Product Innovation : What are the best methods. *PDMA Visions Magazine, 32*(1), 12–17.

Cooper, R. G., Edgett, S., & Kleinschmidt, E. (2001). Portfolio management for new product development : results of an industry practices study. *R&D Management, 31*(4), 361–380. Retrieved from http://onlinelibrary.wiley.com/doi/10.1111/1467-9310.00225/abstract;jsessionid=00B9F6A061878F423EE2799B63386B23.f02t04.

COUNTER. (2015). No Title. Retrieved from http://www.projectcounter.org/about.html.

Coyne, K. P., Clifford, P. G., & Dye, R. (2007). Thinking from Inside the Box. *Harvard Business Review, 85*(12), 70–78.

D'Aveni, R. A., & Gunther, R. E. (1994). *Hypercompetition: Managing the Dynamics of Strategic Maneuvering*. New York: The Free Press.

Dahlander, L., & Magnusson, M. (2008). How do Firms Make Use of Open Source Communities? *Long Range Planning, 41*(6), 629–649. https://doi.org/10.1016/j.lrp.2008.09.003.

Dahlander, L., Mahony, S. O., & Gann, D. M. (2014). One foot in, One foot out: How does individuals' external search breadth affect innovation outcomes? *Strategic Management Journal*. https://doi.org/10.1002/smj.

Dahlander, L., & Wallin, M. W. (2006). A man on the inside: Unlocking communities as complementary assets. *Research Policy, 35*(8), 1243–1259. https://doi.org/10.1016/j.respol.2006.09.011.

Daily, C. M., McDougall, P. P., Covin, J. G., & Dalton, D. R. (2002). Governance and Strategic Leadership in Entrepreneurial Firms. *Journal of Management, 28*(3), 387–412.

Danese, P., Manfè, V., & Romano, P. (2018). A Systematic Literature Review on Recent Lean Research: State-of-the-art and Future Directions. *International Journal of Management Reviews, 20*(2), 579–605. https://doi.org/10.1111/ijmr.12156.

Daneshkhu, S. (2015). Most consumer 'innovations' fail taste test. *Financial Times*. Retrieved from http://www.ft.com/cms/s/0/a36320ac-9915-11e5-9228-87e603d47bdc.html?ftcamp=crm/ email/2015123/nbe/GlobalBusiness/product#axzz3tF6Au07x.

Danneels, E. (2011). Trying to become a different type of company: dynamic capability at Smith Corona. *Strategic Management Journal*, *32*(1), 1–31. https://doi.org/10.1002/smj.

Daum, K. (2016). 37 Quotes From Thomas Edison That Will Inspire Success. Retrieved from Inc. website: https://www.inc.com/kevin-daum/37-quotes-from-thomas-edison-that-will-bring-out-your-best.html.

Davenport, T. H. (2019a). The Business Value of Digital Workflows. *Workflow Quarterly*, (Spring).

Davenport, T. H. (2019b). The World's Most Innovative Companies. *Workflow Quarterly*. Retrieved from https://workflow.servicenow.com/quarterly/issue/1/.

Davenport, T. H., & Spanyi, A. (2019, October 8). Digital Transformation Should Start With Customers. *Sloan Blog*.

Davis, J. P., Eisenhardt, K. M., & Bingham, C. B. (2009). Optimal Structure, Market Dynamism, and the Strategy of Simple Rules. *Administrative Science Quarterly*, *54*(3), 413–452. https://doi.org/10.2189/asqu.2009.54.3.413.

Day, G. S. (2007). Is It Real? Can We Win? Is It Worth Doing? Managing Risk and Reward in an Innovation Portfolio. *Harvard Business Review*, *85*(12), 110–120.

Day, G. S., & Schoemaker, P. J. H. (2004a). Driving Through the Fog: Managing at the Edge. *Long Range Planning*, *37*(2), 127–142.

Day, G. S., & Schoemaker, P. J. H. (2004b). Peripheral Vision: Sensing and Acting on Weak Signals. *Long Range Planning*, *37*(2), 117–121. https://doi.org/10.1016/j.lrp.2004.01.003.

Day, G. S., & Schoemaker, P. J. H. (2006). Peripheral Vision: Detecting the Weak Signals That Will Make or Break Your Company. In *Harvard Business School Press*. Boston: Harvard Business School Press.

Day, G. S., & Schoemaker, P. J. H. (2019). *See Sooner, Act Faster: How Vigilant Leaders Thrive in an Era of Digital Turbulence*. Cambridge, MA: The MIT Press.

de Geus, A. P. (1988). Planning as Learning. *Harvard Business Review*, *66*(March-April),70–74.

Desyllas, P., & Hughes, A. (2010). Do high technology acquirers become more innovative? *Research Policy*, *39*(8), 1105–1121. https://doi.org/10.1016/j.respol.2010.05.005.

Deszca, G., Munro, H., & Noori, H. (1999). Developing breakthrough products : challenges and options for market assessment. *Journal of Operations Management*, *17*, 613–630.

Dierickx, I., & Cool, K. (1989). Asset Stock Accumulation and Sustainability of Competitive Advantage. *Management Science*, *35*(12), 1504–1511.

Dobbs, R., Manyika, J., & Woetzel, J. (2015). *No Ordinary Disruption*. New York: Perseus.

Dodgson, M., & Gann, D. M. (2014). Technology and Innovation. In M. Dodgson, D. M. Gann, & N. Phillips (Eds.), *The Oxford Handbook of Innovation Management* (pp. 375–393). https://doi.org/10.1093/oxfordhb/9780199694945.013.033.

Dodgson, M., Gann, D. M., & Salter, A. (2007). "In Case of Fire, Please Use the Elevator": Simulation Technology and Organization in Fire Engineering. *Organization Science*, *18*(5), 849–864. https://doi.org/10.1287/orsc.1070.0287.

Dodgson, M., Gann, D., & Salter, A. (2005). *Think, Play, Do*. Oxford: OUP.

Dougherty, D. (1992). Interpretive Barriers to Successful Product Innovation in Large Firms. *Organization Science*, *3*(2), 179–202.

Downes, L., & Nunes, P. E. (2013). Big Bang Disruption. *Harvard Business Review*, *91*(3), 44–56.

Drover, W., Wood, M. S., & Payne, G. T. (2014). The Effects of Perceived Control on Venture Capitalist Investment Decisions: A Configurational Perspective. *Entrepreneurship: Theory and Practice*, *38*(4), 833–862. https://doi.org/10.1111/etap.12012.

Drucker, P F. (1954). The practice of management. In *Business Horizons*. Retrieved from http:// www.amazon.ca/exec/obidos/redirect?tag=citeulike09-20&path=ASIN/0887306136.

Drucker, Peter F. (1954). *The practice of management*. New York: Harper & Brothers.

Drucker, Peter F. (1985). Innovation and Entrepreneurship. In *Insight in Innovation* (Classic Dr, Vol. 31). Retrieved from http://www.sciencedirect.com/science?_ob=ArticleURL&_udi= B842K-4MSBBY7-3&_user=10&_coverDate=06/25/2007&_alid=1703463697&_rdoc=65&_ fmt=high&_orig=search&_origin=search&_zone=rslt_list_item&_cdi=33929&_sort=r&_st= 4&_docanchor=&view=c&_ct=413&_acct=C000050221&_version=1&_urlVersion=0&_userid= 10&md5=5b1db4147f6de8c5973de646181d0873&searchtype=a.

Duncan, R. B. (1976). The ambidextrous organization: Designing dual structures for innovation. In R. H. Kilman, L. R. Pondy, & D. Slevin (Eds.), *The management of organization design* (pp. 167–188). New York: North Holland.

Dyer, J. H., Furr, N. R., & Lefrandt, C. (2019). *Innovation Capital: How to compete and win like the world's most innovative leaders*. Cambridge, MA: Harvard Business Review Press.

Dyer, J. H., Gregersen, H. B., & Christensen, C. M. (2009). The Innovator's DNA. *Harvard Business Review, 87*(12), 60–67.

Dyer, J. H., Gregersen, H. B., & Christensen, C. M. (2019). *The Innovator's DNA: Mastering the Five Skills of Disruptive Innovators* (Updated). Cambridge, MA: Harvard Business Review Press.

Dyer, J. H., Kale, P., & Singh, H. (2004). When to Ally & When to Acquire. *Harvard Business Review, 82*(7/8), 108–115.

Economist. (2019). The great experiment. *Economist*.

Eggers, J. P. (2012). All experience is not created equal: learning, adapting, and focusing in product portfolio management. *Strategic Management Journal, 33*(3), 315–335. https://doi.org/ 10.1002/smj.

Eggers, J. P., & Kaplan, S. (2009). Cognition and Renewal: Comparing CEO and Organizational Effects on Incumbent Adaptation to Technical Change. *Organization Science, 20*(2), 461–477. https://doi.org/10.1287/orsc.1080.0401.

Eggers, J. P., & Park, K. F. (2018). Incumbent adaptation to technological change: The past, present, and future of research on heterogeneous incumbent response. *Academy of Management Annals, 12*(1), 357–389.

Eisenhardt, K. M., & Bourgeois, L. J. (1988). Politics of Strategic Decision Making in High-Velocity Environments: Toward a Midrange Theory. *Academy of Management Journal, 31*(4), 737–770.

Eisenhardt, K. M., & Martin, J. A. (2000). Dynamic capabilities: what are they? *Strategic Management Journal, 21*(10–11), 1105–1121. https://doi.org/10.1002/1097-0266(200010/11) 21:10/11<1105::AID-SMJ133>3.0.CO;2-E.

Eisenhardt, K. M., & Sull, D. N. (2001). Strategy as simple rules. *Harvard Business Review, 79*(1), 106–116. https://doi.org/Article.

Ernst, H., & Vitt, J. (2000). The influence of corporate acquisitions on the behavior of key inventors. *R&D Management, 30*, 105–119.

Ferguson, N. (2011). *Civilization* (2nd ed.). London: Penguin.

Financial Times. (2019, March 7). Relx/librarians: silent witness. *Financial Times*. Retrieved from https://www.ft.com/content/19361070-40eb-11e9-9bee-efab61506f44.

Fleming, L. (2001). Recombinant Uncertainty in Technological Search. *Management Science, 47*(1), 117–132.

Foss, N. J., & Lyngsie, J. (2015). Organizational design correlates of entrepreneurship: The roles of decentralization and formalization for opportunity discovery and realization. *Strategic Organization, 13*(1), 32–60. https://doi.org/10.1177/1476127014561944.

Frambach, R. T., Prabhu, J., & Verhallen, T. M. M. (2003). The influence of business strategy on new product activity : The role of market orientation. *International Journal of Research in Marketing, 20*(4), 377–397. https://doi.org/10.1016/j.ijresmar.2003.03.003.

Franke, N. (2014). User-Driven Innovation. In M. Dodgson, D. M. Gann, & N. Phillips (Eds.), *The Oxford Handbook of Innovation Management* (pp. 83–101). https://doi.org/10.1093/oxfordhb/9780199694945.013.036.

Franke, N., & Piller, F. (2004). Value Creation by Toolkits for User Innovation and Design: The Case of the Watch Market. *Journal of Product Innovation Management, 21*(6), 401–415.

Freedman, L. (2013). *Strategy: A History*. Oxford: OUP.

Frey, C. B., & Osborne, M. A. (2013). *The Future of Employment: How Susceptible Are Jobs to Computerisation?* Oxford.

Frow, P., & Payne, A. (2008). The value proposition concept: evolution, development and application in marketing. *Proceedings of the Academy of Marketing Conference, Aberdeen.*, Aberdeen.

Fuld, L. (2003). Be Prepared. *Harvard Business Review, 81*(11), 20–21.

Füller, J. (2010). Refining Virtual Co-Creation from a Consumer Perspective. *California Management Review, 52*(2), 98–122. https://doi.org/10.1525/cmr.2010.52.2.98.

Füller, J., Bartl, M., Ernst, H., & Mühlbacher, H. (2006). Community based innovation: How to integrate members of virtual communities into new product development. *Electronic Commerce Research, 6*(1), 57–73. https://doi.org/10.1007/s10660-006-5988-7.

Furr, N. R., & Dyer, J. H. (2014). *The Innovator's Method*. Boston, MA: Harvard Business School Press.

Gans, J. S. (2016a). Keep Calm and Manage Disruption. *MIT Sloan Management Review, 57*(3), 83–90.

Gans, J. S. (2016b). *The Disruption Dilemma*. Cambridge, MA: The MIT Press.

Gans, J. S. (2016c). The Other Disruption. *Harvard Business Review, 94*(3), 78–94.

Gardiner, P., & Rothwell, R. (1985). Tough customers: good designs. *Design Studies, 6*(1), 7–17. https://doi.org/10.1016/0142-694X(85)90036-5.

Garud, R., & Kumaraswamy, A. (1993). Changing Competitive Dynamics in Network Industries: An Exploration of Sun Microsystems' Open Systems Strategy. *Strategic Management Journal, 14*(5), 351–369.

Garud, R., & Munir, K. (2008). From transaction to transformation costs: The case of Polaroid's SX-70 camera. *Research Policy, 37*(4), 690–705. https://doi.org/10.1016/j.respol.2007.12.010.

Gawer, A., & Cusumano, M. A. (2014). Industry platforms and ecosystem innovation. *Journal of Product Innovation Management, 31*(3), 417–433. https://doi.org/10.1111/jpim.12105

Gibson, C. B., & Birkinshaw, J. (2004). The Antecedents, Consequences, and Mediating Role of Organizational Ambidexterity. *Academy of Management Journal, 47*(2), 209–226.

Gimeno, J., & Woo, C. Y. (1996). Hypercompetition in a Multimarket Environment: The Role of Strategic Similarity and Multimarket Contact in Competitive De-Escalation. *Organization Science, 7*(3), 322–341.

Goffin, K., Lemke, F., & Koners, U. (2010). *Identifying Hidden Needs*. London: Palgrave Macmillan.

Gopalakrishnan, S., & Damanpour, F. (1997). A review of innovation research in economics, sociology and technology management. *Omega, 25*(1), 15–28. https://doi.org/10.1016/S0305-0483(96)00043-6.

Govindarajan, V., & Trimble, C. (2012). *Reverse Innovation*. Boston, MA: Harvard Business School Press.

Graebner, M. E., & Eisenhardt, K. M. (2004). The Seller's Side of the Story: Acquisition as Courtship and Governance as Syndicate in Entrepreneurial Firms. *Administrative Science Quarterly, 49*(3), 366–403.

Gratton, L., & Ghoshal, S. (2005). Beyond Best Practice. *Sloan Management Review, 46*(3), 49–57.

Grichnik, D., Smeja, A., & Welpe, I. (2010). The importance of being emotional : How do emotions affect entrepreneurial opportunity evaluation and exploitation? *Journal of Economic Behavior and Organization, 76*(1), 15–29. https://doi.org/10.1016/j.jebo.2010.02.010.

Grönroos, C. (2008). Service logic revisited: who creates value? And who co-creates? *European Business Review, 20*(4), 298–314.

Gruber, M., de Leon, N., George, G., & Thompson, P. (2015). Managing by Design. *Academy of Management Journal, 58*(1), 1–7.

Gruber, M., Harhoff, D., & Hoisl, K. (2013). Boundaries : Scientists vs. Engineers Knowledge Recombination Across Technological Boundaries : Scientists vs. Engineers. *Management Science, 59*(4), 837–851.

Gulati, R. (1998). Alliances and Networks. *Strategic Management Journal, 19*(4), 293–317.

Haas, M. R., & Ham, W. (2015). Microfoundations of Knowledge Recombination: Peripheral Knowledge and Breakthrough Innovation in Teams. In G. Gavetti & W. Ocasio (Eds.), *Advances in Strategic Management: Cognition and Strategy, Vol. 32* (pp. 47–87). Retrieved from http://emeraldinsight.com/doi/pdfplus/10.1108/S0742-332220150000032002.

Habgood, A., & Engstrom, E. (2014). *Reed Elsevier Results for the Year to December 2013*. Retrieved from http://www.reedelsevier.com/mediacentre/pressreleases/2014/Documents/reed-elsevier-results-2013-announcement.pdf.

Haeckel, S. H. (2004). Peripheral Vision: Sensing and Acting on Weak Signals. *Long Range Planning, 37*(2), 181–189. https://doi.org/10.1016/j.lrp.2004.01.006.

Haeckel, S. H. (2008). Adaptiveness: Finding Meaning in Apparent Noise. In *Adaptive Enterprise: Creating and Leading Sense and Respond Organizations*. Boston, MA: Harvard Business School Press.

Hagedoorn, J. (2002). Inter-firm R & D partnerships : an overview of major trends and patterns since 1960. *Research Policy, 31*(4), 477–492.

Hansen, M. T. (1999). The Search-Transfer Problem : The Role of Weak Ties in Sharing Knowledge across Subunits Organization. *Administrative Science Quarterly, 44*(1), 82–111.

Hansen, M. T. (2009). *Collaboration*. Cambridge, MA: Harvard Business Review Press.

Hargadon, A. B. (2002). Brokering Knowledge: Linking learning and Innovation. *Research in Organizational Behavior, 24*, 41–85. https://doi.org/10.1016/S0191-3085(02)24003-4.

Hargadon, A. B. (2003). *How Breakthroughs Happen*. Boston, MA: Harvard Business School Press.

Hargadon, A. B., & Sutton, R. (1997). Technology Brokering and Innovation in a Product Development Firm. *Administrative Science Quarterly, 42*(4), 716–749.

Harreld, J. B., O'Reilly, C. A., & Tushman, M. L. (2007). Capabilities at IBM. *California Management Review, 49*, 21–44. Retrieved from http://findpdfbooks.org/ebook/ http://www.exed.hbs.edu/assets/Documents/dynamic-capabilities.pdf.

Haynie, J. M., Shepherd, D. A., & McMullen, J. S. (2009). An Opportunity for Me? The Role of Resources in Opportunity Evaluation Decisions. *Journal of Management Studies, 46*(3), 337–361.

Heising, W. (2012). The integration of ideation and project portfolio management – A key factor for sustainable success. *International Journal of Project Management, 30*(5), 582–595. https://doi.org/10.1016/j.ijproman.2012.01.014.

Helfat, C. E., & Raubitschek, R. S. (2000). Product Sequencing: Co-evolution of Knowledge, Capabilities and Products. *Strategic Management Journal, 21*, 961–979.

Henderson, R. M., & Clark, K. B. (1990). Architectural Innovation: The Reconfiguration of Existing Product Technologies and the Failure of Established Firms. *Administrative Science Quarterly, 35*(1), 9–30. https://doi.org/Article.

Higgins, M. J., & Rodriguez, D. (2006). The outsourcing of R & D through acquisitions in the pharmaceutical industry. *Journal of Financial Economics, 80*(2), 351–383. https://doi.org/10.1016/j.jfineco.2005.04.004.

Hill, S. A., & Birkinshaw, J. (2008). Strategy–organization configurations in corporate venture units: Impact on performance and survival. *Journal of Business Venturing*, *23*(4), 423–444. https://doi.org/10.1016/j.jbusvent.2007.04.001.

Hill, S. A., & Birkinshaw, J. (2012). *Ambidexterity and survival in corporate venture units*. *40*(7), 1899–1931. https://doi.org/10.1177/0149206312445925.

Hitt, M. A., Hoskisson, R. E., & Harrison, J. S. (1991). Effects of Acquisitions on R&D Inputs and Outputs. *Academy of Management Journal*, *34*(3), 693–707.

Hitt, M. A., Hoskisson, R. E., Johnson, R. A., & Moesel, D. D. (1996). The Market for Corporate Control and Firm Innovation. *Academy of Management Journal*, *39*(5), 1084–1119.

Huchzermeier, A., & Loch, C. H. (2001). Project Management Under Risk: Using the Real Options Approach to Evaluate Flexibility in R&D. *Management Science*, *47*(1), 85–101.

Ihrig, M., & Macmillan, I. C. (2017). How To Get Ecosystem Buy-in: A Toolkit of assessing the way an innovation will affect each stakeholder. *Harvard Business Review*, *95*(2), 102–108.

Ilinitch, A. Y., D'Aveni, R. A., & Lewin, A. Y. (1996). New Organizational Forms and Strategies for Managing in Hypercompetitive Environments. *Organization Science*, *7*(3), 211–221.

Ireland, R. D., Hitt, M. A., & Sirmon, D. G. (2003). A Model of Strategic Entrepreneurship: The Construct and its Dimensions. *Journal of Management*, *29*(6), 963–989. https://doi.org/10.1016/S0149-2063(03)00086-2.

Israel, P. (1998). *Edison*. New York: Wiley.

Iyer, D. N., & Miller, K. D. (2008). Performance Feedback, Slack, and the Timing of Acquisitions. *Academy of Management Journal*, *51*(4), 808–822.

Jacobides, M. G. (2018). Towards a theory of ecosystems. *Strategic Management Journal*, *39*(8), 2255–2276. https://doi.org/10.1002/smj.2904.

Jaruzelski, B., Chwalik, R., & Goehle, B. (2018). What the Top Innovators Get Right. *Strategy+*, (93).

Jaruzelski, B., Staack, V., & Goehle, B. (2014). *The Global Innovation 1000: Proven Paths to Innovation Success*. Retrieved from http://www.strategyand.pwc.com/media/file/Proven-Paths-to-Innovation-Success.pdf.

Jaworski, B. J., & Kohli, A. K. (1993). Market Orientation: Antecedents and Consequences. *Journal of Marketing*, *57*(3), 53–70.

Jeppesen, L. B., & Lakhani, K. R. (2010). Marginality and Problem-Solving Effectiveness in Broadcast Search. *Organization Science*, *21*(5), 1016–1033. https://doi.org/10.1287/orsc.1090.0491.

Johnson, G. (1988). Rethinking incrementalism. *Strategic Management Journal*, *9*(1), 75–91.

Johnson, R., Watkinson, A., & Mabe, M. (2018). The STM Report: An overview of scientific and scholarly publishing, 5th Edition. In *The STM Report*. https://doi.org/10.1017/CBO9781107415324.004.

Kalbach, J. (2020). *The Jobs to be Done Playbook*. New York: Two Waves.

Kane, G. C., Palmer, D., Phillips, A. N., Kiron, D., & Buckley, N. (2018). Coming of Age Digitally. In *MIT Sloan Management Review and Deloitte Insights*.

Kane, G. C., Palmer, D., Phillips, A. N., Kiron, D., & Buckley, N. (2019). *Accelerating Digital Innovation Inside and Out: Agile Teams, Ecosystems, and Ethics*. Cambridge MA.

Kaplan, R. S., & Norton, D. P. (2001). Transforming the Balanced Scorecard from Performance Measurement to Strategic Management: Part I. *Accounting Horizons*, *15*(1), 87–104. https://doi.org/10.2308/acch.2001.15.1.87.

Kaplan, R. S., Norton, D. P., & Sher, G. (2005). The office of strategy management. *Harvard Business Review*, *83*(10), 72–80.

Kaplan, S. (2008). Cognition, Capabilities, and Incentives: Assessing Firm Response to the Fiber-Optic Revolution Author(s): *Academy of Management Journal*, *51*(4), 672–695.

Kaplan, S., & Henderson, R. M. (2005). Inertia and Incentives : Bridging Organizational and Organizational Theory Economics. *Organization Science*, *16*(5), 509–521.

Kaplan, S., & Orlikowski, W. J. (2013). Temporal Work in Strategy Making. *Organization Science*, *24*(4), 965–995.

Kapoor, R., & Adner, R. (2011). What Firms Make vs. What They Know : How Firms' Production and Knowledge Boundaries Affect Competitive Advantage in the Face of Technological Change. *Organization Science*, 1–22. https://doi.org/10.1287/orsc.1110.0686.

Kapoor, R., & Lim, K. (2007). The impact of acquisitions on the productivity of inventors at semiconductor firms: A synthesis of knowledge-based and incentive-based perspectives. *Academy of Management Journal*, *50*(5), 1133–1155.

Kaul, A. (2012). Technology and Corporate Scope: Firm and Rival Innovation as Antecedents of Corporate Transactions. *Strategic Management Journal*, *33*(4), 347–367. https://doi.org/10.1002/smj.

Kelley, T. (2001). *The Art of Innovation*. London: Harper Collins.

Kelley, T. (2006). *The Ten Faces of Innovation* (2nd ed.). London: Profile Books.

Killen, C. P., & Hunt, R. A. (2013). Robust project portfolio management: capability evolution and maturity. *International Journal of Managing Projects in Business*, *6*(1), 131–151.

Killing, P., Malnight, T., & Keys, T. (2005). *Must Win Battles*. Harlow: Pearson.

Kim, W. C., & Mauborgne, R. (1999). Strategy, value innovation, and the knowledge economy. *Sloan Management Review*, *40*(3), 41–54.

Kim, W. C., & Mauborgne, R. (2005). *Blue Ocean Strategy*. Boston, MA: Harvard Business School Press.

King, D. R., Slotegraaf, R. J., & Kesner, I. (2008). Performance Implications of Firm Resource Interactions in the Acquisition of R&D-Intensive Firms. *Organization Science*, *19*(2), 327–340.

King, A. A., & Baatartogtokh, B. (2015). How Useful Is the Theory of Disruptive Innovation? *Sloan Management Review, 57*(1), 77–90. Retrieved from http://sloanreview.mit.edu/article/how-useful-is-the-theory-of-disruptive-innovation/.

Kirzner, I. M. (2009). The alert and creative entrepreneur : a clarification. *Small Business Economics*, *32*(2), 145–152. https://doi.org/10.1007/s11187-008-9153-7.

Klein, P. G., & Foss, N. J. (2010). Entrepreneurial Alertness and Opportunity Discovery: Origins, Attributes, Critique. In H. Landström & F. Lohrke (Eds.), *The Historical Foundations of Entrepreneurship Research* (pp. 98–120). Aldershot, UK: Edward Elgar.

Klingebiel, R., & Rammer, C. (2014). Resource allocation strategy for innovation portfolio management. *Strategic Management Journal*, *35*, 246–268. https://doi.org/10.1002/smj.

Knight, F. H. (1921). *Risk, Uncertainty, and Profit*. New York: Harper.

Kohli, A. K., & Jaworski, B. J. (1990). Market Orientation : The Construct, Research Propositions, and Managerial Implications. *Journal of Marketing*, *54*(2), 1–18.

Kozinets, R. V. (2002). The Field Behind the Screen : Using Netnography for Marketing Research in Online Communities. *Journal of Marketing Research*, *39*(1), 61–72.

Kozinets, R. V. (2015). *Netnography: Redefined* (2015th ed.). London: Sage.

Kozinets, R. V., Hemetsberger, A., & Schau, H. J. (2008). The Wisdom of Consumer Crowds: Collective Innovation in the Age of Networked Marketing. *Journal of Macromarketing*, *28*(4), 339–354. https://doi.org/10.1177/0276146708325382.

Kumaraswamy, A., Garud, R., & Ansari, S. (Shaz). (2018). Perspectives on Disruptive Innovations. *Journal of Management Studies*, *55*(7), 1025–1042. https://doi.org/10.1111/joms.12399.

Kupiainen, E., Mäntylä, M. V, & Itkonen, J. (2015). Using metrics in Agile and Lean Software Development – A systematic literature review of industrial studies. *Information and Software Technology*, *62*, 143–163. https://doi.org/10.1016/j.infsof.2015.02.005.

Laamanen, T., & Wallin, J. (2009). Cognitive Dynamics of Capability Development Paths. *Journal of Management Studies*, *46*(6), 950–981. https://doi.org/10.1111/j.1467-6486.2009.00823.x.

Lafley, A. G., & Martin, R. L. (2013). *Playing To Win*. Boston: Harvard Business School Press.

Laursen, K., & Salter, A. (2006). Open for innovation: The role of openness in explaining innovation performance among U.K. manufacturing firms. *Strategic Management Journal*, *27*(2), 131–150. https://doi.org/10.1002/smj.507.

Leifer, R., O'Connor, G. C., & Rice, M. (2001). Implementing radical innovation in mature firms: The role of hubs. *Academy of Management Executive*, *15*(3), 102–113. https://doi.org/10.5465/AME.2001.5229646.

Leiponen, A., & Helfat, C. E. (2010). Innovation Objectives, Knowledge Sources, and the Benefits of Breadth. *Strategic Management Journal*, *31*(2010), 224–236. https://doi.org/10.1002/smj.

Leiponen, A., & Helfat, C. E. (2011). Location, Decentralization, and Knowledge. *Organization Science*, *22*(3), 641–658. https://doi.org/10.1287/orsc.1100.0526.

Leonard-Barton, D. (1992). Core capabilities and core rigidities: A paradox in managing new product development. *Strategic Management Journal*, Vol. 13, pp. 111–125. https://doi.org/10.1016/0024-6301(93)90313-5.

Leonard, D. A., & Barton, M. (2014). Knowledge and the Management of Creativity and Innovation. In M. Dodgson, D. M. Gann, & N. Phillips (Eds.), *The Oxford Handbook of Innovation Management* (pp. 121–138). https://doi.org/10.1093/oxfordhb/9780199694945.013.005.

Leonardi, P. M. (2011). New Technology Concepts Innovation Blindness : Culture, Frames, and Cross-Boundary Problem Construction in the Development of New Technology Concepts. *Organization Science*, *22*(2), 347–369. https://doi.org/10.1287/orsc.1100.0529.

Lepore, J. (2014, June 23). The Disruption Machine. *The New Yorker*. Retrieved from http://www.newyorker.com/magazine/2014/06/23/the-disruption-machine

Levinthal, D. A., & March, J. G. (1993). The myopia of learning. *Strategic Management Journal*, *14*(2), 95–112.

Levitt, T. (1975). Marketing Myopia. *Harvard Business Review*, *53*(5), 26–181.

Levitt, T. (1980). Marketing success through differentiation - of anything. *Harvard Business Review*, *58*(1), 83–91.

Li, H., & Atuahene-Gima, K. (2001). Product Innovation Strategy and the Performance of New Technology Ventures in China. *Academy of Management Journal*, *44*(6), 1123–1134.

Li, Q., Maggitti, P. G., Smith, K. G., Tesluk, P. E., & Katila, R. (2013). Top management attention to innovation: The role of search selection and intensity in new product introductions. *Academy of Management Journal*, *56*(3), 893–916.

Lilien, G. L. (2016). The B2B Knowledge Gap. *International Journal of Research in Marketing*, *33*(3), 543–556. https://doi.org/10.1016/j.ijresmar.2016.01.003.

Lilien, G. L., Morrison, P. D., Searls, K., Sonnack, M., & von Hippel, E. (2002). Performance Assessment User of the Lead Process New for Product Development. *Management Science*, *48*(8), 1042–1059.

Lindgreen, A., Hingley, M. K., Grant, D. B., & Morgan, R. E. (2012). Value in business and industrial marketing : Past, present, and future. *Industrial Marketing Management*, *41*(1), 207–214. https://doi.org/10.1016/j.indmarman.2011.11.025.

Lumpkin, G. T., & Dess, G. (1996). Clarifying the Entrepreneurial Orientation Construct and Linking It to Performance. *Academy of Management Review*, *21*(1), 135–172.

Lusch, R. F., & Vargo, S. L. (2011). Advancing Service Dominant Logic. *European Journal of Marketing*, *45*, 1298–1309.

Lüthje, C., & Herstatt, C. (2004). The Lead User method : an outline of empirical findings and issues for future research. *R&D Management*, *34*(5), 553–568.

Macdonald, E. K., Wilson, H. N., Martinez, V., & Toossi, A. (2011). Assessing value-in-use: A conceptual framework and exploratory study. *Industrial Marketing Management*, *40*, 671–682.

MacMillan, I. C. (1988). Controlling Competitive Dynamics by Taking Strategic Initiative. *Academy of Management Executive, 2*(2), 111–118.

Maggitti, P. G., Smith, K. G., & Katila, R. (2013). The complex search process of invention. *Research Policy, 42*(1), 90–100. https://doi.org/10.1016/j.respol.2012.04.020.

March, J. G. (1991). Exploration and Exploitation in Organizational Learning. *Organization Science, 2*(1), 71–87.

Markides, C. C., & Geroski, P. A. (2004). Racing to be Second. *Business Strategy Review, 15*, 25–31. Retrieved from http://doi.wiley.com/10.1111/j.0955-6419.2004.00336.x%5Cnpapers2://publication/doi/10.1111/j.0955-6419.2004.00336.x.

Markides, C. C., & Geroski, P. A. (2005). *Fast Second*. San Francisco: Jossey-Bass.

Markides, C. C., & Oyon, D. (2010). What to Do Against Disruptive Business Models (When and How to Play Two Games at Once). *MIT Sloan Management Review, 51*(4), 27–32. Retrieved from http://scholar.google.com/scholar?hl=en&btnG=Search&q=intitle:What+to+Do+Against+Disruptive+Business+Models+(+When+and+How+to+Play+Two+Games+at+Once+)#0.

McGrath, R. G. (1997). A Real Options Logic for Initiating Technology Positioning Investments. *Academy of Management Review, 22*(4), 974–996.

McGrath, R. G. (2011). Failing By Design. *Harvard Business Review, 89*(4), 76–84.

McGrath, R. G. (2013a). *The End of Competitive Advantage*. Boston, MA: Harvard Business School Press.

McGrath, R. G. (2013b). Transient Advantage. *Harvard Business Review, 91*(6), 62–70.

McGrath, R. G., & Kim, J. (2014). Innovation, Strategy, and Hypercompetition. In M. Dodgson, D. M. Gann, & N. Phillips (Eds.), *The Oxford Handbook of Innovation Management*. https://doi.org/10.1093/oxfordhb/9780199694945.013.010.

McGrath, R. G., & MacMillan, I. C. (2009). How to Rethink Your Business During Uncertainty. *Sloan Management Review, 50*(3), 25–30.

McGrath, R. G., & Nerkar, A. (2004). Real options reasoning and a new look at the R&D investment strategies of pharmaceutical firms. *Strategic Management Journal, 25*(1), 1–21. https://doi.org/10.1002/smj.358.

McKelvie, A., Haynie, J. M., & Gustavsson, V. (2011). Unpacking the uncertainty construct: Implications for entrepreneurial action. *Journal of Business Venturing, 26*(3), 273–292. https://doi.org/10.1016/j.jbusvent.2009.10.004.

Menon, T., & Pfeffer, J. (2003). Valuing Internal vs. External Knowledge : Explaining the Preference for Outsiders. *Management Science, 49*(4), 497–513.

Miller, D. J. (2004). Firms' technological resources and the performance effects of diversification: a longitudinal study. *Strategic Management Journal, 25*(11), 1097–1119.

Mintzberg, H. (1987). Crafting Strategy. *Harvard Business Review, 65*(4), p66–75.

Mintzberg, H. (1990). The design school: reconsidering the basic premises of strategic management. *Strategic Management Journal, 11*(3), 171–195.

Monteiro, F., & Birkinshaw, J. (2016). The external knowledge sourcing process in multinational corporations. *Strategic Management Journal, 51*(2), 315–334. https://doi.org/10.1002/smj.

Moore, G. A. (1998). *Crossing the Chasm: Marketing and Selling High-Tech Products to Mainstream Customers* (2nd ed.). Chichester: Capstone.

Mudambi, R., & Swift, T. (2014). Knowing when to leap: Transitioning between exploitative and explorative R&D. *Strategic Management Journal, 35*(1), 126–145. https://doi.org/10.1002/smj.

Murmann, J. P., & Tushman, M. L. (1998). *Dominant Designs, Technology Cycles, and Organizational Outcomes*.

Nagji, B., & Tuff, G. (2012). Managing Your Innovation Portfolio. *Harvard Business Review, 90*(5), 66–74.

Nickerson, J. A., & Zenger, T. R. (2004). A Knowledge-Based Theory of the Firm: The Problem-Solving Perspective. *Organization Science*, *15*(6), 617–632. https://doi.org/10.1287/orsc.0.

Nieto, M. (2003). From R & D management to knowledge management. An overview of studies of innovation management. *Technological Forecasting and Social Change*, *70*(2), 135–161.

Nonaka, I., & Takeuchi, H. (1995). The Knowledge Creating Company: \nHow Japanese Companies Create the Dynamics of Innovation. In *How Japanese companies create the dynamics of innovation* (Vol. 69). Retrieved from http://books.google.com/books?id=B-qxrPaU1-MC.

O'Reilly, C., & Tushman, M. L. (1997). *Winning through Innovation*. Boston, MA: Harvard Business School Press.

Ocasio, W. (1997). Toward an Attention-Based View of The Firm. *Strategic Management Journal*, *18*, 187–206.

Ocasio, W. (2011). Attention to attention. *Organization Science*, *22*(5), 1286–1296.

Ocasio, W., Laamanen, T., & Vaara, E. (2018). Communication and attention dynamics: An attention-based view of strategic change. *Strategic Management Journal*, *39*(1), 155–167. https://doi.org/10.1002/smj.2702.

Ogawa, S., & Piller, F. T. (2006). Reducing the Risks of New Product Development. *Sloan Management Review*, *47*(2), 65–71.

Ohno, T. (1988). *Toyota Production System: Beyond Large-Scale Production*. New York: Productivity Press.

Oliver, C. (1997). Sustainable competitive advantage: combining institutional and resource-based views. *Strategic Management Journal*, *18*(9), 697–713.

Ortt, J. R. (2010). Understanding the Pre-diffusion Phases. In J. Tidd (Ed.), *Gaining Momentum: Managing the Diffusion of Innovations* (pp. 47–80). London: Imperial College Press.

Osterwalder, A., & Pigneur, Y. (2010). *Business Model Generation*. Hoboken, New Jersey: Wiley.

Osterwalder, A., Pigneur, Y., Bernarda, G., & Smith, A. (2014). *Value Proposition Design*. Hoboken, New Jersey: Wiley.

Osterwalder, A., Pigneur, Y., Etiemble, F., & Smith, A. (2020). *The Invincible Company*. Hoboken, New Jersey: Wiley.

Ottum, B. D., & Moore, W. L. (1997). The Role of Market Information in Newproduct Success/Failure. *Journal of Product Innovation Management*, *14*(4), 258–273.

Owen-Smith, J., & Powell, W. W. (2004). Science Organization Knowledge Networks as Channels and Conduits: The Effects of Spillovers in the Boston Biotechnology Community. *Organization Science*, *15*(1), 5–21. https://doi.org/10.1287/orsc.1030.0054.

Parise, S., Whelan, E., & Todd, S. (2015). How Twitter Users Can Generate Better Ideas. *Sloan Management Review*, *56*(4), 56411.

Payne, A., & Frow, P. (2013). Deconstructing the value proposition of an innovation exemplar. *European Journal of Marketing*, *48*(1), 237–270. https://doi.org/10.1108/EJM-09-2011-0504

Payne, A., & Frow, P. (2014). Developing superior value propositions: a strategic marketing imperative. *Journal of Service Management*, *25*(2), 213–227. https://doi.org/10.1108/JOSM-01-2014-0036.

Phillips, W., Noke, H., & Bessant, J. (2006). Beyond the Steady State: Managing Discontinuous Product and Process Innovation. *International Journal of Innovation Management*, *10*(2), 175–196.

Pisano, G. P. (2015). You Need An Innovation Strategy. *Harvard Business Review*, *93*(6), 44–54.

Podolny, J. M., & Stuart, T. E. (1995). A Role-Based Ecology of Technological Change'. *American Journal of Sociology*, *100*(5), 1224–1260.

Poetz, M. K., & Schreier, M. (2012). The Value of Crowdsourcing: Can Users Really Compete with Professionals in Generating New Product Ideas? *Journal of Product Innovation Management*, *29*(2), 245–256. https://doi.org/10.1111/j.1540-5885.2011.00893.x.

Porter, M. E. (1981). The Contributions of Industrial Organization to Strategic Management. *Academy of Management Review, 6*(4), 609–620.

Porter, M. E. (1985). *On Competition*. Boston, MA: Harvard Business School Press.

Porter, M. E. (1990). *The Competitive Advantage of Nations*. London: Macmillan.

Powell, W. W., Koput, K. W., & Smith-Doerr, L. (1996). Interorganizational and the Collaboration Locus of Innovation : Networks of Learning in Biotechnology. *Administrative Science Quarterly, 41*(1), 116–145.

Powell, W. W., White, D. R., Koput, K. W., & Owen-Smith, J. (2005). Network Dynamics and Field Evolution: The Growth of Interorganizational Collaboration in the Life Sciences. *American Journal of Sociology, 110*(4), 1132–1205.

Prabhu, J. (2014). Marketing and Innovation. In M. Dodgson, D. M. Gann, & N. Phillips (Eds.), *The Oxford Handbook of Innovation Management* (pp. 53–68). https://doi.org/10.1093/oxfordhb/9780199694945.013.023.

Prahalad, C. K. (2004a). The Blinders of Dominant Logic. *Long Range Planning, 37*(2), 171–179. https://doi.org/10.1016/j.lrp.2004.01.010.

Prahalad, C. K. (2004b). *The Fortune at the Bottom of the Pyramid*. New Jersey: Prentice hall.

Prior, D. D., & Miller, L. M. (2012). Webethnography: towards a typology for quality in research design. *International Journal of Market Research, 54*(4), 503–519. https://doi.org/10.2501/IJMR-54-4-503-520.

Puri, A. (2009). Webnography: its evolution and implications for market research. *International Journal of Market Research, 51*(2), 273–275. https://doi.org/10.2501/S1470785309200487.

Radjou, N., & Prabhu, J. C. (2015). *Frugal Innovation: How to do more with less*. London: Profile Books.

Radjou, N., Prabhu, J. C., & Ahuja, S. (2012). *Jugaad Innovation: Think Frugal, be flexible,Generate Breakthrough Innovation*. San Francisco: Jossey Bass.

Reeves, M., Haanæs, K., & Sinha, J. (2015). *Your Strategy Needs a Strategy: How to Select and Execute the Right Approach to Strategy*. Boston, MA: Harvard Business Review Press.

Reeves, M., Love, C., & Mathur, N. (2012). *The Most Adaptive Companies 2012: Winning in an Age of Turbulence*. Retrieved from https://www.bcgperspectives.com/Images/BCG_Most_Adaptive_Companies_2012_tcm80-112829.pdf

Reid, S. E., & de Brentani, U. (2004). The fuzzy front end of new product development for discontinuous innovations: A theoretical model. *Journal of Product Innovation Management, 21*(3), 170–184. https://doi.org/10.1111/j.0737-6782.2004.00068.x.

Ries, E. (2011). *The Lean Start Up*. London: Penguin.

Ries, E. (2017). *The Startup Way*. New York: Currency.

Rigby, D. K., Sutherland, J., & Noble, A. (2018). Agile At Scale. *Harvard Business Review, 96*(3), 88–96.

Ring, P. S., Doz, Y. L., & Olk, P. M. (2005). Managing Formation Processes in R&D Consortia. *California Management Review, 47*(4), 137–156.

Robins, J., & Wiersema, M. F. (1995). A Resource-based Approach to the Multibusiness Firm: Empirical Analysis of Portfolio Interrelationships and Corporate Financial Performance. *Strategic Management Journal, 16* (April1993), 277–299.

Rogers, E. M. (2003). Diffusion of Innovations, 5th Edition. In *Book*. Retrieved from http://www.amazon.com/Diffusion-Innovations-5th-Everett-Rogers/dp/0743222091.

Rohrbeck, R., & Kum, M. E. (2018). Corporate foresight and its impact on firm performance: A longitudinal analysis. *Technological Forecasting and Social Change, 129*(January), 105–116. https://doi.org/10.1016/j.techfore.2017.12.013.

Rosenkopf, L., & Nerkar, A. (2001). Beyond local search: Boundary-spanning, exploration,and impact in the optical disk industry. *Strategic Management Journal*, *22*, 287–306. https://doi.org/10.1002/SMJ.160.

Ross, J. W. (2019). Digital Success Requires Breaking Rules. Retrieved from MIT Sloan Blogs website: https://sloanreview.mit.edu/article/digital-success-requires-breaking-rules/?utm_source=newsletter&utm_medium=email&utm_content=Read the new article now»&utm_campaign=0730DCS.

Ross, J. W., Beath, C. M., & Mocker, M. (2019). Creating Digital Offerings Customers Will Buy. *Sloan Management Review*, *61*(1), 64–69.

Rothaermel, F. T., & Alexandre, M. T. (2009). Ambidexterity in Technology Sourcing : The Moderating Role of Absorptive Capacity. *Organization Science*, *20*(4), 759–780.

Rothwell, R. (1977). The characteristics of successful innovators and technically progressive firms (with some comments on innovation. *R&D Management*, *7*(3), 191–206.

Rothwell, R. (1992). Successful industrial innovation : critical factors for the 1990s. *R&D Management*, *22*(3), 221–239.

Rowlands, I., Nicholas, D., Russell, B., Canty, N., & Watkinson, A. (2011). Social media use in the research workflow. *Learned Publishing*, *24*(3), 183–195. https://doi.org/10.1087/20110306.

Rumelt, R. P. (2011). *Good Strategy/Bad Strategy*. London: Profile Books.

Schilling, M. A., & Steensma, H. K. (2002). Disentangling the Theories of Firm Boundaries: A Path Model and Empirical Test. *Organization Science*, *13*(4), 387–401.

Schmidt, E., & Cohen, J. (2013). *The New Digital Age*. London: John Murray.

Schoemaker, P. J. H. (2011). *Brilliant Mistakes: Finding Success on the Far Side of Failure*. Philadelphia: Wharton Digital Press.

Schoemaker, P. J. H., & Day, G. S. (2009). How to Make Sense of Weak Signals. *MIT Sloan Management Review*, *50*(3), 81–89.

Schoemaker, P. J. H., Day, G. S., & Snyder, S. A. (2013). Integrating organizational networks, weak signals, strategic radars and scenario planning. *Technological Forecasting and Social Change*, *80*(4), 815–824. https://doi.org/10.1016/j.techfore.2012.10.020.

Schoemaker, P. J. H., Heaton, S., & Teece, D. J. (2018). Innovation, Dynamic Capabilities, and Leadership. *California Management Review*, *61*(1), 15–42. https://doi.org/10.1177/0008125618790246.

Schoemaker, P. J. H., & Krupp, S. (2015). The Power of Asking Pivotal Questions. *Sloan Management Review*, *56*(2), 39–47. Retrieved from http://mitsmr.com/1wGfFEB.

Schumpeter, J. A. (1942a). *Can Capitalism Survive* (2009th ed.). New York: Harper Collins.

Schumpeter, J. A. (1942b). *Capitalism, Socialism, and Democracy*. New York: Harper & Row.

Schwab, K. (2017). *The Fourth Industrial Revolution*. New York: Crown Business.

Serrador, P., & Pinto, J. K. (2015). Does Agile work? – A quantitative analysis of agile project success. *International Journal of Project*, *33*(5), 1040–1051. https://doi.org/10.1016/j.ijproman.2015.01.006.

Shane, S. A., & Venkataram, S. (2000). The Promise of Entrepreneurship as a Field of Research. *Academy of Management Review*, *25*(1), 217–226.

Shenhar, A. J. (2001). One Size Does Not Fit All Projects : Exploring Classical Contingency Domains. *Management Science*, *47*(3), 394–414.

Shepherd, D. A., & Gruber, M. (2020). The Lean Startup Framework: Closing the Academic–Practitioner Divide. *Entrepreneurship: Theory and Practice*, 1–31. https://doi.org/10.1177/1042258719899415.

Shepherd, D. A., Patzelt, H., & Baron, R. A. (2013). "I care about nature, but . . . .": Disengaging values in assessing opportunities that cause harm. *Academy of Management Journal*, *56*(5), 1251–1273.

Sia, S. K., Soh, C., & Weill, P. (2016). How DBS bank pursued a digital business strategy. *MIS Quarterly Executive*, *15*(2), 105–121.

Simon, H. (1947). *Administrative Behavior: A Studyof Decision-making Processes in Administrative Organizations*. Chicago IL: Macmillan.

Singh, J., & Fleming, L. (2010). Lone Inventors as Sources of Breakthroughs: Myth or Reality? *Management Science*, *56*(1), 41–56. https://doi.org/10.1287/mnsc.1090.1072.

Sommer, A. F., Hedegaard, C., Dukovska-Popovska, I., & Steger-Jensen, K. (2015). Improved Product Development Performance through Agile/Stage-Gate Hybrids. *Research Technology Management*, *58*(1), 34–45. https://doi.org/10.5437/08956308X5801236

Sood, A., & Tellis, G. J. (2011). Demystifying Disruption: A New Model for Understanding and Predicting Disruptive Technologies. *Marketing Science*, *30*(2), 339–354. https://doi.org/10.1287/mksc.1100.0617.

Statista. (2018). Retrieved November 7, 2019, from file:///C:/Users/wer202/Downloads/study_id10490_smartphones-statista-dossier(1).pdf.

Strategyzer. (2019). Business Model Environment. Retrieved October 19, 2019, from https://www.strategyzer.com/blog/posts/2015/10/14/how-to-scan-through-your-environments-disruptive-threats-and-opportunities.

Stuart, T. E., & Podolny, J. M. (1996). Local Search and the Evolution of Technological Capabilities. *Strategic Management Journal*, *17*, 21–38.

Sull, D. N. (2003). Managing By Commitments. *Harvard Business Review*, *81*(6), 82–91.

Sull, D. N. (2004). Disciplined Entrepreneurship. *Sloan Management Review*, *46*(1), 71–77.

Sull, D. N. (2009). *The Upside of Turbulence*. New York: HarperCollins.

Sull, D. N., & Eisenhardt, K. M. (2012). Simple Rules for a Complex World. *Harvard Business Review*, *90*(9), 69–74.

Sull, D. N., & Eisenhardt, K. M. (2015). *Simple Rules: How to Thrive in a Complex World*. John Murray.

Swift, T. (2016). The perilous leap between exploration and exploitation. *Strategic Management Journal*, *37*(8), 1688–1698. https://doi.org/10.1002/smj.

Taylor, F. W. (1911). *The Principles of Scientific Management*. New York: Norton.

Teece, D. J., & Pisano, G. P. (1994). The Dynamic Capabilities of Firms: an Introduction. *Industrial and Corporate Change*, *3*(3), 537–556.

Teece, D. J., Pisano, G. P., & Shuen, A. (1997). Dynamic capabilities and strategic management. *Strategic Management Journal*, *18*, 509–533. https://doi.org/10.1002/(SICI)1097-0266 (199708)18:7<509::AID-SMJ882>3.0.CO;2-Z.

Tellis, G. J. (2013). *Unrelenting Innovation*. San Francisco: Jossey-Bass.

Thomke, S. H. (1998). Managing Experimentation in the Design of New Products Managing. *Management Science*, *44*(6), 743–762.

Thomke, S. H., & Fujimoto, T. (2000). The Effect of "Front-Loading" Problem-Solving on Product Development Performance. *Journal of Product Innovation Management*, *17*(2), 128–142.

Thomke, S. H., & Manzi, J. (2014). The Discipline of Business Experimentation. *Harvard Business Review*, *92*(12), 70–79.

Thomke, S. H., & Reinertsen, D. G. (2012). Six Myths Of Product Development. *Harvard Business Review*, *90*(5), 84–94.

Tidd, J. (2010). From Models to the Management of Diffusion. In J. Tidd (Ed.), *Gaining Momentum: Managing the Diffusion of Innovations* (pp. 3–45). London: Imperial College Press.

Tidd, J., & Bessant, J. (2018). *Managing Innovation: Integrating Technological, Market and Organizational Change* (6th ed.). Hoboken: John Wiley & Sons.

Tripsas, M., & Gavetti, G. (2000). Capabilities, Cognition, and Inertia: Evidence from Digital Imaging. *Strategic Management Journal*, *21*(10), 1147–1161.

Tuff, G., & Goldbach, S. (2018). *Detonate*. Hoboken, New Jersey: Wiley.

Turner, N., Swart, J., & Maylor, H. (2012). Mechanisms for Managing Ambidexterity: A Review and Research Agenda. *International Journal of Management Reviews*, *15*, no-no. https://doi.org/10.1111/j.1468-2370.2012.00343.x.

Turner, S. F., Mitchell, W., & Bettis, R. A. (2012). Strategic Momentum: How Experience Shapes Temporal Consistency of Ongoing Innovation. *Journal of Management*, *39*(7), 1855–1890. https://doi.org/10.1177/0149206312458704.

Tushman, M. L., & Anderson, P. (1986). Technological Discontinuities and Organizational Environments. *Administrative Science Quarterly*, *31*(3), 439–465.

Tushman, M. L., & O'Reilly, C. A. (1996). Ambidextrous Organizations: *California Management Review*, *38*(4), 8–30.

Tushman, M. L., Smith, W. K., Wood, R. C., Westerman, G., & O'Reilly, C. A. (2010). Organizational designs and innovation streams. *Industrial and Corporate Change*, *19*(5), 1331–1366. https://doi.org/10.1093/icc/dtq040.

Ulwick, A. W. (2002). Turn Customer Input Into Innovation. *Harvard Business Review*, *80*(1), 91–97. Retrieved from http://www.ncbi.nlm.nih.gov/pubmed/12964470.

Ulwick, A. W. (2005). *What Customers Want: Using Outcome-Driven Innovation to Create Breakthrough Products and Services*. New York: McGraw Hill.

UNESCO. (2015). *UNESCO Science Report: towards 2030*. Retrieved from http://uis.unesco.org/sites/default/files/documents/unesco-science-report-towards-2030-part1.pdf.

UNESCO. (2019). UNESCO Institute for Statistics. Retrieved December 19, 2019, from http://uis.unesco.org/apps/visualisations/research-and-development-spending/.

United Nations. (2019). World Population Prospects 2019: Highlights. Retrieved November 7, 2019, from World Population Prospects 2019: Highlights website: https://population.un.org/wpp/Publications/Files/WPP2019_10KeyFindings.pdf.

Urban, G. L., & von Hippel, E. (1988). Lead User Analyses for the Development of New Industrial Products. *Management Science*, *34*(5), 569–582.

Urhahn, C., & Spieth, P. (2014). Governing the Portfolio Management Process for Product Innovation – A Quantitative Analysis on the Relationship Between Portfolio Management Governance, Portfolio Innovativeness, and Firm Performance. *IEEE Transactions on Engineering Management*, *61*(3), 522–533.

Utterback, J. M. (1994). *Mastering the Dynamics of Innovation*. Boston, MA: Harvard Business School Press.

Utterback, J. M., & Abernathy, W. J. (1975). A Dynamic Model of Process and Product Innovation. *Omega*, Vol. 3, pp. 639–656.

Van de Ven, A. H., Polley, D. E., Garud, R., & Venkataraman, S. (1999). *The Innovation Journey*. New York: OUP.

Vargo, S. L., & Lusch, R. F. (2004). Evolving to a New Dominant Logic for Marketing. *Journal of Marketing*, *68*(1), 1–17. https://doi.org/10.1509/jmkg.68.1.1.24036.

Vargo, S. L., & Lusch, R. F. (2010). It's all B2B . . . and beyond: Toward a systems perspective of the market. *Industrial Marketing Management*, *40*, 181–187. https://doi.org/10.1016/j.indmarman.2010.06.026.

Verganti, R. (2016). *Overcrowded: designing meaningful products in a world awash with ideas*. Cambridge, MA: The MIT Press.

Verworn, B., Herstatt, C., & Nagahira, A. (2008). The fuzzy front end of Japanese new product development projects: Impact on success and differences between incremental and radical projects. *R and D Management*, *38*(1), 1–19. https://doi.org/10.1111/j.1467-9310.2007.00492.x.

Villalonga, B., & McGahan, A. M. (2005). The choice among acquisitions, alliances, and divestitures. *Strategic Management Journal*, *26*(13), 1183–1208. https://doi.org/10.1002/smj.493.

von Hippel, E. (1986). Lead Users: A Source of Novel Product Concepts. *Management Learning, 32*(7), 791–805.

von Hippel, E. (1988). *The Sources of Innovation*. Cambridge MA: MIT Press.

von Hippel, E. (1998). Economics of Product Development by Users: The Impact of "Sticky" Local Information. *Management Science, 44*(5), 629–644.

von Hippel, E. (2001). User toolkits for innovation. *Journal of Product Innovation Management, 18*, 247–257.

von Hippel, E. (2005). *Democratizing Innovation*. Cambridge MA: MIT Press.

von Hippel, E., & Katz, R. (2002). Shifting Innovation to Users via Toolkits. *Management Science, 48*(7), 821–833.

von Hippel, E., Thomke, S. H., & Sonnack, M. (1999). Creating Breakthroughs at 3M. *Harvard Business Review, 77*(5), 47–57. https://doi.org/10.1038/nbt1001-921.

von Hippel, E., & von Krogh, G. (2003). Open Source Software and the "Private-Collective" Innovation Model: Issues for Organization Science. *Organization Science, 14*(2), 209–224.

von Krogh, G., Netland, T., & Wörter, M. (2018). Winning With Open Process Innovation. *Sloan Management Review, 59*(2), 53–56.

Ware, M., & Mabe, M. (2015). The STM Report. In *The STM Report*. Retrieved from http://www.stm-assoc.org/2009_10_13_MWC_STM_Report.pdf.

Weinstein, O., & Gallouja, F. (1997). Innovation in services. *Innovation in Services, 26*, 537–556.

Whelan, E., Parise, S., Valk, J. De, & Aalbers, R. (2011). Creating Employee Networks That Deliver Open Innovation. *Sloan Management Review, 53*(1), 37–44.

Williams, D. W., & Wood, M. S. (2015). Rule-based reasoning for understanding opportunity evaluation. *Academy of Management Perspectives, 29*(2), 218–236.

Wilson, A., Zeithaml, V. A., Bitner, M. J., & Gremler, D. D. (2012). *Services Marketing* (2nd ed.). Maidenhead: McGraw Hill.

Winter, S. G., & Nelson, R. R. (1982). *An Evolutionary Theory of Economic Change*. Retrieved from http://papers.ssrn.com/sol3/papers.cfm?abstract_id=1496211.

Wissema, H. (2002). Driving through red lights: How warning signals are missed or ignored. *Long Range Planning, 35*, 521–539.

Womack, J. P., Jones, D. T., & Roos, D. (1990). *The Machine That Changed the World* (First). New York: Rawson Associates.

Wood, M. S., & McKelvie, A. (2015). Opportunity Evaluation as Future Focused Cognition: Identifying Conceptual Themes and Empirical Trends. *International Journal of Management Reviews, 17*, 256–277. https://doi.org/10.1111/ijmr.12053.

Wood, M. S., & Williams, D. W. (2014). Opportunity Evaluation as Rule-Based Decision Making. *Journal of Management Studies, 51*(4), 573–602. https://doi.org/10.1111/joms.12018.

Wunker, S., Wattman, J., & Farber, D. (2016). *Jobs to be Done: A roadmap for customer-centered innovation*. New York: AMACOM.

Xie, C., Bagozzi, R. P., & Troye, S. V. (2008). Trying to prosume : toward a theory of consumers as co-creators of value. *Journal of the Academy of Marketing Science, 36*(1), 109–122. https://doi.org/10.1007/s11747-007-0060-2.

Yip, M. H., Phaal, R., & Probert, D. R. (2014). Stakeholder Engagement in Early Stage Product-Service System Development for Healthcare Informatics. *Engineering Management Journal, 26*(3), 52–62.

Yusuf, Y. Y., Sarhadi, M., & Gunasekaran, A. (1999). Agile manufacturing : The drivers, concepts and attributes. *International Journal of Production Economics, 62*(1), 33–43.

Zaccai, G. (2012, October 18). Why Focus Groups Kill Innovation, From The Designer Behind Swiffer. *Fast Company*. Retrieved from https://www.fastcompany.com/1671033/why-focus-groups-kill-innovation-from-the-designer-behind-swiffer.

About the author

Dr Bill Russell leads teaching at Masters level at the University of Exeter in the UK. He is a specialist in the management of innovation within disrupting ecosystems, with a special focus on the development of competitive offerings. In his teaching and consultancy activities he advocates the design and operationalization of a portfolio of innovation activity across core, adjacent and breakthrough environments.

Before joining the University of Exeter in 2012, Bill worked in globally focused marketing, commercial and Board positions for 27 years. He was a Board Director of Emerald Group Publishing Ltd for 12 years, responsible for sales and marketing activities.

He secured a strong grounding in B2B marketing and branding working with Castrol Oil. Highlights included managing Castrol's international motorsport programme with Jaguar, Mercedes, Toyota and Honda, and operating as Sales and Marketing Director for Castrol Spain in Madrid. He has also been a Sales Director for the US based Hallmark group.

https://doi.org/10.1515/9783110657326-009

List of figures

https://doi.org/10.1515/9783110657326-010

List of tables

https://dol.org/10.1515/9783110657326-011

Index

https://doi.org/10.1515/9783110657326-012